Company's Coming

Kids Do SNACKS

Creampon

Monsieur Auk-Auk

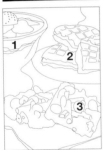

1. Yum-Yum Yogurt Layers, page 27
2. Ham & Cheese Wafflewich, page 53
3. Hokey Pokey Squares, page 120

We gratefully acknowledge the following suppliers for their generous support of our Test and Photography Kitchens:

Broil King Barbecues
Corelle®
Hamilton Beach® Canada
Lagostina®
Proctor Silex® Canada
Tupperware®

Our special thanks to the following businesses for providing props for photography:

Casa Bugatti
Cherison Enterprises Inc.
Chintz & Company
Danesco Inc.
Le Gnome

...exclude the adult of the house from participating, though. We recommend that an adult always look over the recipe that is going to be prepared, and make sure it is suitable for the skill level of the young chef-in-training. We also suggest that an adult be on hand to supervise, in case any questions or concerns arise (think of this as an excellent *fun* learning opportunity).

Now, a little about how this book is structured: Company's Coming believes children need to feel good about themselves when they do something well, so we've created recipes that work for kids with various cooking skills. As the chapters progress throughout the book, the skills required to complete the

Nutrition Information Guidelines

Each recipe is analyzed using the most current version of the Canadian Nutrient File from Health Canada, which is based on the United States Department of Agriculture (USDA) Nutrient Database.

- If more than one ingredient is listed (such as "butter or hard margarine"), or if a range is given (1 – 2 tsp., 5 – 10 mL), only the first ingredient or first amount is analyzed.

- For meat, poultry and fish, the serving size per person is based on the recommended 4 oz. (113 g) uncooked weight (without bone), which is 2 – 3 oz. (57 – 85 g) cooked weight (without bone)— approximately the size of a deck of playing cards.

- Milk used is 2% M.F. (milk fat), unless otherwise stated.

- Cooking oil used is canola oil, unless otherwise stated.

- Ingredients indicating "sprinkle," "optional," or "for garnish" are not included in the nutrition information.

- The fat in recipes and combination foods can vary greatly depending on the sources and types of fats used in each specific ingredient. For these reasons, the amount of saturated, monounsaturated and polyunsaturated fats may not add up to the total fat content.

Vera C. Mazurak, Ph.D.
Nutritionist

Top Chef Tools

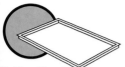

Baking Sheet
Looks like a cookie sheet but it has sides—so things won't roll on to the floor!

Dry Measures
Use these to measure dry ingredients. To measure dry stuff properly, spoon it into your cup, and then level off any extra with the straight side of a table knife.

Grater
Perfect for grating carrots or cheese. Go slowly so you don't accidentally grate your fingers!

Ladle
Great for spooning out soups.

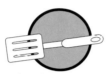

Liquid Measures
You guessed it—these measure liquids. Pour in your liquid and set on an even surface. Check at eye level to see if the liquid reaches the mark.

Measuring Spoons
Make sure ingredients are levelled off, unless the recipe calls for a "heaping" spoonful.

Muffin Pan
Good for making muffins or holding Dixie cups in place when you have to fill a lot of them. Mini-muffin pans look sort-of the same—except the cups are mini-sized.

Pancake Lifter
Slides under pancakes without tearing them.

Pastry Brush
Use this to put liquid on pastry.

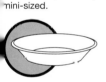

Pie Plate
A circular tin for baking.

Ramekins
Little cups that can be put in the oven.

Rolling Pin
Great for getting pastry flat.

Saucepan
Sometimes called a pot. Always use the size called for in the recipe.

Serrated Knife
Great for cutting softer things like bread.

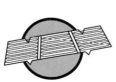

Strainer
An easy way to drain liquid— always use it over a sink.

Oven with Rack Positions
It's important to follow the recipe instructions for rack positions.

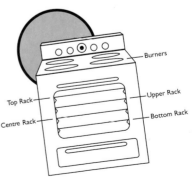

Whisk
A tool that mixes ingredients really well and breaks up lumps.

Wire Rack
Good for cooling baked items by letting air flow underneath.

Blend It!

If you're new to cooking, or you just love to turn solid things into liquid, this is the section for you. In *Blend It!* you don't need a knife for cutting, you just need to know how to measure and, of course, work your blender.

find 20 vegetables

```
G  X  Z  Q  M  N  C  O  R  N  Z  R  E
R  R  M  O  O  R  H  S  U  M  E  J  C
E  Z  E  I  C  L  O  E  G  W  Q  A  U
E  T  N  E  E  E  G  K  O  V  S  S  T
N  O  U  E  N  A  L  L  R  P  X  Q  T
B  M  K  I  B  O  F  E  A  A  G  U  E
E  U  K  B  L  I  N  R  R  Z  P  A  L
A  E  A  H  L  O  A  I  K  Y  I  S  B
N  C  T  U  X  G  C  E  O  X  N  H  E
A  Z  A  N  U  G  D  C  J  N  R  K  E
S  C  P  S  C  A  R  R  O  T  U  P  T
O  T  A  T  O  P  A  E  P  R  T  Z  M
B  E  A  N  S  P  R  O  U  T  B  F  M
```

ASPARAGUS   BEANSPROUT   BEET
BROCCOLI   CABBAGE   CARROT
CAULIFLOWER   CELERY   CORN
GREENBEAN   GREENONION   LEEK
LETTUCE   MUSHROOM   OKRA
ONION   PEA   POTATO
SQUASH   TURNIP

Berry Me Alive, below

Berry Me Alive

Sound scary? It is! If you don't drink it quick, it will get so thick you'll have to dig yourself out with a spoon!

Get It Together: liquid measures, measuring spoons, dry measures, blender, 2 glasses

1.			
Milk	1 1/4 cups	300 mL
Frozen mixed berries	1 cup	250 mL
Raspberry yogurt	1 cup	250 mL
Orange juice	1/3 cup	75 mL
Instant vanilla pudding powder	2 tbsp.	30 mL

1. Put all 5 ingredients into blender. Cover with lid. Blend until smooth. Pour into glasses. Makes about 3 1/2 cups (875 mL)—enough for 2 kids.

1 serving: 279 Calories; 4.5 g Total Fat (trace Mono, trace Poly, 2.9 g Sat); 20 mg Cholesterol; 49 g Carbohydrate; 3 g Fibre; 11 g Protein; 358 mg Sodium

Pictured above.

Blend It!   9

Man-Go-Go Smoothie

Grab some mango when it's time to go-go and you'll have all the energy you need!

Get It Together: liquid measures, dry measures, blender, tall glass

1.	Frozen chopped mango	1 cup	250 mL
	Apple juice	3/4 cup	175 mL
	Vanilla frozen yogurt	1/2 cup	125 mL

1. Put all 3 ingredients into blender. Cover with lid. Blend until smooth. Pour into glass. Makes about 1 3/4 cups (425 mL)—enough for 1 thirsty kid.

1 serving: 330 Calories; 5.0 g Total Fat (0.2 g Mono, 0.1 g Poly, 3.1 g Sat); 15 mg Cholesterol; 71 g Carbohydrate; 3 g Fibre; 4 g Protein; 56 mg Sodium

Pictured on front cover and on page 11.

Milky Way Blue Lemonade

Pucker up, kiddo! When life gives you blueberries, make lemonade milk!

Get It Together: dry measures, liquid measures, measuring spoons, blender, glass

1.	Frozen blueberries	1/2 cup	125 mL
	Milk	1/3 cup	75 mL
	Frozen concentrated lemonade	3 tbsp.	50 mL
	Ice cubes	3	3

1. Put all 4 ingredients into blender. Cover with lid. Blend until smooth. Pour into glass. Makes about 1 1/4 cups (300 mL)—a refreshing drink, just for you.

1 serving: 178 Calories; 2.3 g Total Fat (0 g Mono, trace Poly, 1.0 g Sat); 7 mg Cholesterol; 39 g Carbohydrate; 2 g Fibre; 3 g Protein; 44 mg Sodium

Pictured on page 11.

Q: When do you stop at green and go at red?

A: When you're eating a watermelon.

1. Marshmallow Fruit Soda Pop, page 12
2. Fruit Sludgies, page 12
3. Milky Way Blue Lemonade, page 10
4. Man-Go-Go Smoothie, page 10

11

Marshmallow Fruit Soda Pop

Ever try drinking a marshmallow? Here's your chance! Use other frozen fruit if you like.

Get It Together: dry measures, liquid measures, blender, 2 large glasses, spoon

1.	Frozen strawberries	2 1/2 cups	625 mL
	Orange juice	1 cup	250 mL
2.	Jar of marshmallow creme	7 oz.	198 g
3.	Club soda	1 cup	250 mL

1. Put strawberries and orange juice into blender. Cover with lid. Blend until almost smooth. There should still be some tiny chunks of strawberry.

2. Add marshmallow creme. Blend until mixed. Pour into glasses.

3. Add 1/2 cup (125 mL) club soda to each glass. Stir. Makes about 3 1/3 cups (835 mL)—enough for you and a friend.

1 serving: 442 Calories; 0 g Total Fat (0 g Mono, 0 g Poly, 0 g Sat); 0 mg Cholesterol; 110 g Carbohydrate; 4 g Fibre; 2 g Protein; 90 mg Sodium

Pictured on page 11.

Fruit Sludgies

Everybody likes to drink sludge, don't they? Not sure? Give it a go and you'll be a sludge eater in no time!

Get It Together: can opener, dry measures, ice cream scoop, liquid measures, blender, 2 glasses

1.	Can of fruit cocktail, drained	14 oz.	398 mL
	Lime sherbet	2/3 cup	150 mL
	Milk	1/2 cup	125 mL

1. Put all 3 ingredients into blender. Cover with lid. Blend until almost smooth. Pour into glasses. Makes about 2 1/4 cups (550 mL)—enough for 2 sludge eaters.

1 serving: 239 Calories; 2.4 g Total Fat (0.3 g Mono, 0.1 g Poly, 0.4 g Sat); 8 mg Cholesterol; 56 g Carbohydrate; 3 g Fibre; 3 g Protein; 66 mg Sodium

Pictured on page 11.

(continued on next page)

Cookbot 3000 Tip: Use a different flavour of sherbet to change the flavour and colour of your sludgie! Or make it into a slushie by adding 2 or 3 ice cubes with the other ingredients before blending.

Chocolate Galaxies

This chocolate and vanilla-swirled treat is out of this world—and ready in less than 10 minutes!

Get It Together: liquid measures, dry measures, blender, 2 dessert dishes, measuring spoons, table knife

1. Milk	1 cup	250 mL
Instant chocolate pudding powder (half of 4-serving size box)	1/3 cup	75 mL
2. Vanilla yogurt	1/4 cup	60 mL

1. Put milk into blender. Add pudding powder. Cover with lid. Blend until smooth. Pour pudding mixture into dessert dishes.

2. Spoon 2 tbsp. (30 mL) yogurt on top of each bowl of pudding. Stir pudding and yogurt together with tip of knife to make spirals. Wait for about 5 minutes until thickened. Makes about 2 1/3 cups (575 mL) —enough for you and a friend.

1 serving: 214 Calories; 3.4 g Total Fat (0.9 g Mono, 0.2 g Poly, 1.9 g Sat); 11 mg Cholesterol; 41 g Carbohydrate; 1 g Fibre; 6 g Protein; 628 mg Sodium

Pictured below and on back cover.

Chocolate Galaxies, above

Butterscotch Me Up Dip

Give fruit, graham crackers, cookies or even raisin toast a dunk in this sweet dip.

Get It Together: liquid measures, dry measures, blender, spoon, small bowl

1.			
Milk	1/2 cup	125 mL
Vanilla yogurt	1/2 cup	125 mL
Instant butterscotch pudding powder	1/3 cup	75 mL
(half of 4-serving size box)		

1. Put all 3 ingredients into blender. Cover with lid. Blend until mixture is smooth and thickened. Spoon into bowl. Makes about 1 1/4 cups (300 mL)—enough for you and a friend to go dip crazy.

1 serving: 168 Calories; 2.0 g Total Fat (0 g Mono, 0 g Poly, 1.3 g Sat); 9 mg Cholesterol; 31 g Carbohydrate; 1 g Fibre; 6 g Protein; 201 mg Sodium

Pictured on page 15.

Cookbot 3000 Tip: Mix it up a bit and try other pudding flavours. Make a healthier snack by using sugar-free pudding and low-fat yogurt.

I'm A Little Nutty Dip

Go nuts for this smooth dip that's great with fruit, veggies and crackers.

Get It Together: liquid measures, dry measures, blender, small bowl, spoon

1.			
Vanilla yogurt	1 cup	250 mL
Peanut butter	1/3 cup	75 mL

1. Put yogurt and peanut butter into blender. Cover with lid. Blend until smooth. Spoon into bowl. Makes about 1 1/3 cups (325 mL)—enough dip for 2 nutty kids.

1 serving: 325 Calories; 23.4 g Total Fat (10.4 g Mono, 5.9 g Poly, 5.4 g Sat); 8 mg Cholesterol; 16 g Carbohydrate; 2 g Fibre; 16 g Protein; 87 mg Sodium

Pictured on page 15.

Blend It!

1. I'm A Little Nutty Dip, page 14
2. Butterscotch Me Up Dip, page 14
3. Confusing Dip, page 16
4. 4 O'Clock Fiesta Salsa, page 16

15

Confusing Dip

Is it sweet or is it sour? This confusing dip is both but, thankfully, it's delicious, too! Munch with veggies.

Cookbot 3000 Tip: To soften cream cheese, let it sit on the counter for about 30 minutes.

Get It Together: liquid measures, measuring spoons, dry measures, blender, spoon, small bowl

1.			
Apricot jam	1/2 cup	125 mL	
Cream cheese, softened	4 oz.	125 g	
Apple cider vinegar	2 tbsp.	30 mL	
Soy sauce	2 tbsp.	30 mL	
Hoisin sauce	1 tsp.	5 mL	

1. Put all 5 ingredients into blender. Cover with lid. Blend until smooth. Spoon into bowl. Makes about 1 1/3 cups (325 mL)—enough for 2 confused kids.

1 serving: 411 Calories; 20.3 g Total Fat (0.1 g Mono, 0.1 g Poly, 14.0 g Sat); 60 mg Cholesterol; 57 g Carbohydrate; trace Fibre; 6 g Protein; 1065 mg Sodium

Pictured on page 15.

4 O'Clock Fiesta Salsa

It's a fine time for a pre-dinner fiesta. This beany salsa is great on tortilla chips, crackers or even toast!

Get It Together: can opener, dry measures, liquid measures, measuring spoons, food processor, spoon, small dish

1.			
Canned white kidney beans, rinsed and drained	1 cup	250 mL	
Salsa	1/4 cup	60 mL	
Spreadable cream cheese	1/4 cup	60 mL	
Lime juice	1 tbsp.	15 mL	

1. Put all 4 ingredients into food processor. Cover with lid. Process until almost smooth. If necessary, stop food processor and scrape down sides. Spoon into dish. Makes about 1 1/3 cups (325 mL)—enough for you and a friend.

1 serving: 217 Calories; 11.0 g Total Fat (0 g Mono, 0 g Poly, 7.0 g Sat); 30 mg Cholesterol; 21 g Carbohydrate; 6 g Fibre; 8 g Protein; 381 mg Sodium

Pictured on page 15.

Cookbot 3000 Tip: The remaining beans can be frozen for another time, or added to a soup, salad or stew.

Mix It!

We've mixed it up in this chapter. You'll need to do cutting for some of the recipes—but not all of them. You'll also need to know how to grate.

Q1: What do corn wear to bed?

Q2: What do you take before every meal?

Q3: Why did the chicken cross the playground?

Answers: **Q1:** Silk **Q2:** A seat **Q3:** To get to the other slide

Swimming Fruit Sipper

It's fruit overboard in this ginger ale and fruit drink!

Get It Together: liquid measures, sharp knife, cutting board, tall glass, mixing spoon

1.	Ginger ale	1/2 cup	125 mL
	White grape (or white cranberry) juice	1/2 cup	125 mL
2.	Fresh strawberries, quartered	2	2
	Seedless green grapes, halved	6	6
	Canned mandarin orange segments, halved	8	8

1. Pour ginger ale and juice into glass. Mix gently.

2. Carefully drop in 4 strawberry pieces, 6 grape halves and 8 halved orange segments. Repeat with remaining fruit. Makes about 1 1/2 cups (375 mL)—enough for 1 kid.

1 serving: 174 Calories; 0.2 g Total Fat (0 g Mono, trace Poly, 0.1 g Sat); 0 mg Cholesterol; 43 g Carbohydrate; 1 g Fibre; 1 g Protein; 17 mg Sodium

Pictured on page 19.

Creampuff Tip: Use any combination of your favourite fruit. Watermelon, pineapple, apple, pear, kiwi, honeydew or cantaloupe—they all work!

Apple Of My Iced Tea

Time for a tea party! Wow a friend with this extreme iced tea that has an amazing apple taste!

Get It Together: liquid measures, measuring spoons, pitcher, mixing spoon, 2 large glasses

1.	Apple juice	1 cup	250 mL
	Cold water	3/4 cup	175 mL
	Lemon iced tea crystals	2 tbsp.	30 mL
2.	Ice cubes		

1. Pour apple juice and water into pitcher. Add crystals. Stir until crystals are dissolved. Pour into glasses.

(continued on next page)

Mix It!

2. Add ice cubes. Makes about 2 cups (500 mL)—enough for you and the apple of your eye.

1 serving: 95 Calories; 0 g Total Fat (0 g Mono, 0 g Poly, 0 g Sat); 0 mg Cholesterol; 24 g Carbohydrate; 0 g Fibre; 0 g Protein; 5 mg Sodium

Pictured below.

Creampuff Tip: Experiment with other juices like cranberry peach.

Left: Swimming Fruit Sipper, page 18 Right: Apple Of My Iced Tea, page 18

Left: Curry Fury Dip, below Right: Cheese Puck, page 21

Curry Fury Dip

Are you mad about curry? This dip will satisfy your curry craving in no time!
Eat with your favourite deli meats—just roll them up and dip. Or try with fruit
or veggie sticks.

Get It Together: measuring spoons, small bowl, whisk

1.	Mayonnaise	2 tbsp.	30 mL
	Prepared mustard	2 tbsp.	30 mL
	Syrup	4 tsp.	20 mL
	Curry powder	1/2 tsp.	2 mL
	Salt, sprinkle		

1. Put all 5 ingredients into bowl. Stir with whisk until smooth.
   Makes about 1/3 cup (75 mL)—enough for 1 kid.

1 serving: 238 Calories; 15.5 g Total Fat (8.7 g Mono, 5.0 g Poly, 1.1 g Sat); 8 mg Cholesterol;
25 g Carbohydrate; 1 g Fibre; 2 g Protein; 523 mg Sodium

Pictured above.

Creampuff Tip: This dip can be served immediately or
covered with plastic wrap and chilled for you to eat later on.

Mix It!

Cheese Puck

Score off the ice with this spicy cheese puck. Spread on crackers, pita chips or tortilla chips.

Get It Together: dry measures, measuring spoons, grater, sharp knife, cutting board, small bowl, fork, mixing spoon, plate

1.			
Cream cheese, softened	1/4 cup	60 mL
Grated medium Cheddar cheese	2 tbsp.	30 mL
Grated Monterey Jack cheese	2 tbsp.	30 mL
Cajun seasoning	1/2 tsp.	2 mL
2.		
Finely chopped ham	3 tbsp.	50 mL
Crushed pecans	2 tbsp.	30 mL

1. Put cream cheese into bowl. Mash with fork until smooth. Add next 3 ingredients. Mix well.

2. Add ham and pecans. Mix well. Shape into a flattened ball using your hands. Place on plate. Makes enough for 2 hungry sports fans.

1 serving: 231 Calories; 20.8 g Total Fat (4.2 g Mono, 1.8 g Poly, 10.6 g Sat); 56 mg Cholesterol; 2 g Carbohydrate; 1 g Fibre; 10 g Protein; 334 mg Sodium

Pictured on page 20.

Creampuff Tip: To soften cream cheese, let it sit on the counter for about 30 minutes.

To crush pecans, place nuts in a resealable sandwich bag and roll a rolling pin over top until the nuts are crushed.

Q: What starts with t, ends with t and is filled with t?

A: A teapot.

4 X 4 Dipping Adventure

With 4 layers, this dip is 4 times the fun! Eat with veggies, tortilla chips or Micro-Chips, page 44.

Get It Together: measuring spoons, sharp knife, cutting board, grater, small bowl, fork, spoon, plate

1.	Spreadable cream cheese	3 tbsp.	50 mL
	Sour cream	2 tbsp.	30 mL
	Pepper, sprinkle		
2.	Salsa	2 tbsp.	30 mL
3.	Chopped green pepper	2 tbsp.	30 mL
	Chopped fresh tomato	1 tbsp.	15 mL
4.	Grated mozzarella cheese	2 tbsp.	30 mL

1. Put first 3 ingredients into bowl. Mix with fork until smooth. Spoon onto centre of plate. Spread cheese mixture into a 4 inch (10 cm) wide circle.

2. Spoon salsa over cream cheese mixture.

3. Sprinkle green pepper and tomato over salsa.

4. Sprinkle cheese on top. Makes enough for 2 adventurous kids.

1 serving: 130 Calories; 11.7 g Total Fat (1.2 g Mono, 0.2 g Poly, 7.8 g Sat); 34 mg Cholesterol; 3 g Carbohydrate; trace Fibre; 4 g Protein; 180 mg Sodium

Pictured on page 23.

Creampuff Tip: To make it spicier, add 1 chopped hot pepper ring to the cream cheese mixture. You could also use a spicier salsa or a grated jalapeño cheese blend instead of the mozzarella cheese.

Q: What did the grape say when he was sat on?

A: Nothing—he just let out a little whine.

p: Rice Cream Cones, page 24
ottom: 4 X 4 Dipping Adventure, page 22

Rice Cream Cones

Don't worry about this cone melting all over—it's filled with rice and veggies. What a neat treat!

Get It Together: measuring spoons, liquid measures, dry measures, sharp knife, cutting board, grater, vegetable peeler, medium bowl, mixing spoon, ice cream scoop

1.	Mayonnaise	1/4 cup	60 mL
	Apple cider vinegar	1 tsp.	5 mL
	Granulated sugar	1 tsp.	5 mL
	Prepared mustard	1 tsp.	5 mL
	Cold cooked rice	1 cup	250 mL
2.	Finely chopped deli turkey breast slices	1/3 cup	75 mL
	Finely grated peeled carrot	2 tbsp.	30 mL
	Finely grated unpeeled English cucumber	2 tbsp.	30 mL
3.	Ice cream cones (flat-bottom)	2	2

1. Put first 4 ingredients into bowl. Stir. Add rice. Mix well.
2. Add next 3 ingredients. Stir.
3. Fill cones with rice mixture, packing down gently. Pack ice cream scoop with rice mixture. Place scoop on top of rice mixture in cone. Repeat with the remaining rice mixture and cone. Makes 2 fun snacks.

1 serving: 314 Calories; 15.0 g Total Fat (8.1 g Mono, 4.9 g Poly, 1.1 g Sat); 17 mg Cholesterol; 37 g Carbohydrate; 1 g Fibre; 7 g Protein; 440 mg Sodium

Pictured on page 23.

Q: What is green and goes to a summer camp?

A: A Brussels' scout.

Mix It!

Lickety-Split Sundae

This super sundae's not just for Sundays—eat it any day of the week!

Get It Together: sharp knife, cutting board, liquid measures, dry measures, ice cream scoop, small cereal bowl, small bowl, mixing spoon

1.	**Medium banana**	1/2	1/2
2.	**Applesauce, chilled**	1/2 cup	125 mL
	Canned fruit cocktail, drained	1/4 cup	60 mL
3.	**Vanilla frozen yogurt**	1/2 cup	125 mL
4.	**Maraschino cherry**	1	1

1. Cut banana into 4 long pieces. Arrange banana pieces standing up against sides of cereal bowl.

2. Put applesauce and fruit cocktail into small bowl. Mix well. Spoon half of applesauce mixture into cereal bowl.

3. Spoon half of frozen yogurt over top. Repeat with remaining applesauce and frozen yogurt.

4. Place cherry on top. Eat immediately. Makes 1 stunning sundae.

1 serving: 327 Calories; 5.0 g Total Fat (trace Mono, 0.1 g Poly, 3.1 g Sat); 15 mg Cholesterol; 70 g Carbohydrate; 4 g Fibre; 4 g Protein; 53 mg Sodium

Pictured below.

Lickety-Split Sundae, above

Left: Bumpy Peanut Butter Balls, below Right: Yum-Yum Yogurt Layers, page 27

Bumpy Peanut Butter Balls

Don't go bowling with these bumpy balls—eat them instead!

Get It Together: dry measures, measuring spoons, small bowl, mixing spoon, small plate

1.	Crunchy peanut butter	1/4 cup	60 mL
	Liquid honey	2 tbsp.	30 mL
	Skim milk powder	2 tbsp.	30 mL
	Graham cracker crumbs	1/3 cup	75 mL
2.	Medium sweetened coconut	2 tbsp.	30 mL

1. Put first 3 ingredients into bowl. Stir. Add graham cracker crumbs. Mix well. Divide peanut butter mixture into 4 equal portions. Roll portions between your hands to make balls.

2. Spread coconut on plate. Roll balls in coconut until coated. Makes 4 sweet treats, enough for you and a pal to share.

1 serving: 365 Calories; 18.9 g Total Fat (8.5 g Mono, 5.3 g Poly, 4.2 g Sat); 1 mg Cholesterol; 41 g Carbohydrate; 3 g Fibre; 12 g Protein; 292 mg Sodium

Pictured above.

Yum-Yum Yogurt Layers

Be a layer slayer and devour this sweet treat made with cookies,
fruit and almonds.

Get It Together: sharp knife, cutting board, measuring spoons,
liquid measures, dry measures, tall glass, small bowl, mixing spoon

1.	Chocolate chip cookies	2	2
2.	Berry yogurt	1/2 cup	125 mL
	Sliced natural almonds	1 tbsp.	15 mL
3.	Banana slices, about 1/4 inch (6 mm) thick	6	6
	Sliced fresh strawberries	1/2 cup	125 mL

1. Break cookies into small pieces. Put into glass.

2. Put yogurt and almonds into bowl. Mix well. Spoon half of yogurt mixture over broken cookies.

3. Put 3 banana slices on top of yogurt. Put half of strawberries on top of banana slices. Repeat layers 1 more time with remaining yogurt mixture, banana slices and strawberries. Makes 1 tasty treat.

1 serving: 293 Calories; 9.1 g Total Fat (2.0 g Mono, 0.9 g Poly, 2.3 g Sat); 13 mg Cholesterol; 49 g Carbohydrate; 3 g Fibre; 6 g Protein; 102 mg Sodium

Pictured on divider and on page 26.

Creampuff Tip: Try using your favourite flavour of yogurt.
Also, try experimenting with different kinds of nuts and fruits.

Q: What do you call cheese that doesn't belong to you?

A: Nacho cheese.

Boastin' Toastin' Choco-Treats

You'll have lots to boast about when you make these chocolatey sweet waffle treats, piled high with strawberries and bananas.

Get It Together: measuring spoons, dry measures, sharp knife, cutting board, 2 serving plates, small bowl, fork, mixing spoon, table knife

1.	Cream cheese, softened	3 tbsp.	50 mL
	Prepared chocolate frosting	1/3 cup	75 mL
2.	Frozen waffles	2	2
3.	Sliced fresh strawberries	1/2 cup	125 mL
	Sliced banana	1/4 cup	60 mL

1. Put cream cheese into bowl. Mash with fork until smooth. Add frosting. Mix well.

2. Toast waffles. Place on plates. Spread frosting mixture on waffles.

3. Arrange strawberries and banana slices on top. Makes enough for you and a friend.

1 serving: 382 Calories; 18.7 g Total Fat (4.2 g Mono, 1.1 g Poly, 8.6 g Sat); 33 mg Cholesterol; 52 g Carbohydrate; 2 g Fibre; 5 g Protein; 379 mg Sodium

Pictured on page 29.

Creampuff Tip: To soften cream cheese, let it sit on the counter for about 30 minutes.

If you don't have waffles, use toasted bread instead.

The Tower Of Trifle

The goodies are piled high in this sweet treat with cake, pudding, strawberries and bananas. Use any kind of cake you like.

Get It Together: sharp knife, cutting board, liquid measures, dry measures, 2 small bowls, mixing spoon, whisk, 2 tall glasses, spoons

1.	Sliced banana	1/2 cup	125 mL
	Sliced fresh strawberries	1/2 cup	125 mL
2.	Milk	1 cup	250 mL
	Instant chocolate pudding powder (half of 4-serving size box)	1/3 cup	75 mL

(continued on next page)

Mix It!

3.	Small cake cubes	1 cup	250 mL
	Frozen whipped topping, thawed	1/2 cup	125 mL

1. Put banana and strawberries into 1 bowl. Stir. Set aside.

2. Put milk and pudding powder into other bowl. Stir with whisk for about 2 minutes until mixture is smooth and thick.

3. Put half of cake cubes into each glass. Spoon pudding mixture over cake. Spoon fruit mixture over pudding mixture. Spoon whipped topping on top. Makes 2 towering treats.

1 serving: 320 Calories; 8.7 g Total Fat (0.9 g Mono, 0.8 g Poly, 6.0 g Sat); 10 mg Cholesterol; 56 g Carbohydrate; 3 g Fibre; 6 g Protein; 531 mg Sodium

Pictured below.

Left: Boastin' Toastin' Choco-Treats, page 28 Right: The Tower Of Trifle, page 28

Toss It!

Tossing is a form of mixing—but it has way more pizzazz! When you toss food you can do it in a plastic baggie or you can do it by gently lifting and turning food with spoons. But don't go all crazy and start tossing things on the ceiling—this is a delicate procedure!

find 19 fruits

```
E A Y R R E H C Z Q N U Y V R
A G P V B L U E B E R R Y H A
T N N P M Z P N D E R H U R N
I L O A L A Q J M E L B W F A
E M N L R E J I B W A I A X N
A G R G E O L N N R K W Q M A
O P U A Y M A B B B D D I E H B
H C R Q E R R M U L P K N P Z
G R L I C P P E A C H X I P N
B X A Y C P B J T P X U R U U
Y H N D M O E P R A M O A M L
T T C R R M T T E Z W G T P E
Q I Y R R E B W A R T S C K M
O U N L X X Z U V L P N E I O
L K L Y J G F B E Q Y I N N N
```

APPLE
BLUEBERRY
GRAPE
LIME
ORANGE
PLUM
STRAWBERRY

APRICOT
CHERRY
KIWI
MANGO
PEACH
PUMPKIN
WATERMELON

BANANA
CRANBERRY
LEMON
NECTARINE
PEAR

Countdown Fruit Salad

Counting, measuring and dividing are involved in this mathematical masterpiece. Add up the ingredients and the sum is a yummy salad. Save any leftover fruit to make smoothies or put in yogurt.

Get It Together: sharp knife, cutting board, measuring spoons, medium bowl, mixing spoons, small cup

1.	Seedless grapes	10	10
	Banana slices	9	9
	Pecan halves	8	8
	Cantaloupe cubes	7	7
	Cheddar cheese cubes	6	6
2.	Orange segments	5	5
	Apple slices	4	4
	Sweetened shredded coconut	3 tbsp.	50 mL
3.	Frozen concentrated orange juice, thawed	2 tbsp.	30 mL
	Water	1 tbsp.	15 mL

1. Put first 5 ingredients into bowl.

2. Cut each orange segment into 3 pieces. Add to fruit mixture. Cut each apple slice into 4 pieces. Add to fruit mixture. Sprinkle coconut over top. Use mixing spoons to toss fruit mixture.

3. Put concentrated orange juice and water into cup. Stir. Drizzle over fruit mixture. Toss. Makes about 2 cups (500 mL)—the perfect amount for sharing with a friend.

1 serving: 248 Calories; 12.0 g Total Fat (3.1 g Mono, 1.6 g Poly, 5.1 g Sat); 11 mg Cholesterol; 34 g Carbohydrate; 4 g Fibre; 5 g Protein; 93 mg Sodium

Pictured below. **Countdown Fruit Salad, above**

Mix-Master Snacks-A-Lot

You'll be the master mixer with this sweet and salty snack.

Get It Together: dry measures, measuring spoons, medium bowl, mixing spoons

1.
Small pretzels	1 cup	250 mL
"O"-shaped toasted oat cereal	1/2 cup	125 mL
Honey-roasted almonds	1/4 cup	60 mL
Candy-coated chocolates	2 tbsp.	30 mL
Raisins	2 tbsp.	30 mL

1. Put all 5 ingredients into bowl. Use mixing spoons to toss until combined. Makes about 2 cups (500 mL)—enough for 2 snacks.

1 serving: 496 Calories; 20.1 g Total Fat (9.5 g Mono, 2.7 g Poly, 7.2 g Sat); 6 mg Cholesterol; 73 g Carbohydrate; 5 g Fibre; 9 g Protein; 640 mg Sodium

Pictured on page 33.

Monsieur Auk-Auk Tip: If you can't find honey-roasted almonds, use honey-roasted peanuts instead.

Cannibals won't eat clowns—they taste funny.

Toss It!

Left: Ham & Corn Feed Bag, below Right: Mix-Master Snacks-A-Lot, page 32

Ham & Corn Feed Bag

Your salad's in the bag. Make it in the bag and eat it out
of the bag—talk about easy cleanup!

Get It Together: sharp knife, cutting board, dry measures, measuring
spoons, resealable sandwich bag

1.			
Frozen kernel corn, thawed	1/3 cup	75 mL
Diced ham	1/4 cup	60 mL
Frozen peas, thawed	1/4 cup	60 mL
Cherry tomatoes, halved	3	3
Croutons	2 tbsp.	30 mL
Ranch dressing	1 tbsp.	15 mL
Chili powder, sprinkle		

1. Put all 7 ingredients into bag. Seal bag. Toss until coated. Makes about
   1 cup (250 mL)—enough for 1 kid.

*1 serving: 245 Calories; 11.9 g Total Fat (0.9 g Mono, 0.3 g Poly, 1.3 g Sat); 18 mg Cholesterol;
22 g Carbohydrate; 4 g Fibre; 15 g Protein; 122 mg Sodium*

Pictured above.

Toss It!   33

Bronco Bull Eggs

Didn't think bulls laid eggs? Well, they don't but we figured if you crossed an ornery bull and a chicken, you might end up with this spicy egg spread!

Get It Together: sharp knife, cutting board, measuring spoons, small bowl, mixing spoons

1.	Large hard-cooked egg, chopped	1	1
	Ranch dressing	1 tbsp.	15 mL
	Hot pepper sauce	1/4 tsp.	1 mL
2.	Crackers	4	4

1. Put first 3 ingredients into bowl. Use mixing spoons to toss until coated.
2. Spoon egg mixture onto crackers. Makes 4 cracker snacks for you to enjoy.

1 serving: 203 Calories; 14.5 g Total Fat (2.9 g Mono, 0.9 g Poly, 3.0 g Sat); 216 mg Cholesterol; 10 g Carbohydrate; trace Fibre; 8 g Protein; 365 mg Sodium

Pictured on page 35.

Monsieur Auk-Auk Tip: Do you know how to cook the perfect hard-cooked egg? First place an egg in a small saucepan. Add cold water until about 1 inch (2.5 cm) above the egg. Bring to a boil on medium-high. Remove the saucepan from the heat. Cover with lid. Wait for 20 minutes. Drain. Cover the egg with cold water. Change the water each time it warms up until the egg is cool. Remove the shell. There you have it—the perfect hard-cooked egg!

Q: What did the spoon say to the knife?

A: Lookin' sharp.

Toss It!

Tomato Tossle

Like Italian food? If you do, you'll love this tomato-tossed snack!

Get It Together: sharp knife, cutting board, dry measures, grater, measuring spoons, small bowl, mixing spoons

1.			
Chopped tomato	1/3 cup	75 mL
Grated mozzarella cheese	2 tbsp.	30 mL
Fresh basil leaf, torn into small pieces	1	1
(or 1/8 tsp., 0.5 mL, dried basil)		
Olive (or cooking) oil	1/2 tsp.	2 mL
Granulated sugar	1/4 tsp.	1 mL
Garlic powder, sprinkle		
Salt, sprinkle		
2. Bread slice, toasted	1	1

1. Put first 7 ingredients into bowl. Use mixing spoons to toss until combined.

2. Cut toast into 4 pieces. Spoon tomato mixture over toast pieces. Drain remaining juice in bottom of bowl. Makes 4 tossles for you to taste.

1 serving: 143 Calories; 6.5 g Total Fat (2.8 g Mono, 0.9 g Poly, 2.4 g Sat); 12 mg Cholesterol; 16 g Carbohydrate; 1 g Fibre; 5 g Protein; 192 mg Sodium

Pictured below.

Top: Tomato Tossle, above Bottom: Bronco Bull Eggs, page 34

Luau Wow-Wow

Who cares if you're not on a beach in Hawaii? Make your own mini-luau with this sweet and crunchy pineapple salad.

Get It Together: can opener, sharp knife, cutting board, dry measures, vegetable peeler, grater, measuring spoons, small bowl, mixing spoons, 2 cereal bowls

1.			
Canned pineapple tidbits, drained	1/2 cup	125 mL
Chopped celery	1/2 cup	125 mL
Grated peeled carrot	1/2 cup	125 mL
Raisins	1/4 cup	60 mL
Mayonnaise	2 tbsp.	30 mL
Pineapple juice	1 tsp.	5 mL

1. Put all 6 ingredients into small bowl. Use mixing spoons to toss until coated. Spoon into cereal bowls. Makes about 1 1/2 cups (375 mL)—enough for a 2-kid luau.

1 serving: 179 Calories; 7.4 g Total Fat (4.0 g Mono, 2.5 g Poly, 0.6 g Sat); 4 mg Cholesterol; 29 g Carbohydrate; 3 g Fibre; 2 g Protein; 138 mg Sodium

Pictured on page 37.

Take 1–It's A Wrap!

This chicken wrap tastes just like Chinese takeout!

Get It Together: sharp knife, cutting board, dry measures, measuring spoons, small bowl, mixing spoons, plate

1. Chopped or torn lettuce, lightly packed	1 cup	250 mL
Sesame ginger dressing	2 tbsp.	30 mL
2. Flour tortilla (9 inch, 22 cm, diameter)	1	1
Chopped cooked chicken	1/2 cup	125 mL
Dry chow mein noodles	2 tbsp.	30 mL
3. Sesame ginger dressing	2 tbsp.	30 mL

1. Put lettuce into bowl. Add first amount of dressing. Use mixing spoons to toss until coated. Set aside.

(continued on next page)

Toss It!

2. Place tortilla on plate. Spoon chicken in a line across middle of tortilla, leaving a small edge uncovered on both sides. Sprinkle noodles over chicken. Spoon lettuce mixture over noodles. Fold small edges over filling. Roll up from bottom to enclose filling. Cut tortilla in half.

3. Serve with second amount of dressing for dipping. Makes 1 totally wrapped up snack.

1 serving: 654 Calories; 34.5 g Total Fat (5.6 g Mono, 3.6 g Poly, 6.2 g Sat); 66 mg Cholesterol; 54 g Carbohydrate; 3 g Fibre; 29 g Protein; 1044 mg Sodium

Pictured below.

Top: Luau Wow-Wow, page 36   Bottom: Take 1—It's A Wrap!, page 36

Hickory Sticks Coleslaw

Hickory sticks may be good on their own but they're a sure hit in coleslaw!

Get It Together: measuring spoons, sharp knife, cutting board, dry measures, small bowl, mixing spoons

1.			
Sour cream	2 tbsp.	30 mL
Water	2 tsp.	10 mL
White vinegar	2 tsp.	10 mL
Granulated sugar	1 tsp.	5 mL
Chopped fresh dill	1/2 tsp.	2 mL
(or 1/8 tsp., 0.5 mL, dried dillweed)		
Cooking oil	1/4 tsp.	1 mL
Salt, sprinkle		
Pepper, sprinkle		
2.			
Coleslaw mix	1/2 cup	125 mL
Diced marble cheese	1/4 cup	60 mL
Hickory sticks	1/4 cup	60 mL

1. Put first 8 ingredients into bowl. Stir.
2. Add remaining 3 ingredients. Use mixing spoons to toss until coated. Serve immediately. Makes about 2/3 cup (150 mL)—a fun snack for 1.

1 serving: 278 Calories; 18.9 g Total Fat (4.8 g Mono, 0.8 g Poly, 9.3 g Sat); 42 mg Cholesterol; 18 g Carbohydrate; 2 g Fibre; 10 g Protein; 213 mg Sodium

Pictured below.

Left: Hickory Sticks Coleslaw, above Right: Turkey-Lurkey Happy Wraps, page 39

Turkey-Lurkey Happy Wraps

Made with rice paper, this wrap sure is different! You'll be happy you made it. Good on its own or try with 4 O'Clock Fiesta Salsa, page 16, or Confusing Dip, page 16.

Get It Together: grater, vegetable peeler, dry measures, measuring spoons, small bowl, mixing spoons, pie plate, 2 plates, plastic wrap

1.	Cooked rice	1 cup	250 mL
	Grated peeled carrot	1/4 cup	60 mL
	Grated unpeeled English cucumber	1/4 cup	60 mL
	Raisins	1/4 cup	60 mL
	Mayonnaise	2 tbsp.	30 mL
	Salt	1/4 tsp.	1 mL
	Pepper	1/8 tsp.	0.5 mL
2.	Very warm water		
3.	Rice paper rounds	4	4
	(6 inch, 15 cm, diameter)		
4.	Thin deli turkey breast slices	4	4

1. Put first 7 ingredients into bowl. Use mixing spoons to toss until coated.

2. Pour very warm water (as hot as you can handle) into pie plate until about 1/2 inch (12 mm) deep.

3. Dip 1 rice paper round into water for about 30 seconds until softened. Place rice paper on 1 plate.

4. Place 1 turkey slice on rice paper round. Spoon about 1/3 cup (75 mL) rice mixture onto centre of turkey slice. Spread rice in a line across middle of turkey slice, leaving a small edge uncovered on both sides. Fold small edges of rice paper round over filling. Roll up from bottom to enclose filling. Place, seam-side down, on other plate. Cover with plastic wrap. Repeat with remaining rice paper rounds, turkey slices and rice mixture. Makes 4 wraps—enough for 2 hungry kids.

1 serving: 629 Calories; 8.6 g Total Fat (4.2 g Mono, 2.6 g Poly, 1.4 g Sat); 14 mg Cholesterol; 124 g Carbohydrate; 2 g Fibre; 14 g Protein; 2007 mg Sodium

Pictured on page 38.

Zap It!

Now you're cooking! In this chapter you're dealing with hot stuff, but there's one thing to keep in mind—microwaves come in many different powers. Some cook very fast, others take a little bit longer. We tested our recipes in a 900 Watt microwave and that's how we determined our cooking times. If your microwave has more power, you need to keep an eye on your food so it doesn't overcook. If your microwave has less power, you may need to cook your food a little longer than our recommended time.

18 things you find in a kitchen

```
I  N  A  W  A  K  P  S  B  D  J  B  B  D  E
K  C  Q  L  N  L  T  N  I  M  J  A  Z  G  S
N  F  E  I  U  N  K  S  I  H  W  K  D  M  P
I  H  F  C  E  T  H  U  M  B  T  I  C  S  O
S  E  A  V  R  W  A  B  D  H  R  N  P  E  O
Q  N  O  V  A  E  R  P  O  F  X  G  A  P  N
G  L  A  S  S  D  A  E  S  W  T  S  N  R  H
Y  Y  H  X  P  H  P  M  X  Q  L  H  R  E  K
W  E  F  O  R  K  Y  L  S  I  D  E  E  T  K
R  H  T  P  U  C  N  Y  A  C  M  E  N  S  R
N  Y  V  Z  W  G  C  Y  A  T  O  T  W  A  J
B  B  T  T  W  Z  I  F  K  C  E  O  Z  O  L
D  S  C  O  T  B  I  S  V  T  F  K  P  T  X
E  J  G  V  F  X  N  I  B  S  Q  Q  F  Z  T
E  V  A  W  O  R  C  I  M  Z  O  K  L  C  V
```

BAKING SHEET	BOWL	CUP
DISHWASHER	FORK	FRIDGE
GLASS	ICE CREAM SCOOP	KNIFE
MICROWAVE	MIXER	OVEN
PAN	PLATE	POT
SINK	SPATULA	SPOON

The Great Apple & Cheese Squeeze, below

The Great Apple & Cheese Squeeze

Put the squeeze on hunger with this apple and cheese-filled snack.

Get It Together: grater, measuring spoons, dry measures, sharp knife, cutting board, microwave-safe plate

1.
Flour tortilla (6 inch, 15 cm, diameter)	**1**	**1**
Grated medium Cheddar cheese	**2 tbsp.**	**30 mL**
Thinly sliced apple	**1/3 cup**	**75 mL**
Grated medium Cheddar cheese	**2 tbsp.**	**30 mL**

1. Place tortilla on plate. Sprinkle first amount of cheese on 1 half of tortilla. Arrange apple over cheese. Sprinkle second amount of cheese over top. Fold uncovered side of tortilla over filling. Press down lightly. Microwave on high (100%) for about 30 seconds until cheese is melted. Cut tortilla in half. Makes enough for 1 kid.

1 serving: 226 Calories; 11.5 g Total Fat (3.8 g Mono, 0.6 g Poly, 6.5 g Sat); 30 mg Cholesterol; 21 g Carbohydrate; 1 g Fibre; 10 g Protein; 314 mg Sodium

Pictured above.

Zap It!

Fruit Island

You certainly won't go hungry if you're ever stranded on this island!

Get It Together: sharp knife, cutting board, dry measures, measuring spoons, liquid measures, small microwave-safe dish, mixing spoon, 2 small bowls

1.	Mixed dried fruit, chopped	1/4 cup	60 mL
	Apple juice	1 tbsp.	15 mL
	Water	1 tbsp.	15 mL
2.	Vanilla yogurt	1 cup	250 mL

1. Put first 3 ingredients into dish. Microwave, covered, on high (100%) for 1 minute. Stir. Microwave, uncovered, on high (100%) for another 30 to 60 seconds until fruit is soft and liquid is evaporated. Stir.

2. Spoon yogurt into bowls. Spoon half of fruit mixture in centre of each bowl. Makes 2 tasty snacks.

1 serving: 138 Calories; 1.5 g Total Fat (0 g Mono, 0 g Poly, 1.3 g Sat); 10 mg Cholesterol; 23 g Carbohydrate; 1 g Fibre; 6 g Protein; 113 mg Sodium

Pictured on page 43.

Cookbot 3000 Tip: There are many varieties of mixed dried fruit. Are you in the mood for mango mania, sweet papaya, sticky pineapple or tart cranberries? Mix it up as much as you like, just make sure you keep the amount the same.

Buffoon's Macaroons

You won't find an easier way to make these chewy chocolate treats.

Get It Together: dry measures, measuring spoons, medium bowl, small bowl, whisk, mixing spoon, parchment paper, scissors, 2 microwave-safe dinner plates

1.	Egg white product (or 1 egg white)	2 tbsp.	30 mL
2.	Icing (confectioner's) sugar	1/3 cup	75 mL
	Cocoa, sifted if lumpy	1 tsp.	5 mL
3.	Medium unsweetened coconut	3/4 cup	175 mL

(continued on next page)

Zap It!

1. Put egg white into medium bowl. Beat with the whisk until bubbly on top.

2. Put icing sugar and cocoa into small bowl. Stir. Add to egg white. Mix well.

3. Add coconut. Stir. Cut two 6 inch (15 cm) pieces of parchment paper. Place a parchment sheet on each plate. Using a rounded tablespoon of coconut mixture for each, spoon 4 mounds onto each sheet. Make sure the mounds are spaced about 1 1/2 inches (3.8 cm) apart. Place 1 plate in the microwave. Microwave on high (100%) for about 90 seconds until the mixture is firm. Remove the plate from the microwave. Let cool for 5 minutes. Repeat with the second plate. Makes 8 macaroons—enough to share if you're feeling generous.

1 serving: 271 Calories; 18.0 g Total Fat (0.8 g Mono, 0.2 g Poly, 16.0 g Sat); 0 mg Cholesterol; 27 g Carbohydrate; 5 g Fibre; 4 g Protein; 38 mg Sodium

Pictured below.

Top: Fruit Island, page 42 Bottom: Buffoon's Macaroons, page 42

Left: Ex-Cous Me Peas, page 45 Right: Micro-Chips, below

Micro-Chips

These crisp pita chips are great for dipping!

Get It Together: measuring spoons, cutting board, pastry brush, paper towel, sharp knife

1.	Pita bread (8 inch, 20 cm, diameter)	1	1
	Cooking oil	1/4 tsp.	1 mL
2.	Salt, sprinkle		

1. Place pita bread on cutting board. Brush cooking oil on one side of pita bread.
2. Sprinkle with salt. Cut pita bread into 8 triangles. Place paper towel in microwave. Lay pita pieces on top in a single layer. Microwave on high (100%) for 1 minute. Wait for about 2 minutes until crisp and cool enough to handle. Makes enough for 1 cyber chef.

1 serving: 175 Calories; 1.9 g Total Fat (0.7 g Mono, 0.7 g Poly, 0.2 g Sat); 0 mg Cholesterol; 33 g Carbohydrate; 1 g Fibre; 5 g Protein; 322 mg Sodium

Pictured above.

(continued on next page)

Zap It!

CINNAMON MICRO-CHIPS: Instead of salt, sprinkle with 1/2 tsp. (2 mL) granulated sugar and 1/8 tsp. (0.5 mL) ground cinnamon before cooking.

HERBED MICRO-CHIPS: Add a sprinkle of Italian seasoning with the salt before cooking.

SALT AND PEPPER MICRO-CHIPS: Add a sprinkle of pepper with the salt before cooking.

SEASONED MICRO-CHIPS: Instead of salt, use a sprinkle of seasoned salt before cooking.

Ex-Cous Me Peas

You don't need an excuse to try something new. Couscous is actually tiny bits of pasta—and this version is good and spicy!

Get It Together: measuring spoons, liquid measures, dry measures, grater, small microwave-safe bowl, mixing spoon, fork

1.	Prepared chicken broth	1/4 cup	60 mL
	Chunky salsa	2 tbsp.	30 mL
	Frozen peas	2 tbsp.	30 mL
	Chili powder	1/8 tsp.	0.5 mL
2.	Couscous	1/4 cup	60 mL
3.	Grated mild Cheddar cheese	1 tbsp.	15 mL

1. Put first 4 ingredients into bowl. Stir. Microwave, covered, on high (100%) for about 2 minutes until boiling.

2. Add couscous. Stir. Cover with lid. Wait for about 5 minutes until couscous is tender and liquid is soaked up. Stir with fork.

3. Sprinkle cheese over top. Cover with lid. Wait for about 1 minute until cheese is melted. Makes about 1 cup (250 mL)—enough for 1 kid.

1 serving: 232 Calories; 3.0 g Total Fat (0.8 g Mono, 0.3 g Poly, 1.6 g Sat); 7 mg Cholesterol; 41 g Carbohydrate; 3 g Fibre; 9 g Protein; 652 mg Sodium

Pictured on page 44.

Sea Wolf BBQ Sub

Are you hungry enough to wolf down this saucy meatball sub? If you have a leftover hamburger, cut it into pieces and use it instead of meatballs.

Get It Together: measuring spoons, grater, dry measures, sharp knife, cutting board, table knife, microwave-safe plate, paper towel

1.	Barbecue sauce	2 tbsp.	30 mL
	Submarine bun (8 inch, 20 cm), split	1	1
	Grated medium Cheddar cheese	1/3 cup	75 mL
	Refried beans	2 tbsp.	30 mL
2.	Lettuce leaf	1	1
	Dill pickle, sliced	1	1
3.	Frozen (or leftover) cooked meatballs	5	5
4.	Barbecue sauce	2 tbsp.	30 mL

1. Spread barbecue sauce on top half of submarine bun. Sprinkle cheese over barbecue sauce. Spread refried beans on bottom half of submarine bun.

2. Place lettuce over refried beans. Arrange pickle slices over lettuce.

3. Place meatballs on plate. Cover loosely with paper towel. Microwave on high (100%) for about 2 minutes until meatballs are hot. Cut meatballs in half. Arrange meatball halves over pickle slices. Place the other half of submarine bun over meatballs, cheese-side down.

4. Serve with second amount of barbecue sauce for dipping. Makes 1 submarine sandwich—enough to feed 2 hungry sea cadets.

1 serving: 396 Calories; 17.8 g Total Fat (6.5 g Mono, 1.7 g Poly, 7.8 g Sat); 79 mg Cholesterol; 35 g Carbohydrate; 4 g Fibre; 23 g Protein; 1497 mg Sodium

Pictured on page 47.

Cookbot 3000 Tip: Store the remaining refried beans in an airtight container in the fridge for up to 1 week, or freeze in smaller amounts to use in other recipes.

Top: Sea Wolf BBQ Sub, above
Bottom: Folded Pizza Subwich, page 48

Zap It!

Folded Pizza Subwich

Tastes like a pizza and looks like one too—until you fold it over and it becomes a sub!

Get It Together: measuring spoons, sharp knife, cutting board, grater, dry measures, microwave-safe plate, spoon

1.	**Pizza sauce**	**2 tbsp.**	**30 mL**
	Hot dog bun, split	**1**	**1**
2.	**Pepperoni slices**	**3**	**3**
	Thinly sliced red pepper rings, cut in half	**3**	**3**
	Grated medium Cheddar cheese	**1/2 cup**	**125 mL**

1. Spread pizza sauce on bun halves. Place them, side-by-side, on plate.
2. Arrange pepperoni slices over sauce. Arrange red pepper over pepperoni. Sprinkle with cheese. Microwave on high (100%) for about 1 minute until cheese is melted. Let cool for 3 minutes. Place 1 bun half on top of other, cheese-sides facing each other, to make a sandwich. Makes 1 really tasty subwich.

1 serving: 531 Calories; 35.6 g Total Fat (12.8 g Mono, 3.0 g Poly, 17.7 g Sat); 85 mg Cholesterol; 26 g Carbohydrate; 2 g Fibre; 26 g Protein; 1360 mg Sodium

Pictured on page 47.

Space Pod Soup

Green space pods float in a galaxy of chicken noodle soup!

Get It Together: liquid measures, sharp knife, cutting board, dry measures, medium microwave-safe bowl, mixing spoon, ladle, 2 soup bowls

1.	**Package of instant noodles with chicken seasoning packet**	**3 oz.**	**85 g**
	Water	**2 cups**	**500 mL**
2.	**Sugar snap peas, trimmed and cut in half**	**3/4 cup**	**175 mL**
	Diced cooked chicken	**1/2 cup**	**125 mL**

(continued on next page)

1. Break noodles into 6 pieces. Put them into medium bowl. Set seasoning packet aside. Pour water over noodles. Microwave, covered, on high (100%) for 3 minutes. Stir.

2. Add peas and chicken. Stir. Microwave, covered, on high (100%) for about 2 minutes until peas start to soften. Add seasoning packet. Stir. Spoon into soup bowls. Makes about 3 cups (750 mL)—enough for 2 hungry astronauts.

1 serving: 230 Calories; 3.1 g Total Fat (0.9 g Mono, 0.6 g Poly, 0.7 g Sat); 31 mg Cholesterol; 31 g Carbohydrate; 2 g Fibre; 18 g Protein; 490 mg Sodium

Pictured below.

Cookbot 3000 Tip: Not sure how to trim sugar snap peas? It's easy! Just snap or break the stem end of the pea and pull the string that comes with it all the way down the length of the pea. Throw the stringy part away.

Space Pod Soup, page 48

Fry It!

Hear that sizzle? You will soon! Get your frying pan and your pancake lifter ready and you're good-to-go.

> **Q1:** Why did the tomato turn red?
>
> **Q2:** What kind of soda would you never drink?

Answers: **Q1:** It saw salad dressing **Q2:** Baking soda

Hit-The-Trail Mix

Has your get-up-and-go got-up-and-went? Give yourself enough energy to make it through to dinnertime with this fruit and nut mix.

Get It Together: dry measures, measuring spoons, small frying pan, wooden spoon, small bowl

1.	**Whole natural almonds**	1/4 cup	60 mL
2.	**Unsalted sunflower seeds**	2 tbsp.	30 mL
3.	**Dried papaya chunks**	1/4 cup	60 mL
	Dried pineapple chunks	1/4 cup	60 mL
	Raisins	1/4 cup	60 mL

1. Put almonds into frying pan. Heat and stir with wooden spoon on medium for 3 to 4 minutes until lightly browned. Transfer almonds to bowl.

2. Put sunflower seeds into same frying pan. Heat and stir on medium for 1 to 2 minutes until golden. Add to almonds.

3. Add remaining 3 ingredients to almond mixture. Stir. Let cool for 5 minutes. Makes about 1 1/2 cups (375 mL)—enough for 2 happy campers.

1 serving: 325 Calories; 13.4 g Total Fat (6.6 g Mono, 4.9 g Poly, 1.2 g Sat); 0 mg Cholesterol; 51 g Carbohydrate; 8 g Fibre; 7 g Protein; 15 mg Sodium

Pictured below.

Creampuff Tip: If you can't find dried papaya chunks, use dried mango, apricots, dates or figs. Any one of these is a great-tasting substitution.

Hit-The-Trail Mix, above

Stir-Crazy Granola

Feeling a little bored? Well then, hop to it and stir-fry yourself some granola!

Get It Together: measuring spoons, dry measures, small frying pan, wooden spoon, plate

1.			
	Butter	1 tbsp.	15 mL
	Sesame seeds	2 tbsp.	30 mL
	Honey	1 tbsp.	15 mL
2.	Large flake rolled oats	1/2 cup	125 mL
	Sliced almonds	2 tbsp.	30 mL
	Medium sweetened coconut	1 tbsp.	15 mL
	Ground cinnamon, sprinkle		

1. Melt and spread butter in frying pan on medium. Add sesame seeds and honey. Cook, stirring often with wooden spoon, for about 2 minutes until sesame seeds are golden.

2. Add remaining 4 ingredients. Cook, stirring often, for 2 to 3 minutes until oatmeal mixture is golden. Spoon oatmeal mixture onto plate. Spread out evenly with wooden spoon. Let cool for about 5 minutes until dry. Break apart larger pieces. Makes about 1 1/3 cups (325 mL) —enough for you and a stir-crazy friend.

1 serving: 261 Calories; 15.1 g Total Fat (5.1 g Mono, 2.9 g Poly, 5.1 g Sat); 15 mg Cholesterol; 26 g Carbohydrate; 4 g Fibre; 6 g Protein; 47 mg Sodium

Pictured on page 53.

Creampuff Tip: Make sure everything is measured beforehand and ready to add to the pan so the sesame seeds don't burn. Although you might be tempted to sample your creation right away, be sure to wait until it's cool so you don't burn yourself!

Q: Who grants wishes to cows?

A: Dairy godmothers.

Stir-Crazy Granola, page 52

Ham & Cheese Wafflewich

Forget the bread—ham and cheese taste so much better in a waffle sandwich!

Get It Together: measuring spoons, grater, small frying pan with lid, table knife, pancake lifter

1.	**Butter**	2 tsp.	10 mL
2.	**Prepared mustard**	1/2 tsp.	2 mL
	Slice of deli ham, cut to fit waffle	1	1
	Frozen waffles	2	2
	Grated medium Cheddar cheese	2 tbsp.	30 mL

1. Melt and spread butter in frying pan on medium.

2. Spread mustard on one side of ham. Place 1 waffle in pan. Sprinkle cheese over waffle. Place ham over cheese. Place second waffle on top of ham. Cover with lid. Cook for about 2 minutes until waffle is browned on bottom. Use lifter to check. Press top waffle with lifter so it will stick to melting cheese. Carefully turn wafflewich over. Cover with lid. Cook for another 2 minutes until both sides of wafflewich are browned and cheese is melted. Makes 1 wafflewich for 1 lucky kid.

1 serving: 335 Calories; 18.6 g Total Fat (3.3 g Mono, 0.4 g Poly, 9.3 g Sat); 65 mg Cholesterol; 30 g Carbohydrate; 1 g Fibre; 13 g Protein; 914 mg Sodium

Pictured on divider.

Fry It!

UFO

What's that up in the sky? It's an Unidentified Frying Object! Serve this alien edible with a slice of toast or on a toasted English muffin half for a more filling snack.

Get It Together: measuring spoons, table knife, can opener, grater, small frying pan with lid, pancake lifter

1.	**Cooking oil**	**1/4 tsp.**	**1 mL**
	Deli ham slice, cut to fit pineapple slice	**1**	**1**
	Canned pineapple slice	**1**	**1**
2.	**Grated medium Cheddar cheese**	**2 tbsp.**	**30 mL**
	Pepper, sprinkle		

1. Heat cooking oil in frying pan on medium for 3 minutes. Put ham and pineapple slice in pan beside each other. Cook for about 2 minutes until both are starting to brown on bottom. Use lifter to check. Turn ham and pineapple slice over. Cook for 1 minute. Place pineapple slice on top of ham slice.

2. Sprinkle cheese and pepper over pineapple. Cover with lid. Turn down heat to medium-low. Cook for about 2 minutes until cheese is melted. Makes 1 tasty treat.

1 serving: 132 Calories; 6.1 g Total Fat (2.0 g Mono, 0.5 g Poly, 3.1 g Sat); 25 mg Cholesterol; 12 g Carbohydrate; 1 g Fibre; 8 g Protein; 398 mg Sodium

Pictured on page 55.

1. Kooky Zooky Coins, page 56
2. UFO, above
3. Cluckin' 'Za, page 57

Creampuff Tip: Keep the remaining pineapple slices in an airtight container in the refrigerator for up to 5 days. Pineapple slices make a great snack—and don't forget to drink the juice!

Kooky Zooky Coins

These crispy, golden zucchini coins are delicious on their own or with
4 O'Clock Fiesta Salsa, page 16.

Get It Together: dry measures, measuring spoons, sharp knife, cutting
board, large resealable freezer bag, medium bowl, whisk, mixing spoon,
plate, large frying pan, pancake lifter

1.	Fine dry bread crumbs	1/3 cup	75 mL
	Celery salt	1/2 tsp.	2 mL
	Pepper	1/4 tsp.	1 mL
	Ground cinnamon	1/8 tsp.	0.5 mL
2.	Large egg	1	1
	Unpeeled zucchini slices, about 1/2 inch (12 mm) thick	20	20
3.	Cooking oil	2 tbsp.	30 mL

1. Put first 4 ingredients into freezer bag. Seal bag. Shake well.

2. Break egg into bowl. Beat with whisk until egg is bubbly on top.
    Add zucchini. Stir until coated. Transfer half of zucchini into bag.
    Seal bag. Shake until coated. Remove zucchini from bag and place
    on plate. Repeat with remaining zucchini and crumb mixture.

3. Heat cooking oil in frying pan on medium for 3 minutes. Arrange zucchini
    in pan in a single layer. Cook for 3 to 5 minutes until golden on bottom.
    Use lifter to check. Turn zucchini slices over. Cook for another 3 to
    5 minutes until golden on both sides. Makes 20 coins for 2 wealthy kids.

1 serving: 229 Calories; 17.1 g Total Fat (9.5 g Mono, 4.6 g Poly, 2.0 g Sat); 93 mg Cholesterol;
14 g Carbohydrate; 1 g Fibre; 5 g Protein; 436 mg Sodium

Pictured on page 55.

Q: What did one
fish say to another?

A: If we keep our
mouths closed, we
won't get caught.

Fry It!

Cluckin' 'Za

Just like pizza but with an egg and potato twist!

Get It Together: measuring spoons, dry measures, sharp knife, cutting board, grater, medium non-stick frying pan with lid, mixing spoon, small bowl, whisk

1.	**Butter**	2 tsp.	10 mL
	Frozen shredded hash brown potatoes	1/2 cup	125 mL
	Finely chopped green onion	1 tbsp.	15 mL
2.	**Large egg**	1	1
	Dried oregano	1/8 tsp.	0.5 mL
	Salt, sprinkle		
	Pepper, sprinkle		
3.	**Deli pepperoni slices**	3	3
	Grated mozzarella cheese	3 tbsp.	50 mL
4.	**Pizza sauce**	1 tbsp.	15 mL

1. Melt and spread butter in frying pan on medium. Add potatoes and onion. Cook for about 5 minutes, stirring occasionally, until potatoes are lightly browned. Spread potatoes evenly in pan.

2. Break egg into bowl. Beat with whisk until egg is bubbly on top. Add next 3 ingredients. Stir. Pour egg mixture evenly over potatoes in pan. Do not stir.

3. Arrange pepperoni slices over top. Sprinkle with cheese. Turn down heat to medium-low. Cover with lid. Cook for 2 to 3 minutes until cheese is melted and egg is firm. Remove pan from heat.

4. Spoon pizza sauce over top. Makes enough for 1 pizza-craving kid.

1 serving: *437 Calories; 36.9 g Total Fat (14.6 g Mono, 3.2 g Poly, 16.4 g Sat); 249 mg Cholesterol; 17 g Carbohydrate; 1 g Fibre; 19 g Protein; 960 mg Sodium*

Pictured on page 55.

Q: Why do fish live in salt water?

A: Because pepper makes them sneeze.

Fry It!

1. Fried Funky Monkey, page 60
2. *El Queso Grande*, page 59
3. *Quelle Surprise!*, page 61

58

El Queso Grande

The name means "big cheese," so if you like cheese and a little spicy Mexican heat, you'll love this sandwich.

Get It Together: measuring spoons, dry measures, table knife, 2 small shallow bowls, whisk, spoon, medium frying pan with lid, pancake lifter

1.	Butter	2 tsp.	10 mL
	Bread slices	2	2
	Grated Mexican cheese blend	1/4 cup	60 mL
2.	Large egg	1	1
	Milk	2 tbsp.	30 mL
	Grated Parmesan cheese	2 tsp.	10 mL
	Pepper, sprinkle		
3.	Fine dry bread crumbs	2 tbsp.	30 mL
	Seasoned salt	1/8 tsp.	0.5 mL
4.	Butter	2 tsp.	10 mL
5.	Salsa	2 tbsp.	30 mL

1. Spread 1 tsp. (5 mL) butter on 1 side of each bread slice. Sprinkle cheese over butter on 1 bread slice. Cover with second bread slice, buttered-side down. Press down firmly on edges to seal.

2. Break egg into 1 bowl. Add milk. Beat with whisk until mixture is bubbly on top. Add Parmesan cheese and pepper. Stir. Dip both sides of sandwich into egg mixture. Let sit in egg mixture for about 2 minutes until all of egg mixture is soaked up into bread.

3. Put bread crumbs and seasoned salt into other bowl. Stir. Gently press both sides of sandwich into crumb mixture until coated.

4. Melt and spread 1 tsp. (5 mL) butter in frying pan on medium. Place sandwich in pan. Turn down heat to medium-low. Cover with lid. Cook for about 5 minutes until golden and crisp on bottom. Use lifter to check. Add remaining butter to pan. Carefully turn sandwich over. Cook for another 6 to 8 minutes until golden and crisp on both sides. Cut sandwich in half.

5. Serve sandwich with salsa for dipping. Makes a big sandwich for 1 hungry kid.

1 serving: 627 Calories; 39.6 g Total Fat (8.3 g Mono, 1.6 g Poly, 20.5 g Sat); 270 mg Cholesterol; 41 g Carbohydrate; 1 g Fibre; 28 g Protein; 1419 mg Sodium

Pictured on page 58.

Fried Funky Monkey

Fried raisin bread with banana and chocolate—does it get any better?

Get It Together: measuring spoons, sharp knife, cutting board, table knife, small frying pan, pancake lifter

1.	Spreadable cream cheese	1 tbsp.	15 mL
	Raisin bread slices	2	2
	Thin banana slices	10	10
	Milk chocolate chips	2 tsp.	10 mL
2.	Butter	2 tsp.	10 mL

1. Spread cream cheese on 1 side of each bread slice. Arrange banana slices over cream cheese on 1 bread slice. Sprinkle chocolate chips over banana slices. Cover with other bread slice, cream cheese-side down.

2. Spread 1 tsp. (5 mL) butter on top side of sandwich. Melt and spread remaining butter in frying pan on medium-low. Carefully place sandwich in pan, buttered-side up. Cook for 3 to 5 minutes until bottom is golden. Use lifter to check. Carefully turn sandwich over. Cook for another 3 to 5 minutes until both sides are golden and chocolate chips are melted. Cut sandwich into 4 pieces. Makes 1 funky monkey.

1 serving: 346 Calories; 17.2 g Total Fat (3.9 g Mono, 0.8 g Poly, 10.2 g Sat); 37 mg Cholesterol; 45 g Carbohydrate; 4 g Fibre; 6 g Protein; 313 mg Sodium

Pictured on page 58.

Creampuff Tip: Try butterscotch chips or peanut butter chips instead of chocolate chips.

Q: What do you call a book about eggs?

A: A yolk book.

Quelle Surprise!

The surprise in this French toast is the raspberry centre!

Get It Together: measuring spoons, small plate, fork, small bowl, whisk, shallow pie plate, large frying pan, pancake lifter, plate, knife

1.	**Cream cheese, softened**	**2 tbsp.**	**30 mL**
	Raspberry jam (not jelly)	**2 tbsp.**	**30 mL**
2.	**Large egg**	**1**	**1**
	Milk	**2 tbsp.**	**30 mL**
3.	**Butter**	**2 tsp.**	**10 mL**
	Bread slices	**2**	**2**
4.	**Icing (confectioner's) sugar**	**2 tsp.**	**10 mL**
	Ground cinnamon, sprinkle		

1. Put cream cheese and jam onto plate. Mash with fork until smooth. Set aside.

2. Break egg into small bowl. Add milk. Beat with whisk until mixture is bubbly on top. Pour into pie plate.

3. Melt and spread butter in frying pan on medium-high. Dip bread slices into egg mixture, coating both sides. Arrange bread slices in pan. Cook for 1 to 2 minutes until the bread slices are browned on bottom. Use lifter to check. Turn bread slices over. Cook for another 1 to 2 minutes until browned on both sides. Remove bread slices to plate. Spread the cream cheese mixture on 1 bread slice. Cover with remaining bread slice. Cut sandwich in half.

4. Sprinkle icing sugar and cinnamon over top. Makes 1 surprising snack.

1 serving: 515 Calories; 26.1 g Total Fat (4.1 g Mono, 1.0 g Poly, 13.7 g Sat); 239 mg Cholesterol; 60 g Carbohydrate; 0 g Fibre; 13 g Protein; 500 mg Sodium

Pictured on page 58.

Creampuff Tip: To soften cream cheese, let it sit on the counter for about 30 minutes.

Use jam, not jelly, because it's thicker and will mix better with the cream cheese. Try different flavours of jam, if you like.

Gold Dust Flapjacks

Thar's gold in these here pancakes (well, applesauce, anyway)! Try them cold with yogurt or applesauce for a dip.

Get It Together: dry measures, liquid measures, measuring spoons, medium bowl, mixing spoon, small bowl, whisk, large frying pan, spoon, pancake lifter, serving plate, foil

1.	Pancake mix	1 1/4 cups	300 mL
2.	Large egg	1	1
	Vanilla yogurt	3/4 cup	175 mL
	Applesauce	1/2 cup	125 mL
3.	Cooking oil	1 tbsp.	15 mL

1. Put pancake mix into medium bowl. Dig a hole in centre of pancake mix with mixing spoon.

2. Break egg into small bowl. Beat with whisk until egg is bubbly on top. Add yogurt and applesauce. Stir well. Pour yogurt mixture into hole in pancake mix. Stir just until pancake mix is moistened. Batter will be lumpy.

3. Heat 1 tsp. (5 mL) cooking oil in frying pan on medium-low for 3 minutes. Measure batter into pan, using about 1/4 cup (60 mL) for each pancake. Use back of spoon to spread batter into a 4 inch (10 cm) wide circle. Cook for about 3 minutes until bubbles form on top and edges of pancakes look dry. Use lifter to turn pancakes over. Cook for another 2 to 3 minutes until bottoms are golden. Use lifter to check. Remove pancakes to serving plate. Cover with foil to keep warm. Repeat with remaining batter, heating more cooking oil in pan before each batch, if necessary, so pancakes won't stick. Makes 8 pancakes—a filling snack for 2 hungry kids.

1 serving: 446 Calories; 11.7 g Total Fat (5.3 g Mono, 2.9 g Poly, 2.2 g Sat); 99 mg Cholesterol; 70 g Carbohydrate; 5 g Fibre; 14 g Protein; 1009 mg Sodium

Pictured on page 64.

Creampuff Tip: Experiment a little! Make these pancakes using different flavours of applesauce and yogurt until you find the combination you like the best.

Fry It!

No Dud Spud Cakes

These spuds in pancake form are super easy to make—
you'll never end up with a dud!

Get It Together: measuring spoons, dry measures, small bowl, whisk,
large frying pan, spoon, pancake lifter

1.	**Large egg**	1	1
	Seasoned salt	1/4 tsp.	1 mL
	Pepper, sprinkle		
	Garlic powder, sprinkle		
2.	**Frozen shredded hash brown potatoes**	1 cup	250 mL
	All-purpose flour	1 tbsp.	15 mL
3.	**Cooking oil**	1 tsp.	5 mL
4.	**Ketchup**	2 tbsp.	30 mL

1. Put first 4 ingredients into bowl. Beat with whisk until mixture is bubbly on top.

2. Add potatoes. Sprinkle flour over top. Stir until potatoes are coated.

3. Heat cooking oil in frying pan on medium for 3 minutes. Spoon potato mixture into 4 mounds in pan. Flatten each mound with back of spoon. Try not to let cakes touch each other. Cook for 3 to 4 minutes until bottoms are golden. Use lifter to check. Turn cakes over. Cook for another 3 to 4 minutes until cakes are golden on both sides.

4. Serve cakes with ketchup for dipping. Makes 4 spud cakes—enough for you to share with a friend.

1 serving: 147 Calories; 9.6 g Total Fat (4.5 g Mono, 1.6 g Poly, 2.8 g Sat); 93 mg Cholesterol; 21 g Carbohydrate; 1 g Fibre; 5 g Protein; 408 mg Sodium

Pictured on page 64.

Creampuff Tip: Instead of ketchup, try other dips like sour cream or salsa.

Q: What does the invisible man drink?

A: Evaporated milk.

Humpty Dumpty Burrito

Don't bother trying to put Humpty Dumpty back together again—just scramble him up and serve him in a burrito! Try with your favourite salsa or with 4 O'Clock Fiesta Salsa, page 16.

Get It Together: grater, measuring spoons, liquid measures, small bowl, whisk, small frying pan with lid, plate, spoon

1.	**Large egg**	1	1
	Milk	1 tsp.	5 mL
	Salt, sprinkle		
	Pepper, sprinkle		
2.	**Butter**	1 tsp.	5 mL
3.	**Grated medium Cheddar cheese**	2 tbsp.	30 mL
4.	**Flour tortilla (6 inch, 15 cm, diameter)**	1	1
	Salsa	1/4 cup	60 mL

1. Break egg into bowl. Add next 3 ingredients. Beat with whisk until mixture is bubbly on top.

2. Melt and spread butter in frying pan on medium. Pour egg mixture into pan. Heat and stir for about 1 minute until egg mixture is almost cooked. It should still be a little soft and creamy.

3. Sprinkle cheese on top. Remove pan from heat. Cover with lid. Wait for about 1 minute until cheese is melted.

4. Place tortilla on plate. Spoon the egg mixture in a line across middle of tortilla, leaving a small edge uncovered on both sides. Fold small edges over filling. Roll up from bottom to enclose filling. Place seam-side down on plate. Serve with salsa. Makes enough for 1 spicy kid.

1 serving: 278 Calories; 15.7 g Total Fat (5.6 g Mono, 1.4 g Poly, 7.5 g Sat); 211 mg Cholesterol; 21 g Carbohydrate; 2 g Fibre; 13 g Protein; 597 mg Sodium

Pictured on page 64.

1. Gold Dust Flapjacks, page 62
2. No Dud Spud Cakes, page 63
3. Humpty Dumpty Burrito, above

Fry It!

Boil It!

They say a watched pot never boils. Put that theory to test in this chapter and have your snacks bubbling on the stovetop in no time.

find 15 flavours of ice cream

```
S  W  E  U  N  C  S  I  A  Z  G  X  U  A  X
U  T  O  L  O  I  N  C  D  T  N  Z  T  L  X
Y  T  R  F  P  O  F  B  N  C  E  Y  Q  L  H
O  R  F  A  M  A  O  I  H  C  A  T  S  I  P
P  E  R  U  W  U  M  Q  I  C  P  E  R  N  F
E  W  P  E  W  B  X  N  H  B  O  D  F  A  M
Z  S  I  U  B  L  E  O  W  N  L  E  B  V  H
H  C  A  E  P  P  C  R  V  N  I  M  U  G  O
M  L  X  A  A  O  S  O  R  I  T  I  C  C  H
E  G  D  T  L  Z  J  A  C  Y  A  L  N  A  T
X  E  M  A  A  Y  X  D  R  O  N  V  O  R  C
Q  D  T  R  A  I  N  B  O  W  N  F  L  A  W
B  E  A  U  A  M  M  M  S  C  V  U  D  M  F
Q  F  C  A  G  O  X  O  F  F  H  E  T  E  Y
J  B  N  E  E  R  Z  H  O  K  K  H  A  L  U
```

CARAMEL	CHOCOLATE	COCONUT
COFFEE	LIME	MAPLE
MINT	NEAPOLITAN	PEACH
PISTACHIO	RAINBOW	RASPBERRY
SPUMONI	STRAWBERRY	VANILLA

Don't Box Me In Pudding

Pudding doesn't come from a box! This is how real chefs make it. If you want to eat this cold, cover with plastic wrap that touches the top of the pudding, and refrigerate for 2 hours.

Get It Together: liquid measures, measuring spoons, small dish, mixing spoon, small saucepan, 2 cereal bowls

1.	**Mashed overripe banana**	1/4 cup	60 mL
	Lemon juice	1/4 tsp.	1 mL
2.	**Egg yolk (large)**	1	1
	Milk	3/4 cup	175 mL
	Granulated sugar	2 tbsp.	30 mL
	Cornstarch	4 tsp.	20 mL
3.	**Butter**	1 tsp.	5 mL
4.	**Chocolate chips**	1 tbsp.	15 mL
	Banana chips	4	4

1. Put banana and lemon juice into dish. Mix well.

2. Put next 4 ingredients into saucepan. Mix well. Cook on medium for about 5 minutes, stirring constantly, until mixture starts to boil and thicken. Add banana mixture. Stir. Cook for about 1 minute, stirring constantly, until mixture is boiling. Cook and stir for 1 minute. Remove pan from heat.

3. Add butter to banana mixture. Stir until melted. Wait for about 5 minutes, stirring occasionally, until slightly cooled. Spoon into bowls.

4. Top each bowl of pudding with half of chocolate chips and banana chips. Makes about 1 cup (250 mL)—enough for 2 kids to enjoy.

1 serving: 245 Calories; 9.2 g Total Fat (1.1 g Mono, 0.4 g Poly, 4.4 g Sat); 107 mg Cholesterol; 36 g Carbohydrate; 1 g Fibre; 5 g Protein; 66 mg Sodium

Pictured on page 68.

Monsieur Auk-Auk Tip: If you don't have an egg separator, you can separate the yolk from the egg white by cracking the egg as close to the middle as possible, being careful not to break the yolk. Hold the half of the shell with the yolk in it in one hand and the other half of the shell in the other hand. Allow as much of the egg white as possible to run out of the shell and into a small bowl. Then, transfer the yolk to the other half of the shell, allowing more of the egg white to run out. Repeat, a few times, until most of the egg white has been removed.

Rock-A-Hula Sauce

This rockin' sweet pineapple sauce is great on pancakes, waffles, yogurt or ice cream.

Get It Together: can opener, liquid measures, measuring spoons, small saucepan, mixing spoon

1.			
Canned crushed pineapple, with juice	3/4 cup	175 mL
Cinnamon honey	2 tbsp.	30 mL
Butter	1 tbsp.	15 mL
Cornstarch	1 tsp.	5 mL

1. Put pineapple with juice into saucepan. Add remaining 3 ingredients. Stir until well mixed. Cook and stir on medium for about 10 minutes until boiling and thickened. Remove pan from heat. Cool. Makes about 1 cup (250 mL)—enough for 2 rockin' kids.

1 serving: 176 Calories; 5.5 g Total Fat (0 g Mono, 0 g Poly, 3.5 g Sat); 15 mg Cholesterol; 31 g Carbohydrate; 1 g Fibre; 0 g Protein; 53 mg Sodium

Pictured on page 68.

Monsieur Auk-Auk Tip: If you don't have cinnamon honey, just use the same amount of regular honey with a sprinkle of ground cinnamon.

Store the leftover crushed pineapple in an airtight container in the refrigerator for up to 1 week.

If you aren't sharing the sauce with a friend, save the other half in an airtight container in the refrigerator for up to 1 week. Reheat the sauce in the microwave, covered, on high (100%) for 30 seconds. Stir. Microwave for another 30 seconds.

1. Don't Box Me In Pudding, page 67
2. Marshmallow Berry Meld, page 70
3. Wonka's Dream Sauce, page 70
4. Rock-A-Hula Sauce, above

Marshmallow Berry Meld

When marshmallow and berries become fused, an unstoppable topping is born!
Great over ice cream or cake.

Get It Together: sharp knife, cutting board, measuring spoons,
dry measures, small saucepan, mixing spoon

1.	Large marshmallows, cut up	3	3
	Milk	2 tbsp.	30 mL
	Butter	1 tbsp.	15 mL
2.	Frozen mixed berries	1/2 cup	125 mL
	Icing (confectioner's) sugar	1/4 cup	60 mL

1. Put first 3 ingredients into saucepan. Cook and stir on low for about
   5 minutes until marshmallows are melted and hot.

2. Add berries and icing sugar. Cook and stir for 2 to 3 minutes until
   berries are softened and warm. Makes about 2/3 cup (150 mL)—
   enough for 1 kid.

1 serving: *322 Calories; 11.7 g Total Fat (trace Mono, trace Poly, 7.4 g Sat); 33 mg Cholesterol;
53 g Carbohydrate; 2 g Fibre; 2 g Protein; 124 mg Sodium*

Pictured on page 68.

Wonka's Dream Sauce

A chocolate and caramel sauce that's perfect for pouring on pancakes
or dipping with fruit or cookies.

Get It Together: dry measures, measuring spoons, small saucepan,
mixing spoon

1.	Brown sugar, packed	1/4 cup	60 mL
	Butter	2 tbsp.	30 mL
	Water	1 tbsp.	15 mL
2.	Whipping cream	3 tbsp.	50 mL
3.	Semi-sweet chocolate chips	2 tbsp.	30 mL

1. Put first 3 ingredients into saucepan. Heat and stir on medium-low
   for 3 to 5 minutes until sugar is dissolved.

(continued on next page)

2. Add whipping cream. Cook, uncovered, for 10 to 12 minutes, stirring occasionally, until boiling and thickened enough to coat spoon when lifted from mixture. Remove pan from heat.

3. Add chocolate chips. Stir until smooth. Makes about 1/2 cup (125 mL)—enough sauce for 2 chocolate-craving kids.

1 serving: 328 Calories; 22.0 g Total Fat (3.3 g Mono, 0.4 g Poly, 13.7 g Sat); 59 mg Cholesterol; 34 g Carbohydrate; 1 g Fibre; 1 g Protein; 110 mg Sodium

Pictured on page 68.

Oodles Of Noodles Soup

Do you go gaga for noodles? Then this is your soup!

Get It Together: liquid measures, dry measures, medium saucepan, mixing spoon

1.	Vegetable cocktail juice	1 cup	250 mL
	Water	1 cup	250 mL
2.	Package of instant noodles with seasoning packet	3 oz.	85 g
	Frozen mixed vegetables	1 cup	250 mL

1. Put vegetable cocktail and water into saucepan. Bring to a boil on medium-high.

2. Break noodles into large chunks. Carefully add noodles with seasoning packet and mixed vegetables to juice mixture. Stir. Turn down heat to medium-low. Cook, uncovered, for 3 to 4 minutes, stirring occasionally, until vegetables start to soften. Makes about 3 cups (750 mL)—oodles of soup for 2 kids.

1 serving: 222 Calories; 0.8 g Total Fat (trace Mono, 0.1 g Poly, 0.1 g Sat); 0 mg Cholesterol; 46 g Carbohydrate; 5 g Fibre; 10 g Protein; 818 mg Sodium

Pictured on page 73.

Monsieur Auk-Auk Tip: Use your favourite flavour of instant noodle soup.

Bandito's Broth

Say *olé* to this creamy Mexican-flavoured cheese and chicken soup. Add extra salsa if you're an extreme bandito.

Get It Together: can opener, liquid measures, sharp knife, cutting board, dry measures, grater, small saucepan, mixing spoon, small cup, ladle, 2 soup bowls

1.	Canned condensed cream of chicken soup (about half of a 10 oz., 284 mL, can)	1/2 cup	125 mL
	Chopped cooked chicken	1/2 cup	125 mL
	Chunky salsa	1/2 cup	125 mL
	Frozen mixed vegetables	1/2 cup	125 mL
	Milk	1/2 cup	125 mL
2.	Grated medium Cheddar cheese	1/2 cup	125 mL
	Tortilla corn chips, broken into large pieces	1/2 cup	125 mL
3.	Tortilla corn chips, broken into large pieces	1/2 cup	125 mL

1. Put first 5 ingredients into saucepan. Mix well. Heat and stir on medium for about 8 minutes until boiling. Turn down heat to medium-low. Cook, uncovered, for another 2 minutes until vegetables are soft.

2. Put 2 tbsp. (30 mL) cheese into cup. Set aside. Add remaining cheese and first amount of chips to soup mixture. Heat and stir for about 30 seconds until cheese is melted and chips are softened. Ladle soup into bowls.

3. Sprinkle half of second amount of tortilla chips and remaining cheese over each bowl of soup. Makes about 2 cups (500 mL)—enough for 2 banditos.

1 serving: 390 Calories; 20.0 g Total Fat (5.0 g Mono, 2.0 g Poly, 8.8 g Sat); 71 mg Cholesterol; 29 g Carbohydrate; 4 g Fibre; 23 g Protein; 1166 mg Sodium

Pictured on page 73.

Monsieur Auk-Auk Tip: Store the remaining condensed soup in an airtight container in the refrigerator for up to 3 days. Use it to make another batch of Bandito's Broth or in another recipe.

Boil It!

1. Bandito's Broth,
   page 72
2. Oodles Of Noodles Soup,
   page 71
3. Smashed Potato Soup,
   page 74

73

Smashed Potato Soup

Mashed potatoes in a soup? It's simply smashing!

Get It Together: vegetable peeler, sharp knife, cutting board, dry measures, liquid measures, measuring spoons, grater, small saucepan, potato masher, mixing spoon

1.	Chopped peeled potato	1 cup	250 mL
	Water	1/2 cup	125 mL
	Chopped onion	1/4 cup	60 mL
2.	Grated mozzarella cheese	1/2 cup	125 mL
	Milk	1/2 cup	125 mL
	Parsley flakes	1 tsp.	5 mL
	Salt, sprinkle		
	Pepper, sprinkle		

1. Put first 3 ingredients into saucepan. Bring to a boil. Turn down heat to medium. Cook, uncovered, for about 10 minutes, stirring occasionally, until potatoes are soft. Remove pan from heat. Mash with potato masher.

2. Add remaining 5 ingredients. Heat and stir on medium-low for about 2 minutes until cheese is melted. Makes about 1 1/2 cups (375 mL)— enough soup for you and a friend.

1 serving: 191 Calories; 7.7 g Total Fat (1.9 g Mono, 0.3 g Poly, 4.6 g Sat); 28 mg Cholesterol; 22 g Carbohydrate; 2 g Fibre; 9 g Protein; 146 mg Sodium

Pictured on page 73.

Ham & Pea Hide-&-Seek

Ham and peas play hide-and-seek in cheesy pasta shells.

Get It Together: liquid measures, measuring spoons, dry measures, sharp knife, cutting board, large saucepan, mixing spoon, strainer

1.	Water	4 cups	1 L
	Salt	1/2 tsp.	2 mL
	Small shell pasta	1 cup	250 mL
	Frozen peas	1 cup	250 mL
2.	Finely chopped ham	1 1/4 cups	300 mL
	Process cheese spread	1/2 cup	125 mL

(continued on next page)

Boil It!

1. Put water and salt into saucepan. Bring to a boil on medium-high. Add pasta. Cook, uncovered, for 8 minutes, stirring occasionally. Add peas. Cook, uncovered, for about 3 minutes, stirring occasionally, until pasta is soft. Use strainer to drain pasta mixture. Return pasta mixture to same pot.

2. Add ham and cheese spread. Turn heat down to medium-low. Heat and stir for about 1 minute until pasta is coated and ham is warm. Makes about 3 1/2 cups (875 mL)—enough for you to share with a friend because playing hide-and-seek alone is no fun.

1 serving: 588 Calories; 22.8 g Total Fat (3.9 g Mono, 1.1 g Poly, 11.6 g Sat); 129 mg Cholesterol; 51 g Carbohydrate; 5 g Fibre; 43 g Protein; 1218 mg Sodium

Pictured below.

Left: Neptune's Num-Nums, page 76 Right: Ham & Pea Hide-&-Seek, page 74

Neptune's Num-Nums

Tuna and cheesy pasta shells make a snack fit for a king, or queen, of the sea!

Get It Together: liquid measures, dry measures, sharp knife, cutting board, measuring spoons, large saucepan with lid, mixing spoon, strainer

1.	Water	4 cups	1 L
	Salt	1/2 tsp.	2 mL
	Small shell pasta	1 cup	250 mL
	Finely chopped celery	1/4 cup	60 mL
2.	Frozen peas	1/4 cup	60 mL
3.	Herb and garlic cream cheese	1/4 cup	60 mL
	Milk	2 tbsp.	30 mL
	Can of chunk light tuna in water, drained	6 oz.	170 g
4.	Process cheese slices	2	2

1. Put water and salt into saucepan. Bring to a boil on medium-high. Add pasta and celery. Cook, uncovered, for 7 minutes, stirring occasionally.

2. Add peas. Cook for about 1 minute, stirring occasionally, until pasta is soft. Use strainer to drain pasta mixture. Return pasta mixture to same pan.

3. Add cream cheese and milk. Cook and stir on medium for about 2 minutes until cream cheese is melted. Add tuna. Stir gently. Turn down heat to medium-low.

4. Place cheese slices over tuna mixture. Cover with lid. Cook for 2 minutes. Heat and stir for about 1 minute until tuna mixture is hot and cheese slices are melted. Be careful not to let the cheese burn. Makes about 2 cups (500 mL)—a good amount for 2 kids to share.

1 serving: 465 Calories; 17.3 g Total Fat (0.2 g Mono, 0.6 g Poly, 10.5 g Sat); 72 mg Cholesterol; 41 g Carbohydrate; 3 g Fibre; 34 g Protein; 525 mg Sodium

Pictured on page 75.

Q: Where does a man-eating fish hang out?

A: At a seafood restaurant.

Abracadabra Omelette

Amaze your friends with your magical skills. All you need is a freezer bag and, abracadabra, a perfect omelette appears!

Get It Together: sharp knife, cutting board, grater, measuring spoons, liquid measures, small resealable freezer bag, medium saucepan, tongs, plate

1.	Large eggs	2	2
	Diced ham	2 tbsp.	30 mL
	Grated medium Cheddar cheese	2 tbsp.	30 mL
2.	Water	5 cups	1.25 L

1. Put first 3 ingredients into freezer bag. Seal bag. Squeeze, squish and shake ingredients in bag until well mixed.

2. Put water into saucepan. Bring to a boil. Turn down heat to medium-low. Place freezer bag in water. Cook, uncovered, for 12 to 14 minutes until egg is firm. Remove bag from water with tongs. Let cool for 1 minute. Carefully open bag. Slide omelette onto plate. Makes 1 perfect omelette.

1 serving: 233 Calories; 15.3 g Total Fat (2.1 g Mono, 0.3 g Poly, 6.5 g Sat); 461 mg Cholesterol; 2 g Carbohydrate; 0 g Fibre; 20.5 g Protein; 228 mg Sodium

Pictured below.

Monsieur Auk-Auk Tip:
Make sure you use a freezer bag and not a sandwich bag because it's stronger for cooking.

Abracadabra Omelette, above

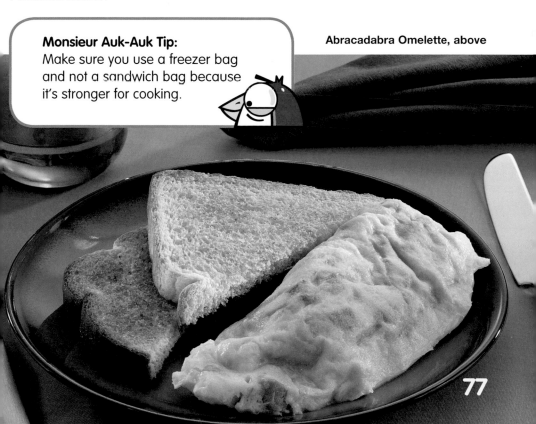

77

Bake It!

Here's where you get to use the oven. Remember—oven mitts are mandatory!

Q1: Say toast 10 times quickly. What do you put in a toaster?

Q2: What do you get when you cross a chili pepper, a shovel and a golden retriever?

Q3: What is a full turkey called?

78

Chillin' Cheese Toast

Chili out! The coolest way to eat chili is on a cheesy slice of toast.

Get It Together: measuring spoons, can opener, grater, baking sheet with sides, table knife, spoon, oven mitts, wire rack

1.			
Texas bread slice	1	1
Spreadable cream cheese	1 tbsp.	15 mL
Canned chili	2 tbsp.	30 mL
Grated medium Cheddar cheese	2 tbsp.	30 mL

1. Place oven rack in centre position. Turn oven on to 375°F (190°C). Place bread slice on baking sheet. Gently spread cream cheese on bread slice. Spoon chili onto centre of bread slice. Sprinkle with cheese. Bake for about 15 minutes until bread is lightly browned. Put baking sheet on wire rack to cool. Let cool for 2 minutes. Turn oven off. Makes 1 tasty toast.

1 serving: 213 Calories; 7.8 g Total Fat (0 g Mono, 0 g Poly, 5.1 g Sat); 21 mg Cholesterol; 26 g Carbohydrate; 2 g Fibre; 9 g Protein; 509 mg Sodium

Pictured below.

Creampuff Tip: Leftover chili can be served on hot dogs or hamburgers to make chili dogs or chili burgers. You can also put it on French fries to make chili fries. If you're not using the leftover chili in the next day or 2, store it in an airtight container in the freezer.

Chillin' Cheese Toast, above

Big Daddy Garlic Toast

Make garlic cheese toast just like they do in restaurants.

Get It Together: measuring spoons, sharp knife, cutting board, grater, foil, baking sheet with sides, table knife, oven mitts, wire rack

1.	Butter	1 tsp.	5 mL
	Bread slice, toasted	1	1
	Garlic clove, cut in half	1	1
2.	Grated mozzarella cheese	2 tbsp.	30 mL

1. Place oven rack in centre position. Turn oven broiler on. Line baking sheet with foil. Spread butter on bread slice. Rub bread slice lightly with cut side of garlic. Discard garlic. Place bread, butter-side up, on baking sheet.

2. Sprinkle with cheese. Broil for about 3 minutes until cheese is melted and starting to brown. Put baking sheet on wire rack to cool. Let cool for 2 minutes. Turn broiler off. Makes 1 toast for 1 lucky kid.

1 serving: 145 Calories; 8.5 g Total Fat (2.0 g Mono, 0.3 g Poly, 4.3 g Sat); 22 mg Cholesterol; 13 g Carbohydrate; 0 g Fibre; 5 g Protein; 217 mg Sodium

Pictured on page 81.

Creampuff Tip: You don't have to peel the garlic clove. Just cut it in half.

Ragin' Cajun Wedges

A little spice is always nice! Serve with ranch dressing or salsa and sour cream for dipping.

Get It Together: measuring spoons, grater, dry measures, baking sheet with sides, foil, cooking spray, fork, paper towel, oven mitts, sharp knife, cutting board, wire rack

1.	Large potato	1	1
2.	Grated jalapeño Monterey Jack cheese	1/2 cup	125 mL
	Cajun seasoning	1/2 tsp.	2 mL

(continued on next page)

. Put oven rack in centre position. Turn oven on to 425°F (220°C). Line baking sheet with foil. Grease foil with cooking spray. Set aside. Poke potato all over with fork. Wrap potato in paper towel. Microwave on high (100%) for 3 minutes. Use oven mitts to turn potato over. Microwave for another 3 minutes. The potato is cooked when you can easily poke it with a fork. Let potato stand for about 5 minutes until cool enough to handle. Cut potato from end to end into 8 long wedges. Spray each wedge with cooking spray. Place wedges side by side and close together on baking sheet.

2. Sprinkle cheese and seasoning over wedges. Bake for about 10 minutes until cheese is melted and wedges are hot. Place baking sheet on wire rack to cool. Let cool for 5 minutes. Turn oven off. Makes enough wedges for 2 kids to share.

1 serving: 241 Calories; 9.2 g Total Fat (0 g Mono, 0.1 g Poly, 5.0 g Sat); 25 mg Cholesterol; 33 g Carbohydrate; 3 g Fibre; 9 g Protein; 335 mg Sodium

Pictured below.

Left: Big Daddy Garlic Toast, page 80 Right: Ragin' Cajun Wedges, page 80

81

Nicely Spicy Crisps

Are you nice enough to share these golden-brown potato moons?

Get It Together: measuring spoons, foil, baking sheet with sides, cooking spray, sharp knife, cutting board, medium bowl, mixing spoons, oven mitts, wire rack

1.	Large potato	1	1
	Cooking oil	1 tsp.	5 mL
2.	Grated Parmesan cheese	1 tbsp.	15 mL
	Chili powder	1/8 tsp.	0.5 mL
	Seasoned salt	1/8 tsp.	0.5 mL

1. Place oven rack in centre position. Turn oven on to 450°F (230°C). Line baking sheet with foil. Grease foil with cooking spray. Set aside. Cut potato in half from end to end. Cut potato halves from side to side into 1/4 inch (6 mm) thick slices. Put potato slices into bowl. Drizzle with cooking oil.

2. Sprinkle next 3 ingredients over potato slices. Use mixing spoons to toss until coated. Arrange potato slices in a single layer on baking sheet. Spray tops of potato slices with cooking spray. Bake for 15 minutes. Turn potato slices over. Bake for another 15 minutes until browned. Put baking sheet on wire rack to cool. Let cool for 5 minutes. Turn oven off. Makes plenty of crisps for 2 hungry kids.

1 serving: 175 Calories; 3.7 g Total Fat (1.5 g Mono, 0.8 g Poly, 1.0 g Sat); 4 mg Cholesterol; 32 g Carbohydrate; 3 g Fibre; 5 g Protein; 130 mg Sodium

Pictured on page 84.

Creampuff Tip: The thinner you slice the potato, the crispier your crisps will be.

Q: What do you call a seed of corn that's planted at night?

A: A nocturnal kernel.

Big Tex's Beef Dippers

For whenever you're a-hankerin' for some big ranch BBQ taste.

Get It Together: measuring spoons, liquid measures, table knife, foil, oven mitts, wire rack, small bowl, mixing spoon

1.	English muffins, split	2	2
	Butter	2 tsp.	10 mL
2.	Prepared mustard	1/2 tsp.	2 mL
	Garlic powder	1/4 tsp.	1 mL
3.	Deli shaved roast beef	4 oz.	113 g
4.	Barbecue sauce	1/4 cup	60 mL
	Prepared beef broth	1/4 cup	60 mL

1. Place oven rack in centre position. Turn oven on to 400°F (205°C). Toast muffin halves until brown and crispy. Spread 1/2 tsp. (2 mL) butter on each muffin half.

2. Spread 1/4 tsp. (1 mL) mustard on 1 half of each muffin. Sprinkle garlic powder on other muffin halves.

3. Place half of roast beef over mustard on each muffin. Place other muffin halves over roast beef, garlic powder-side down. Cut two 9 x 12 inch (22 x 30 cm) pieces of foil. Wrap 1 muffin in each piece of foil. Bake for 10 to 12 minutes until hot. Put foil-wrapped muffins on wire rack to cool. Turn oven off.

4. Put barbecue sauce and broth into bowl. Mix well. Carefully remove foil from muffins. Serve muffins with sauce mixture for dipping. Makes 2 dippers for 2 hungry kids.

1 serving: 241 Calories; 3.0 g Total Fat (0.1 g Mono, 0.1 g Poly, 3.0 g Sat); 42 mg Cholesterol; 29 g Carbohydrate; 2 g Fibre; 16 g Protein; 989 mg Sodium

Pictured on page 84.

Q: What did the cook give his girlfriend?

A: A 14-carrot onion ring.

Bake It!

83

Fully-Loaded Potato Puffs

Loaded up with baked potato fixin's,
these tasty tots are sure to rev up your engine.

Get It Together: measuring spoons, sharp knife, cutting board, 9 inch (22 cm) pie plate, cooking spray, oven mitts, wire rack, spoon

1.	Frozen potato tots (gems or puffs)	16	16
2.	Process Cheddar cheese slices	2	2
	Bacon bits	1 tbsp.	15 mL
	Chopped green onion	1 tbsp.	15 mL
3.	Sour cream	1 tbsp.	15 mL

1. Put oven rack in centre position. Turn oven on to 450°F (230°C). Grease pie plate with cooking spray. Arrange potato tots in pie plate. Bake for 10 to 12 minutes until golden.

2. Cut or tear cheese slices into small pieces. Sprinkle over potato tots. Sprinkle with bacon bits and green onion. Bake for another 3 to 5 minutes until cheese is melted. Put pie plate on wire rack to cool. Turn oven off. Let cool for 5 minutes. Turn oven off.

3. Spoon sour cream on top. Makes enough to share with a friend.

1 serving: 221 Calories; 11.7 g Total Fat (2.6 g Mono, 0.1 g Poly, 5.0 g Sat); 23 mg Cholesterol; 21 g Carbohydrate; 2 g Fibre; 7 g Protein; 722 mg Sodium

Pictured on page 84.

Creampuff Tip: You can sprinkle 1/4 cup (60 mL) grated Mexican cheese blend over the potato tots instead of using the cheese slices.

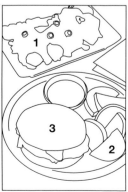

1. Fully-Loaded Potato Puffs, above
2. Nicely Spicy Crisps, page 82
3. Big Tex's Beef Dippers, page 83

NYU Pizza

Not Your Usual Pizza. Combines 2 all-time
favourite snacks in 1—pizza and chips!

Get It Together: measuring spoons, grater, dry measures, baking sheet
with sides, cooking spray, spoon, oven mitts, wire rack, cutting board,
sharp knife

1.	Flour tortilla (9 inch, 22 cm, diameter)	1	1
	Pizza sauce	1 tbsp.	15 mL
2.	Grated mozzarella cheese	1/4 cup	60 mL
	Coarsely crushed potato chips	1/4 cup	60 mL

1. Place oven rack in centre position. Turn oven on to 375°F (190°C).
   Grease baking sheet with cooking spray. Place tortilla on baking sheet.
   Spread pizza sauce on top, leaving about 1/2 inch (12 mm) edge.

2. Sprinkle 2 tbsp. (30 mL) cheese over sauce. Sprinkle with chips.
   Sprinkle remaining cheese over top. Bake for about 10 minutes
   until cheese is bubbling and golden. Put baking sheet on wire rack to
   cool. Let cool for 2 minutes. Turn oven off. Carefully slide pizza onto
   cutting board. Cut into 4 wedges. Makes 1 unusual pizza.

1 serving: 293 Calories; 15.3 g Total Fat (1.0 g Mono, 2.6 g Poly, 6.0 g Sat); 15 mg Cholesterol;
31 g Carbohydrate; 1 g Fibre; 12 g Protein; 635 mg Sodium

Pictured on page 87.

Creampuff Tip: Use your favourite flavour of potato chips—or
mix up a bunch of flavours, if you dare! Try using grated
mozzarella and Cheddar cheese blend with BBQ chips or use
grated mozzarella cheese with salt and vinegar chips.

Q: Why didn't
the chicken cross
the road?

A: He was chicken.

Bake It!

Left: Sandwich Alfredo, below Right: NYU Pizza, page 86

Sandwich Alfredo

Who needs pasta to enjoy alfredo sauce?
Mama mia, it's just as good in a sandwich!

Get It Together: measuring spoons, sharp knife, cutting board, dry measures, grater, baking sheet with sides, cooking spray, table knife, oven mitts, wire rack

1.			
Texas bread slices, toasted	2	2
Alfredo pasta sauce	2 tbsp.	30 mL
Chopped ham	1/4 cup	60 mL
Grated mozzarella cheese	1/4 cup	60 mL

1. Place oven rack in top position. Turn oven broiler on. Grease baking sheet with cooking spray. Place bread slices on baking sheet. Spread 1 tbsp. (15 mL) alfredo sauce on each bread slice. Sprinkle ham over sauce on 1 bread slice. Sprinkle cheese over sauce on other bread slice. Broil for about 5 minutes until cheese is melted and bubbly. Put baking sheet on wire rack to cool. Let cool for 1 minute. Turn broiler off. Place cheese-topped slice over ham-topped slice, cheese-side down. Cut sandwich in half. Makes 1 really tasty sandwich.

1 serving: 429 Calories; 17.5 g Total Fat (3.4 g Mono, 0.5 g Poly, 8.7 g Sat); 67 mg Cholesterol; 44 g Carbohydrate; 2 g Fibre; 22 g Protein; 721 mg Sodium

Pictured above.

Dog 'N' Bean Cups

Wieners and beans are downright purty dressed up in their own bread cups.

Get It Together: sharp knife, cutting board, can opener, measuring spoons, grater, 2 ramekins, baking sheet with sides, oven mitts, wire rack, small bowl, mixing spoon

1.	Bread slices	2	2
2.	Wiener, chopped	1	1
	Canned baked beans in tomato sauce	2 tbsp.	30 mL
	Salsa	1 tbsp.	15 mL
	Grated mozzarella cheese	2 tbsp.	30 mL

1. Place oven rack in centre position. Turn oven on to 350°F (175°C). Cut crusts off bread slices. Press bread slices into bottom and sides of ramekins. It's okay if the corners stick out. Place ramekins on baking sheet. Bake for 10 to 12 minutes until lightly browned. Put baking sheet on wire rack. Turn down heat in oven to 325°F (160°C).

2. Put next 3 ingredients into bowl. Mix well. Spoon wiener mixture into toast cups. Sprinkle cheese over top. Bake for about 15 minutes until hot. Put baking sheet on wire rack to cool. Let cool for 5 minutes. Turn oven off. Makes 2 super snacks.

1 serving: 162 Calories; 7.5 g Total Fat (2.1 g Mono, 0.4 g Poly, 2.5 g Sat); 13 mg Cholesterol; 18 g Carbohydrate; 1 g Fibre; 7 g Protein; 485 mg Sodium

Pictured on page 89

Creampuff Tip: Leftover baked beans can be stored in an airtight container in the freezer, or added to a chili, soup or stew.

Q: Why did the elephant eat a candle?

A: He wanted a light snack.

Top: Dog 'N' Bean Cups, above Bottom: Blackbeard's Treasure Chests, page 90

Bake It!

Blackbeard's Treasure Chests

If you're not afraid of the pirate's curse, you're bound
to find a golden filling in these treasure chests.

Get It Together: sharp knife, cutting board, dry measures, measuring
spoons, small bowl, mixing spoon, small cup, fork, baking sheet with sides,
pastry brush, spoon, oven mitts, wire rack

1.	Chopped cooked chicken	1/2 cup	125 mL
	Plain yogurt	2 tbsp.	30 mL
	Raisins	2 tbsp.	30 mL
	Curry powder	1/2 tsp.	2 mL
	Salt	1/4 tsp.	1 mL
	Pepper	1/8 tsp.	0.5 mL
2.	Large egg	1	1
	Water	1 tbsp.	15 mL
3.	Unbaked tart shells	8	8

1. Place oven rack in centre position. Turn oven on to 400°F (190°C).
   Put first 6 ingredients into bowl. Mix well. Set aside.

2. Break egg into cup. Add water. Beat egg a little with fork.

3. Place 4 tart shells on baking sheet. Spoon 2 tbsp. (30 mL) chicken
   mixture into each tart shell. Brush edges of filled tarts with egg mixture
   using pastry brush. Carefully remove 1 of the remaining tart shells from
   foil liner. Gently place shell, upside-down, over top of a filled tart.
   Press edges gently to seal. Repeat with remaining tart shells.
   Use remaining egg mixture to brush tops of tarts. Bake for about
   15 minutes until golden. Put baking sheet on wire rack to cool.
   Let cool for 5 minutes. Turn oven off. Makes 4 treasure-filled chests
   for 2 brave kids.

1 serving: 487 Calories; 26.3 g Total Fat (10.0 g Mono, 8.7 g Poly, 4.7 g Sat); 139 mg Cholesterol;
43 g Carbohydrate; 1 g Fibre; 18 g Protein; 801 mg Sodium

Pictured on page 89.

According to the
Guinness World
Records, the
largest sandwich
weighed 5,440
lbs. (2,467.5 kg)!

Tutti-Frutti Mini-Crisps

These crispy fruit cups are fruit-errific!

Get It Together: dry measures, measuring spoons, sharp knife, can opener, cutting board, 2 ramekins, cooking spray, baking sheet with sides, 2 small bowls, mixing spoon, oven mitts, wire rack

1.	Quick-cooking rolled oats	1/2 cup	125 mL
	Butter, melted	1/4 cup	60 mL
	All-purpose flour	2 tbsp.	30 mL
	Brown sugar, packed	2 tbsp.	30 mL
	Ground cinnamon	1/8 tsp.	0.5 mL
2.	Canned pineapple tidbits, drained	1/2 cup	125 mL
	Diced banana	1/2 cup	125 mL
	Lemon juice	2 tsp.	10 mL

1. Place oven rack in centre position. Turn oven on to 350°F (175°C). Grease ramekins with cooking spray. Place ramekins on baking sheet. Set aside. Put first 5 ingredients into 1 bowl. Stir until mixture resembles coarse crumbs.

2. Put next 3 ingredients into other bowl. Stir. Spoon fruit mixture into ramekins. Sprinkle oat mixture over top. Bake for about 30 minutes until golden. Put baking sheet on wire rack to cool. Let cool for 5 minutes. Turn oven off. Makes 2 terrific treats.

1 serving: 425 Calories; 23.7 g Total Fat (trace Mono, trace Poly, 14.0 g Sat); 60 mg Cholesterol; 50 g Carbohydrate; 4 g Fibre; 4 g Protein; 192 mg Sodium

Pictured on page 92.

Creampuff Tip: To melt butter, measure into small microwave-safe dish. Microwave on high (100%) for 10 seconds. Stir until melted.

Q: What are the 3 flavours in Neapolitan ice cream?

A: Chocolate, strawberry, vanilla.

Top: Tutti-Frutti Mini-Crisps, page 91 Bottom: Cinnamon Hypnotizers, below

Cinnamon Hypnotizers

Stare too long and you'll be hypnotized by these whirly twirly cinnamon pinwheels.

Get It Together: measuring spoons, baking sheet with sides, cooking spray, small bowl, mixing spoon, pastry brush, oven mitts, wire rack, sharp knife, cutting board

1.	Brown sugar, packed	3 tbsp.	50 mL
	Ground cinnamon	1 tsp.	5 mL
2.	Flour tortillas (9 inch, 22 cm, diameter)	2	2
	Butter, melted	3 tbsp.	50 mL

1. Place oven rack in centre position. Turn oven on to 350°F (175°C). Grease baking sheet with cooking spray. Set aside. Put brown sugar and cinnamon into bowl. Mix well.

2. Brush tortillas with half of butter using pastry brush. Sprinkle half of brown sugar mixture on each tortilla. Roll tortillas up tightly, jelly roll-style. Place rolls, seam-side down, on baking sheet. Brush with remaining butter. Bake for 8 to 10 minutes until rolls are golden. Put baking sheet on wire rack to cool. Let cool for 5 minutes. Turn oven off. Cut rolls into 1/2 inch (12 mm) thick slices. Makes about 28 hypnotizers—enough to get you and a friend really dizzy.

1 serving: 332 Calories; 19.0 g Total Fat (0 g Mono, 0 g Poly, 11.0 g Sat); 45 mg Cholesterol; 37 g Carbohydrate; 1 g Fibre; 2 g Protein; 368 mg Sodium

Pictured above.

Plan It!

We know. You're a busy person. If you prefer to grab your snack and go, this is the chapter for you. Here you whip up a bunch of snacks that you can save to eat whenever you want. And no matter your skill level, there's a big-batch recipe you can make in this section.

Personal food profile

My name is: _____

My favourite vegetable is: _____

My favourite fruit is: _____

My favourite meat is: _____

My favourite dessert is: _____

My favourite drink is: _____

My favourite meal is: _____

My least favourite meal is: _____

I would never eat: _____

If I had a restaurant, I would name it:_____

In my restaurant I would serve: _____

Food trivia

Did you know that a tomato is actually a fruit? Fruits have seeds inside them and vegetables don't!

Do you know that pepper was once the most expensive spice in the world?

Did you know that French fries were actually invented in Belgium? And Belgians often serve their fries with mayonnaise!

Señor Piquante Chili Bites

Yow! These babies have a spicy, fiery bite. Are you brave enough to try?

Get It Together: liquid measures, grater, dry measures, measuring spoons, mini-muffin pan, cooking spray, small bowl, fork, spoon, wooden toothpick, oven mitts, wire rack, table knife, plate

1.			
Large eggs		2	2
Grated jalapeño Monterey Jack cheese		1/2 cup	125 mL
Chunky salsa		1/4 cup	60 mL
Crushed Ritz crackers (about 8 crackers)		1/4 cup	60 mL
Chili powder		1/2 tsp.	2 mL

1. Place oven rack in centre position. Turn oven on to 425°F (220°C). Grease muffin cups with cooking spray. Break eggs into bowl. Beat eggs a little with fork. Add remaining 4 ingredients. Mix well. Spoon about 1 1/2 tbsp. (25 mL) cheese mixture into each muffin cup. Bake for 8 to 10 minutes until toothpick inserted straight down into centre of a bite comes out clean. Put pan on wire rack. Turn oven off. Let cool for 2 minutes. Run knife around inside edge of muffin cups to loosen bites. Transfer to plate. Makes 12 bites.

1 bite: 54 Calories; 3.4 g Total Fat (1.2 g Mono, 0.2 g Poly, 1.3 g Sat); 35 mg Cholesterol; 4 g Carbohydrate; trace Fibre; 2 g Protein; 115 mg Sodium

Pictured on page 96.

Monsieur Auk-Auk Tip: Store bites in resealable sandwich bags in sets of 3 in the refrigerator for up to 5 days. Eat cold or reheat in the microwave on high (100%) for about 15 seconds until hot.

Q: What is a cannibal's favourite game?

A: Swallow the leader.

Plan It!

Surf's Up Pizza Pandemonium

There's enough mini-Hawaiian pizzas here to keep you hangin' ten for over a week!

Get It Together: liquid measures, sharp knife, cutting board, dry measures, can opener, grater, baking sheet with sides, cooking spray, spoon, strainer, oven mitts, wire rack

1.	Tube of refrigerator pizza dough	10 oz.	283 g
2.	Pizza sauce	1/2 cup	125 mL
	Chopped ham	3/4 cup	175 mL
3.	Canned crushed pineapple, drained	1/2 cup	125 mL
	Grated mozzarella cheese	1 cup	250 mL

1. Place oven rack in centre position. Turn oven on to 400°F (205°C). Remove pizza dough from wrapping but do not unroll. Slice pizza dough roll into eight 1 inch (2.5 cm) slices. Press each slice out to 3 1/2 inch (9 cm) wide circle, about 1/8 inch (3 mm) thick. Grease baking sheet with cooking spray. Arrange circles in a single layer on baking sheet.

2. Spread 1 tbsp. (15 mL) sauce on each circle. Sprinkle ham over sauce.

3. Press pineapple in strainer until no more liquid comes out. Spread pineapple over ham. Sprinkle cheese over top. Bake for about 20 minutes until golden. Put baking sheet on wire rack. Turn oven off. Let cool for 5 minutes. Makes 8 mini-pizzas.

1 mini-pizza: 175 Calories; 6.1 g Total Fat (1.5 g Mono, 0.2 g Poly, 2.4 g Sat); 23 mg Cholesterol; 20 g Carbohydrate; 1 g Fibre; 10 g Protein; 327 mg Sodium

Pictured on page 96.

Monsieur Auk-Auk Tip: Leftover crushed pineapple may be stored in an airtight container in the refrigerator for up to 3 days.

Store your pizzas in an airtight container in the freezer for up to 1 month. To reheat, place a frozen pizza on a paper towel-lined plate. Microwave on high (100%) for about 60 seconds until hot.

Plan It! 95

1. Presto Pizzeria Buns,
   page 97
2. Surf's Up Pizza
   Pandemonium,
   page 95
3. Señor Piquante
   Chili Bites, page 94

Presto Pizzeria Buns

Just say "Presto," and you'll change-o these regular rolls into pizza buns.

Get It Together: grater, dry measures, measuring spoons, baking sheet with sides, cooking spray, waxed paper, tea towel, small bowl, mixing spoon, oven mitts, wire rack

1.	Package of frozen unbaked dinner rolls, covered, thawed in refrigerator overnight	1 lb.	454 g
2.	Grated mild Cheddar cheese	1/3 cup	75 mL
	Grated Parmesan cheese	1/3 cup	75 mL
	Pizza sauce	1/4 cup	60 mL

1. Grease baking sheet with cooking spray. Place rolls on baking sheet in 3 rows, 4 across. Press each roll into a 3 1/2 inch (9 cm) wide circle. It's okay if rolls are touching one another. Grease waxed paper with cooking spray. Cover rolls with waxed paper, greased-side down. Place tea towel over top. Let sit in oven with light on and door closed for 30 minutes. Remove baking sheet from oven.

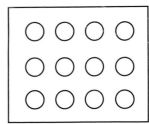

2. Place oven rack in centre position. Turn oven on to 375°F (190°C). Put Cheddar and Parmesan cheese into bowl. Mix well. Spread 1 tsp. (5 mL) pizza sauce on each bun, leaving 1/2 inch (12 mm) border. Sprinkle 1 tbsp. (15 mL) cheese mixture over pizza sauce. Bake for about 18 minutes until lightly browned. Put baking sheet on wire rack. Turn oven off. Let cool for 5 minutes. Makes 12 pizza buns.

1 bun: *180 Calories; 7.0 g Total Fat (1.3 g Mono, 0.1 g Poly, 3.2 g Sat); 13 mg Cholesterol; 18 g Carbohydrate; 1 g Fibre; 10 g Protein; 548 mg Sodium*

Pictured on page 96.

Monsieur Auk-Auk Tip: Store the pizza buns in an airtight container or covered with plastic wrap in the refrigerator for up to 3 days. Store in the freezer for up to 1 month. To reheat, microwave on high (100%) for about 30 seconds.

Samurai Sushi Rolls

Grasshopper, do you have what it takes to tackle sushi?
Actually, it's easier to make this simply super sushi than you may think.

Get It Together: dry measures, liquid measures, measuring spoons,
sharp knife, cutting board, can opener, strainer, medium saucepan
with a lid, mixing spoons, small bowl, waxed paper, fork, plastic wrap

1.	Short grain white rice	1 cup	250 mL
	Water	1 1/2 cups	375 mL
	Salt	1/8 tsp.	0.5 mL
2.	Rice vinegar	2 tbsp.	30 mL
	Granulated sugar	1 tbsp.	15 mL
3.	Cooked chicken, cut into thin strips	1/3 cup	75 mL
	Thick teriyaki basting sauce	2 tbsp.	30 mL
4.	Nori (roasted seaweed) sheets	2	2
5.	Thin strips of red pepper	10	10
6.	Canned pineapple slices, each cut into 4 pieces	2	2

1. Put rice into strainer. Rinse rice under cold water until water runs clear (is no longer cloudy). Put rice into saucepan. Add water and salt. Stir. Bring to a boil. Turn down heat to medium-low. Cover with lid. Cook for about 20 minutes, without lifting lid, until rice is tender. Remove pan from heat. Wait for about 5 minutes until liquid is soaked up.

2. Add rice vinegar and sugar. Mix well. Cool.

3. Put chicken into bowl. Drizzle with teriyaki sauce. Use mixing spoons to toss until coated.

4. Place 1 sheet of nori, shiny-side down, on a sheet of waxed paper with 1 long edge closest to you. Spoon half of rice mixture onto centre of nori. Run fork under water so that it is wet. Spread rice mixture almost to edge of nori using fork, leaving a 2 inch (5 cm) edge on the side farthest from you (see Step A). Lay half of chicken strips across the rice, about 2 inches (5 cm) away from the edge closest to you.

5. Lay half of red pepper slices alongside chicken.

(continued on next page)

5. Lay 4 pieces of pineapple alongside red pepper (see Step B). Dampen 1/2 inch (12 mm) border along edge farthest from you with water. Starting at edge closest to you, roll up tightly, using waxed paper as a guide (see Step C). Repeat with remaining ingredients to make another sushi roll. Cover rolls with plastic wrap. Chill for about 1 hour until cold. Cut each roll into 8 slices (see Step D). Makes 16 slices.

1 slice: 61 Calories; 0.3 g Total Fat (0.1 g Mono, 0.1 g Poly, 0.1 g Sat); 3 mg Cholesterol; 12 g Carbohydrate; trace Fibre; 2 g Protein; 111 mg Sodium

Pictured below.

Monsieur Auk-Auk Tip: Have any leftover chicken strips? They'll work fine in this recipe! If you don't have any leftover, maybe ask a grown-up to cook a couple extra strips for you.

Step A

Step B

Step C

Step D

Bird's Nest Pies

Make your very own chicken pot pies with a golden biscuit top.

Get It Together: dry measures, sharp knife, cutting board, can opener, baking sheet with sides, foil, four 5 inch (12.5 cm) foil pie plates, medium bowl, mixing spoon, small bowl, whisk, pastry brush, oven mitts, wire rack

1.	Crushed soda crackers (about 8 crackers)	1/3 cup	75 mL
2.	Frozen mixed vegetables, thawed	3 cups	750 mL
	Chopped cooked chicken	1 1/2 cups	375 mL
	Can of condensed cream of chicken soup	10 oz.	284 mL
3.	Tube of refrigerator crescent rolls (8 rolls per tube)	8 1/2 oz.	235 g
4.	Large egg	1	1

1. Place oven rack in centre position. Turn oven on to 350°F (175°C). Line baking sheet with foil. Arrange pie plates on baking sheet. Sprinkle cracker crumbs into pie plates.

2. Put next 3 ingredients into medium bowl. Stir. Spoon into pie plates.

3. Unroll dough. Separate into 8 triangles. Lay 2 triangles on a lightly floured surface, with longest edges slightly overlapping. Press together to make a 5 1/4 inch (13 cm) square. Trim corners to make a round shape. Discard trimmings. Repeat with remaining triangles.

4. Break egg into small bowl. Beat with whisk until bubbly on top. Place circles over pie plates. Press edges of dough against sides of pie plates to seal. Brush dough with egg using pastry brush. Cut three 1 inch (2.5 cm) slits in top of each pie to allow steam to escape during baking. Bake for 25 to 30 minutes until tops are golden and filling is hot. Put baking sheet on wire rack. Turn oven off. Let cool for 5 minutes. Makes 4 chicken pies.

1 pie: 513 Calories; 23.1 g Total Fat (4.1 g Mono, 2.2 g Poly, 6.0 g Sat); 99 mg Cholesterol; 53 g Carbohydrate; 6 g Fibre; 26 g Protein; 589 mg Sodium

Pictured on page 101.

(continued on next page)

Plan It!

Monsieur Auk-Auk Tip: Store the baked pies in an airtight container in the refrigerator for up to 2 days or in the freezer for up to 1 month. To thaw, place in the refrigerator overnight. To reheat, bake in 350°F (175°C) oven for about 25 minutes until filling is hot.

Make sure to be careful when breaking the crust. The steam coming from the pie will be hot!

Bird's Nest Pies, page 100

Gold Rush Muffins

Strike it rich with these muffins full of golden apple nuggets.

Get It Together: dry measures, measuring spoons, liquid measures, sharp knife, cutting board, muffin pan, cooking spray, medium bowl, mixing spoon, small bowl, fork, wooden toothpick, oven mitts, wire rack

1.	All-purpose flour	2 cups	500 mL
	Brown sugar, packed	1/2 cup	125 mL
	Baking powder	1 1/2 tsp.	7 mL
	Baking soda	1/2 tsp.	2 mL
	Salt	1/2 tsp.	2 mL
2.	Large egg	1	1
	Vanilla yogurt	1 cup	250 mL
	Syrup	1/4 cup	60 mL
	Applesauce	2 tbsp.	30 mL
	Cooking oil	2 tbsp.	30 mL
3.	Chopped peeled apple	1 cup	250 mL
	Chopped pecans	1/2 cup	125 mL

1. Place oven rack in centre position. Turn oven on to 375°F (190°C). Grease muffin cups with cooking spray. Set aside. Put first 5 ingredients into medium bowl. Stir well. Dig a hole in centre of flour mixture with mixing spoon. Set aside.

2. Break egg into small bowl. Beat egg a little with fork. Add next 4 ingredients. Stir until well mixed. Pour into hole in flour mixture.

3. Add apple and pecans. Stir just until flour mixture is moistened. Fill muffin cups 3/4 full with batter. Bake for 18 to 20 minutes until toothpick inserted straight down into centre of a muffin comes out clean. Put pan on wire rack. Turn oven off. Let cool for 5 minutes. Transfer muffins from pan to wire rack to cool. Makes 12 muffins.

1 muffin: 206 Calories; 6.4 g Total Fat (3.5 g Mono, 1.8 g Poly, 0.7 g Sat); 17 mg Cholesterol; 35 g Carbohydrate; 1 g Fibre; 4 g Protein; 203 mg Sodium

Pictured on page 105.

Monsieur Auk-Auk Tip: Store the muffins in an airtight container or wrapped individually in plastic wrap in the freezer for up to 1 month.

Plan It!

Fanana Of Banana Muffins

Try saying that 5 times fast! If you're a fan of banana and chocolate, these muffins are for you.

Get It Together: dry measures, measuring spoons, liquid measures, fork, plate, muffin pan, cooking spray, large bowl, mixing spoon, medium bowl, wooden toothpick, oven mitts, wire rack

1.			
	All-purpose flour	2 cups	500 mL
	Brown sugar, packed	3/4 cup	175 mL
	Baking powder	1 tsp.	5 mL
	Baking soda	1/2 tsp.	2 mL
	Salt	1/2 tsp.	2 mL
2.	Large egg	1	1
	Mashed overripe banana (about 3 medium)	1 1/2 cups	375 mL
	Milk	1/2 cup	125 mL
	Butter, melted	1/3 cup	75 mL
	Vanilla extract	1 tsp.	5 mL
3.	Mini semi-sweet chocolate chips	1/2 cup	125 mL

1. Place oven rack in centre position. Turn oven on to 375°F (190°C). Grease muffin cups with cooking spray. Set aside. Put first 5 ingredients into large bowl. Stir. Dig a hole in centre of flour mixture with mixing spoon.

2. Break egg into medium bowl. Beat egg a little with fork. Add next 4 ingredients. Stir well. Pour into hole in flour mixture.

3. Add chocolate chips. Stir just until flour mixture is moistened. Fill muffin cups 3/4 full with batter. Bake for about 25 minutes until toothpick inserted straight down into centre of a muffin comes out clean. Put pan on wire rack. Turn oven off. Let cool for 5 minutes. Transfer muffins from pan to wire rack to cool. Makes 12 muffins.

1 muffin: 248 Calories; 8.4 g Total Fat (2.4 g Mono, 0.4 g Poly, 5.1 g Sat); 30 mg Cholesterol; 41 g Carbohydrate; 2 g Fibre; 4 g Protein; 224 mg Sodium

Pictured on page 105.

Monsieur Auk-Auk Tip: To melt butter, measure butter into small microwave-safe dish. Microwave on high (100%) for 10 seconds. Stir until melted.

Store the muffins in an airtight container or wrapped individually in plastic wrap in the freezer for up to 1 month.

No-Fluster Clusters

Hey Buster, don't fluster—these peanut butter and raisin clusters
are E-Z to make.

Get It Together: dry measures, measuring spoons, baking sheet with
sides, waxed paper, large bowl, medium bowl, mixing spoons

1. Cornflakes cereal	2 cups	500 mL
Chopped pecans	1/4 cup	60 mL
Raisins	1/4 cup	60 mL
2. Miniature marshmallows	2 cups	500 mL
Smooth peanut butter	1/4 cup	60 mL
Butter	2 tbsp.	30 mL

1. Line baking sheet with waxed paper. Set aside. Put first 3 ingredients
   into large bowl. Mix well.

2. Put remaining 3 ingredients into medium bowl. Microwave
   on high (100%) for 1 minute. Stir. Microwave for another 1 minute.
   Stir until smooth. Pour over cereal mixture. Stir until coated.
   Drop by tablespoonfuls onto baking sheet. Wait for about
   5 minutes until firm. Makes 18 clusters.

*1 cluster: 84 Calories; 4.3 g Total Fat (1.9 g Mono, 0.9 g Poly, 1.3 g Sat); 3 mg Cholesterol;
10 g Carbohydrate; 1 g Fibre; 1 g Protein; 38 mg Sodium*

Pictured on page 105.

Monsieur Auk-Auk Tip: Clusters can be individually
wrapped in plastic wrap or placed in an airtight container
and left at room temperature for up to 5 days. They can
also be stored in the freezer for up to 1 month.

1. Gold Rush Muffins, page 102
2. Fanana Of Banana Muffins, page 103
3. No-Fluster Clusters, above

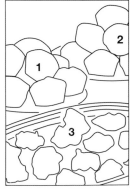

Plan It!

Left: Lemon Pineapple Ice Bombs, page 107 Right: Smoothie-On-A-Stick, below

Smoothie-On-A-Stick

It's a slick trick to lick a smoothie if it's on a stick!

Get It Together: liquid measures, sharp knife, cutting board, measuring spoons, blender, 8 paper cups (5 oz., 142 mL, size), muffin pan, foil, 8 wooden craft sticks

1.	Strawberry yogurt	1 1/2 cups	375 mL
	Sliced banana	1 cup	250 mL
	Milk	3/4 cup	175 mL
	Orange juice	3/4 cup	175 mL
	Vanilla extract	1/2 tsp.	2 mL

1. Put all 5 ingredients into blender. Cover with lid. Blend until smooth. Place 1 paper cup in each muffin cup. Pour yogurt mixture into paper cups until 3/4 full. Cover top of each cup with foil. Cut a small slit in centre of each piece of foil. Insert 1 stick through each slit almost to bottom of cup. Freeze overnight until firm. To loosen, run bottom of each cup under hot water for 3 to 4 seconds. While holding stick, push from bottom of cup to remove smoothie. Makes 8 smoothies.

1 smoothie: 87 Calories; 1.1 g Total Fat (trace Mono, trace Poly, 0.6 g Sat); 5 mg Cholesterol; 17 g Carbohydrate; trace Fibre; 3 g Protein; 37 mg Sodium

Pictured above.

Plan It!

Lemon Pineapple Ice Bombs

Get blown away by the explosion of lemon and pineapple flavour!

Get It Together: can opener, ice cream scoop, dry measures, medium bowl, mixing spoon, 10 paper cups (5 oz., 142 mL, size), muffin pan, foil, 10 wooden craft sticks

1.			
Can of lemon pie filling	19 oz.	540 mL
Butterscotch ripple ice cream, softened	2 cups	500 mL
Can of crushed pineapple, drained	14 oz.	398 mL

1. Put first 3 ingredients into bowl. Mix well. Place 1 paper cup in each muffin cup. Spoon about 1/2 cup (125 mL) ice cream mixture into each paper cup. Cover top of each cup with foil. Cut a small slit in centre of each piece of foil. Insert 1 stick through each slit almost to bottom of cup. Freeze overnight until firm. To loosen, run bottom of each cup under hot water for 3 to 4 seconds. While holding stick, push from bottom of cup to remove ice bomb. Makes 10 ice bombs.

1 ice bomb: 320 Calories; 10.8 g Total Fat (1.6 g Mono, 0.8 g Poly, 5.3 g Sat); 119 mg Cholesterol; 52 g Carbohydrate; 1 g Fibre; 5 g Protein; 72 mg Sodium

Pictured on page 106.

Monsieur Auk-Auk Tip: To soften ice cream, measure the amount you need and let it sit on the counter for about 5 minutes.

Q: Why did the cookie go to the doctor?

A: He was feeling crummy.

Cinnamon Hearts

These heart-shaped treats make a perfect gift when you want to say "I ♥ U."

Get It Together: measuring spoons, small bowl, mixing spoon, baking sheet with sides, cooking spray, oven mitts, wire rack

1.	**Granulated sugar**	**2 tbsp.**	**30 mL**
	Ground cinnamon	**1 1/2 tsp.**	**7 mL**
2.	**Tube of plain bread stick dough**	**11 oz.**	**311 g**

1. Place oven rack in centre position. Turn oven on to 350°F (175°C). Grease baking sheet with cooking spray. Set aside. Put sugar and cinnamon into bowl. Stir.

2. Unroll dough. Sprinkle dough with sugar mixture. Separate dough into 8 strips along perforations. Roll and twist strips to 14 inches (35 cm) long. Form strips into a heart. Pinch dough at top and bottom points of heart.

   Place hearts on baking sheet. Bake for 18 to 20 minutes until golden. Put baking sheet on wire rack. Turn oven off. Let cool for 5 minutes. Makes 8 hearts.

1 heart: 123 Calories; 2.0 g Total Fat (0 g Mono, 0 g Poly, 0 g Sat); 0 mg Cholesterol; 22 g Carbohydrate; 1 g Fibre; 3 g Protein; 290 mg Sodium

Pictured on page 109.

Monsieur Auk-Auk Tip: Store the hearts in an airtight container or wrapped individually in plastic wrap in the freezer for up to 1 month. To reheat, microwave the frozen heart on high (100%) for about 15 seconds until warm.

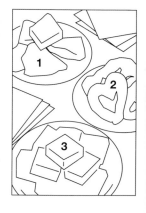

1. Hop Butterscotch Wedges, page 110
2. Cinnamon Hearts, above
3. Fairground Squares, page 111

Plan It!

Hop Butterscotch Wedges

Go triangular and replace your lunchtime granola bar with this deliciously sweet oat wedge!

Get It Together: dry measures, measuring spoons, sharp knife, cutting board, liquid measures, medium bowl, mixing spoon, small bowl, whisk, 9 inch (22 cm) microwave-safe pie plate, cooking spray

1.	Large flake rolled oats	2 cups	500 mL
	Butterscotch chips	1/2 cup	125 mL
	Brown sugar, packed	6 tbsp.	100 mL
	Chopped almonds	2 tbsp.	30 mL
	Salt	1/4 tsp.	1 mL
2.	Large egg	1	1
	Butter, melted	1/4 cup	60 mL
	Corn syrup	1/4 cup	60 mL
	Vanilla extract	1 tsp.	5 mL

1. Put first 5 ingredients into medium bowl. Stir.

2. Break egg into small bowl. Beat with whisk until egg is bubbly on top. Add remaining 3 ingredients. Mix well. Add to oat mixture. Mix well. Grease pie plate with cooking spray. Spread oat mixture evenly in pie plate. Microwave on high (100%) for 6 minutes. Let cool for 5 minutes. Cuts into 8 wedges.

1 wedge: 305 Calories; 12.2 g Total Fat (3.2 g Mono, 1.2 g Poly, 6.8 g Sat); 38 mg Cholesterol; 44 g Carbohydrate; 3 g Fibre; 5 g Protein; 151 mg Sodium

Pictured on page 109.

Monsieur Auk-Auk Tip: To melt butter, measure butter into small microwave-safe dish. Microwave on high (100%) for 10 seconds. Stir until melted.

If you don't have a microwave-safe pie plate, you can use a dinner plate instead.

Keep the wedges in an airtight container or wrap them individually in plastic wrap. Store them at room temperature for up to 3 days or in the freezer for up to 1 month.

Fairground Squares

Just like a caramel apple—but without the stick! Look for the caramel apple wraps in the produce section of your grocery store.

Get It Together: liquid measures, sharp knife, cutting board, dry measures, 9 x 9 inch (22 x 22 cm) pan, cooking spray, medium bowl, mixing spoon, large bowl, oven mitts, wire rack

1.	Diced peeled apple	3 cups	750 mL
	Lemon juice	1/4 cup	60 mL
2.	All-purpose flour	1 1/2 cups	375 mL
	Quick-cooking rolled oats	1 1/4 cups	300 mL
	Brown sugar, packed	1/2 cup	125 mL
	Butter	1 cup	250 mL
3.	Caramel apple wraps	5	5

1. Place oven rack in centre position. Turn oven on to 350°F (175°C). Grease pan with cooking spray. Set aside. Put apple and lemon juice into medium bowl. Stir until coated.

2. Put next 3 ingredients into large bowl. Stir. Rub in butter with your fingers until mixture resembles coarse crumbs. Press 2/3 of oat mixture into bottom of baking pan. Spread apple mixture over top.

3. Place caramel wraps over apple mixture, slightly overlapping. Sprinkle remaining oat mixture over top. Press down gently. Bake for about 30 minutes until golden. Put pan on wire rack. Turn oven off. Let cool for 5 minutes. Cuts into 16 squares.

1 square: 247 Calories; 13.1 g Total Fat (2.9 g Mono, 0.4 g Poly, 8.3 g Sat); 30 mg Cholesterol; 30 g Carbohydrate; 1 g Fibre; 3 g Protein; 117 mg Sodium

Pictured on page 109.

Monsieur Auk-Auk Tip: Store these squares in an airtight container or covered with plastic wrap in the refrigerator for up to 5 days. Or, store them in the freezer for up to 1 month.

Q: Why did the turkey cross the road twice?

A: To prove he wasn't a chicken.

Top: Love That Lemon Squares, page 113 Bottom: I Dream Of Square Cookies, below

I Dream Of Square Cookies

OK, these fluffy treats may not be square cookies, but they are cookie squares.

Get It Together: dry measures, medium bowl, fork, mixing spoon, 8 x 8 inch (20 x 20 cm) pan, foil, sharp knife

1.	Cream cheese, softened	4 oz.	125 g
	Icing (confectioner's) sugar	1/2 cup	125 mL
	Smooth peanut butter	1/2 cup	125 mL
2.	Frozen whipped topping, thawed	2 cups	500 mL
	Crushed chocolate chip cookies	1 cup	250 mL

1. Put cream cheese into bowl. Mash with fork until smooth. Add icing sugar and peanut butter. Stir until smooth.

2. Add whipped topping and cookies. Mix well. Line pan with foil. Spoon cookie mixture into pan. Spread evenly. Freeze for about 2 hours until firm. Cuts into 16 squares.

1 square: 149 Calories; 10.6 g Total Fat (2.0 g Mono, 1.1 g Poly, 5.1 g Sat); 10 mg Cholesterol; 13 g Carbohydrate; trace Fibre; 3 g Protein; 51 mg Sodium

Pictured above.

Monsieur Auk-Auk Tip: To soften cream cheese, let it sit on the counter for about 30 minutes.

Once frozen, cut and wrap squares individually in plastic wrap. Store them in the freezer for a convenient snack.

Love That Lemon Squares

These squares are a way-cool frozen treat with a chocolate crumb crust.

Get It Together: dry measures, liquid measures, small saucepan, mixing spoon, 9 x 9 inch (22 x 22 cm) pan, blender, sharp knife, cutting board

1.	Butter	1/4 cup	60 mL
	Chocolate wafer crumbs	1 1/4 cups	300 mL
	Brown sugar, packed	1/4 cup	60 mL
2.	Frozen whipped topping, thawed	4 cups	1 L
	Milk	1 cup	250 mL
	Box of instant lemon pudding powder (4-serving size)	1	1
3.	Lemon jellied candy slices	8	8

1. Melt butter in saucepan. Add wafer crumbs and brown sugar. Stir well. Remove pan from heat. Press wafer crumb mixture into pan.

2. Put next 3 ingredients into blender. Cover with lid. Blend until smooth. Pour over wafer crumb mixture in pan. Spread evenly. Freeze for at least 4 hours until firm. Cut into 16 squares.

3. Cut candy slices in half. Gently press 1 half on each square. Makes 16 squares.

1 square: 163 Calories; 8.4 g Total Fat (1.2 g Mono, 0.5 g Poly, 6.4 g Sat); 9 mg Cholesterol; 22 g Carbohydrate; trace Fibre; 1 g Protein; 124 mg Sodium

Pictured on page 112.

Monsieur Auk-Auk Tip: Instead of lemon pudding powder, use another flavour such as chocolate or butterscotch. To decorate, use chocolate chips or candy-coated chocolates.

Store the frozen squares in an airtight container or individually wrapped in plastic wrap in the freezer for up to 1 month.

Q: What happens if you tell an egg a joke?

A: It cracks up.

Swirling Dervish Cookies

Round and round these dizzying treats go.

Get It Together: dry measures, measuring spoons, 2 small bowls, mixing spoon, large bowl, rolling pin, waxed paper, table knife, plastic wrap, cutting board, serrated knife, cookie sheets, cooking spray, oven mitts, wire racks

1.	Chocolate hazelnut spread	1/2 cup	125 mL
	Crushed walnuts	1/3 cup	75 mL
2.	All-purpose flour	1 1/4 cups	300 mL
	Baking powder	1/4 tsp.	1 mL
	Salt	1/4 tsp.	1 mL
3.	Butter, softened	1/2 cup	125 mL
	Granulated sugar	1/2 cup	125 mL
	Egg yolk (large)	1	1
	Vanilla extract	1/4 tsp.	1 mL

1. Put chocolate spread and walnuts into 1 small bowl. Mix well.
2. Put next 3 ingredients into other small bowl. Mix well.
3. Put butter and sugar into large bowl. Stir. Add egg yolk. Beat well. Add vanilla. Beat until smooth. Add half of flour mixture. Stir to combine. Add remaining flour mixture. Stir to combine. Shape dough into a ball. Place dough on sheet of waxed paper. Flatten dough into a rectangle. Place second sheet of waxed paper over top. Roll out dough to 8 x 10 inch (20 x 25 cm) rectangle. Discard top sheet of waxed paper. Spread chocolate mixture over dough, leaving a 1/2 inch (12 mm) border at each long edge. Roll up tightly from long side, jelly roll-style, using waxed paper as a guide. Press seam against roll to seal. Wrap with plastic wrap. Chill for about 1 hour until firm. Place oven rack in centre position. Turn oven on to 350°F (175°C). Grease cookie sheets with cooking spray. Set aside. Place roll, seam-side down, on cutting board. Cut with serrated knife into 1/4 inch (6 mm) slices. Arrange slices on cookie sheets, about 1 inch (2.5 cm) apart. Bake for 10 to 12 minutes until golden. Put cookie sheets on wire racks. Turn oven off. Let cool for 5 minutes. Transfer cookies to wire racks to cool. Makes about 36 cookies.

1 cookie: 78 Calories; 4.6 g Total Fat (1.5 g Mono, 0.9 g Poly, 1.9 g Sat); 12 mg Cholesterol; 8 g Carbohydrate; trace Fibre; 1 g Protein; 38 mg Sodium

Pictured on page 115.

(continued on next page)

Top: Swirling Dervish Cookies, above
Bottom: Slammin' Jam Tarts, page 116

Plan It!

Monsieur Auk-Auk Tip: To soften butter, let it sit on the counter for about 1 hour.

If you don't have an egg separator, you can separate the yolk from the egg white by cracking the egg as close to the middle as possible, being careful not to break the yolk. Hold the half of the shell with the yolk in it in one hand and the other half of the shell in the other hand. Allow as much of the egg white as possible to run out of the shell and into a small bowl. Then, transfer the yolk to the other half of the shell, allowing more of the egg white to run out. Repeat, a few times, until most of the egg white has been removed.

For fresh baked cookies anytime, after rolling the dough, wrap the roll in plastic wrap and freeze it. When you want fresh baked cookies, take the roll out of the freezer and wait for 10 minutes. Unwrap the roll and slice as many cookies as you like and bake them as directed.

Slammin' Jam Tarts

With lemon and berry, these tarts are completely jam-packed.

Get It Together: measuring spoons, dry measures, baking sheet with sides, oven mitts, wire rack, spoon

1.	**Unbaked tart shells**	8	8
2.	**Spreadable cream cheese**	8 tsp.	40 mL
3.	**Lemon spread (or curd)**	1/2 cup	125 mL
4.	**Mixed berry jam**	8 tsp.	40 mL

1. Place oven rack in centre position. Turn oven on to 375°F (190°C). Place tart shells on baking sheet. Bake for 10 to 12 minutes until golden. Put baking sheet on wire rack. Turn oven off. Let cool for 5 minutes.

2. Place 1 tsp. (5 mL) cream cheese in each tart. Gently spread cream cheese in bottom of tarts using spoon.

3. Spoon 1 tbsp. (15 mL) lemon spread over cream cheese. Spread evenly.

4. Spoon 1 tsp. (5 mL) jam in centre of each tart. Chill for about 1 hour until firm. Makes 8 tarts.

1 tart: 189 Calories; 9.0 g Total Fat (3.5 g Mono, 1.0 g Poly, 3.5 g Sat); 27 mg Cholesterol; 25 g Carbohydrate; trace Fibre; 2 g Protein; 153 mg Sodium

Pictured on page 115.

Monsieur Auk-Auk Tip: Store the tarts in an airtight container or covered with plastic wrap in the refrigerator for up to 2 days or in the freezer for up to 1 month.

Q: What did the hungry computer eat?

A: Microchips— 1 byte at a time.

Chocolate Dollar Dippers

These mini chocolate pancakes are great for dipping in yogurt, pudding or applesauce.

Get It Together: dry measures, liquid measures, measuring spoons, large bowl, mixing spoon, small bowl, whisk, large frying pan, pancake lifter, large plate, foil

1.	Pancake mix	1 1/4 cups	300 mL
2.	Large egg	1	1
	Chocolate milk	1 cup	250 mL
3.	Cooking oil	1 – 3 tsp.	5 – 15 mL

1. Put pancake mix into large bowl. Dig a hole in centre of pancake mix with mixing spoon.

2. Break egg into small bowl. Add milk. Beat with whisk until mixture is bubbly on top. Pour into hole in pancake mix. Stir just until pancake mix is moistened. The batter will be lumpy.

3. Heat 1 tsp. (5 mL) cooking oil in frying pan on medium-low for 3 minutes. Measure batter into pan, using about 1 tbsp. (15 mL) for each pancake. Cook for about 1 minute until bubbles form on top and edges of pancakes look dry. Use lifter to turn pancakes over. Cook for another 1 minute until bottoms are golden. Use lifter to check. Remove pancakes to plate. Cover with foil to keep warm. Repeat with remaining batter, heating more cooking oil in pan before each batch, if necessary, so pancakes won't stick. Makes about 32 dippers.

1 pancake: 25 Calories; 0.5 g Total Fat (0.2 g Mono, 0.1 g Poly, 0.2 g Sat); 6 mg Cholesterol; 4 g Carbohydrate; trace Fibre; 1 g Protein; 64 mg Sodium

Pictured on page 119.

Monsieur Auk-Auk Tip: Store the cooled pancakes in an airtight container in the fridge for up to 3 days, or in the freezer for up to 1 month. To eat cold, thaw frozen pancakes at room temperature for about 20 minutes. To reheat, place 5 to 10 pancakes on a plate. Microwave on high (100%) for 20 to 30 seconds until warm.

Granola Grab Bags

**Grab these ready-to-eat bags of granola whenever you're on the go.
Eat it right out of the bag or sprinkle it on yogurt or ice cream.**

Get It Together: dry measures, sharp knife, cutting board, measuring spoons, large saucepan, mixing spoons, baking sheet with sides, cooking spray, oven mitts, wire rack, large bowl, 6 resealable sandwich bags

1.	Brown sugar, packed	1/3 cup	75 mL
	Butter	1/4 cup	60 mL
2.	Quick-cooking rolled oats	2 1/2 cups	625 mL
	Chopped walnuts	1/4 cup	60 mL
	Slivered almonds	1/4 cup	60 mL
	Vanilla extract	1/2 tsp.	2 mL
	Ground cinnamon	1/8 tsp.	0.5 mL
3.	Dried cranberries	1/2 cup	125 mL
	Raisins	1/2 cup	125 mL
	Chopped dried apricot	1/4 cup	60 mL
	Semi-sweet chocolate chips	1/4 cup	60 mL

1. Place oven rack in centre position. Turn oven on to 350°F (175°C). Grease baking sheet with cooking spray. Set aside. Put brown sugar and butter into saucepan. Heat and stir on medium until melted and smooth. Remove pan from heat.

2. Add next 5 ingredients. Stir until coated. Spoon oat mixture onto baking sheet. Spread evenly. Bake for 10 to 15 minutes, stirring occasionally, until golden. Put baking sheet on wire rack. Turn oven off. Wait for about 30 minutes until cool. Transfer to bowl.

3. Add remaining 4 ingredients. Use mixing spoons to toss until combined. Spoon about 3/4 cup (175 mL) into each sandwich bag. Makes 6 grab bags.

1 grab bag: *439 Calories; 18.5 g Total Fat (5.0 g Mono, 3.4 g Poly, 6.6 g Sat); 20 mg Cholesterol; 65 g Carbohydrate; 7 g Fibre; 8 g Protein; 67 mg Sodium*

Pictured on page 119.

Monsieur Auk-Auk Tip:
The grab bags can be stored at room temperature for up to 5 days.

Top: Granola Grab Bags, above

Bottom: Chocolate Dollar Dippers, page 117

Hokey Pokey Squares

You put some of this in. You take nothing out.
You put some of that in—and you stir it all about!

Get It Together: dry measures, measuring spoons, large bowl, small saucepan, mixing spoon, 9 x 9 inch (22 x 22 cm) pan, cooking spray, sharp knife

1. Broken stick pretzels	1 1/4 cups	300 mL
Crisp rice cereal	1 cup	250 mL
Candy-coated chocolates	3/4 cup	175 mL
Dry-roasted peanuts	1/4 cup	60 mL
2. Miniature marshmallows	2 1/2 cups	625 mL
Butter	1/4 cup	60 mL
Smooth peanut butter	2 tbsp.	30 mL

1. Put first 4 ingredients into bowl. Mix well.

2. Put remaining 3 ingredients into saucepan. Heat and stir on medium until melted. Pour marshmallow mixture over pretzel mixture. Stir until pretzel mixture is coated. Grease pan with cooking spray. Spoon mixture into pan. Spread evenly and press down with back of spoon. Let cool for about 10 minutes until firm. Cuts into 16 squares.

1 square: 263 Calories; 12.4 g Total Fat (4.2 g Mono, 1.0 g Poly, 6.7 g Sat); 12 mg Cholesterol; 35 g Carbohydrate; 1 g Fibre; 3 g Protein; 163 mg Sodium

Pictured on front cover and on divider.

Monsieur Auk-Auk Tip: For easier packing, after spreading the mixture in the pan, lay a sheet of waxed paper over top and press down evenly with your hands.

Store these squares in an airtight container at room temperature for up to 3 days.

Q: Why did the cow cross the road?

A: It was the chicken's day off.

Measurement Tables

Throughout this book measurements are given in Conventional and Metric measure. To compensate for differences between the two measurements due to rounding, a full metric measure is not always used. The cup used is the standard 8 fluid ounce. Temperature is given in degrees Fahrenheit and Celsius. Baking pan measurements are in inches and centimetres as well as quarts and litres. An exact metric conversion is given below as well as the working equivalent (Metric Standard Measure).

Spoons

Conventional Measure	Metric Exact Conversion Millilitre (mL)	Metric Standard Measure Millilitre (mL)
1/8 teaspoon (tsp.)	0.6 mL	0.5 mL
1/4 teaspoon (tsp.)	1.2 mL	1 mL
1/2 teaspoon (tsp.)	2.4 mL	2 mL
1 teaspoon (tsp.)	4.7 mL	5 mL
2 teaspoons (tsp.)	9.4 mL	10 mL
1 tablespoon (tbsp.)	14.2 mL	15 mL

Cups

Conventional Measure	Metric Exact Conversion Millilitre (mL)	Metric Standard Measure Millilitre (mL)
1/4 cup (4 tbsp.)	56.8 mL	60 mL
1/3 cup (5 1/3 tbsp.)	75.6 mL	75 mL
1/2 cup (8 tbsp.)	113.7 mL	125 mL
2/3 cup (10 2/3 tbsp.)	151.2 mL	150 mL
3/4 cup (12 tbsp.)	170.5 mL	175 mL
1 cup (16 tbsp.)	227.3 mL	250 mL
4 1/2 cups	1022.9 mL	1000 mL (1 L)

Oven Temperatures

Fahrenheit (°F)	Celsius (°C)
175°	80°
200°	95°
225°	110°
250°	120°
275°	140°
300°	150°
325°	160°
350°	175°
375°	190°
400°	205°
425°	220°
450°	230°
475°	240°
500°	260°

Dry Measurements

Conventional Measure Ounces (oz.)	Metric Exact Conversion Grams (g)	Metric Standard Measure Grams (g)
1 oz.	28.3 g	28 g
2 oz.	56.7 g	57 g
3 oz.	85.0 g	85 g
4 oz.	113.4 g	125 g
5 oz.	141.7 g	140 g
6 oz.	170.1 g	170 g
7 oz.	198.4 g	200 g
8 oz.	226.8 g	250 g
16 oz.	453.6 g	500 g
32 oz.	907.2 g	1000 g (1 kg)

Pans

Conventional Inches	Metric Centimetres
8x8 inch	20x20 cm
9x9 inch	22x22 cm
9x13 inch	22x33 cm
10x15 inch	25x38 cm
11x17 inch	28x43 cm
8x2 inch round	20x5 cm
9x2 inch round	22x5 cm
10x4 1/2 inch tube	25x11 cm
8x4x3 inch loaf	20x10x7.5 cm
9x5x3 inch loaf	22x12.5x7.5 cm

Casseroles

CANADA & BRITAIN		UNITED STATES	
Standard Size Casserole	Exact Metric Measure	Standard Size Casserole	Exact Metric Measure
1 qt. (5 cups)	1.13 L	1 qt. (4 cups)	900 mL
1 1/2 qts. (7 1/2 cups)	1.69 L	1 1/2 qts. (6 cups)	1.35 L
2 qts. (10 cups)	2.25 L	2 qts. (8 cups)	1.8 L
2 1/2 qts. (12 1/2 cups)	2.81 L	2 1/2 qts. (10 cups)	2.25 L
3 qts. (15 cups)	3.38 L	3 qts. (12 cups)	2.7 L
4 qts. (20 cups)	4.5 L	4 qts. (16 cups)	3.6 L
5 qts. (25 cups)	5.63 L	5 qts. (20 cups)	4.5 L

Recipe Index

A

4 X 4 Dipping Adventure 22

4 O'Clock Fiesta Salsa 16

Abracadabra Omelette 77

Alfredo, Sandwich 87

Apple & Cheese Squeeze, The Great 41

Apple Of My Iced Tea 18

B

Bake It!

    Big Daddy Garlic Toast 80

    Big Tex's Beef Dippers 83

    Blackbeard's Treasure Chests 90

    Chillin' Cheese Toast 79

    Cinnamon Hypnotizers 92

    Dog 'N' Bean Cups 88

    Fully-Loaded Potato Puffs 85

    Nicely Spicy Crisps 82

    NYU Pizza 86

    Ragin' Cajun Wedges 80

    Sandwich Alfredo 87

    Tutti-Frutti Mini-Crisps 91

Banana Muffins, Fanana Of 103

Bandito's Broth 72

BBQ Sub, Sea Wolf 46

Bean Cups, Dog 'N' 88

Beef Dippers, Big Tex's 83

Berry Me Alive 9

Berry Meld, Marshmallow 70

Beverages

    Apple Of My Iced Tea 18

    Berry Me Alive 9

    Fruit Sludgies 12

    Man-Go-Go Smoothie 10

    Marshmallow Fruit Soda Pop 12

    Milky Way Blue Lemonade 10

    Swimming Fruit Sipper 18

Big Daddy Garlic Toast 80

Big Tex's Beef Dippers 83

Bird's Nest Pies 100

Blackbeard's Treasure Chests 90

Blend It!

    Berry Me Alive 9

    Butterscotch Me Up Dip 14

    Chocolate Galaxies 13

    Confusing Dip 16

    4 O'Clock Fiesta Salsa 16

    Fruit Sludgies 12

    I'm A Little Nutty Dip 14

    Man-Go-Go Smoothie 10

    Marshmallow Fruit Soda Pop 12

    Milky Way Blue Lemonade 10

Boastin' Toastin' Choco-Treats 28

Boil It!

    Abracadabra Omelette 77

    Bandito's Broth 72

    Don't Box Me In Pudding 67

    Ham & Pea Hide-&-Seek 74

    Marshmallow Berry Meld 70

    Neptune's Num-Nums 76

    Oodles Of Noodles Soup 71

    Rock-A-Hula Sauce 69

    Smashed Potato Soup 74

    Wonka's Dream Sauce 70

Bronco Bull Eggs 34

Broth, Bandito's 72

Buffoon's Macaroons 42

Bumpy Peanut Butter Balls 26

Buns, Presto Pizzeria 97

Burrito, Humpty Dumpty 65

Butterscotch Me Up Dip 14

Butterscotch Wedges, Hop 110

C

Cajun Wedges, Ragin' 80

Cheese Puck 21

Cheese Squeeze, The Great Apple & 41

Cheese Toast, Chillin' 79

Cheese Wafflewich, Ham & 53

Chili Bites, Señor Piquante 94

Chillin' Cheese Toast 79

Chips

    Cinnamon Micro- 45

    Herbed Micro-. 45

    Micro- 44

    Salt And Pepper Micro- 45

    Seasoned Micro-. 45

Chocolate Dollar Dippers 117

Chocolate Galaxies. 13

Choco-Treats, Boastin' Toastin' 28

Cinnamon Hearts 108

Cinnamon Hypnotizers 92

Cinnamon Micro-Chips. 45

Cluckin' 'Za 57

Coleslaw, Hickory Sticks. 38

Cones, Rice Cream. 24

Confusing Dip 16

Cookies & Squares

    Buffoon's Macaroons 42

    Bumpy Peanut Butter Balls. 26

    Fairground Squares. 111

    Hokey Pokey Squares. 120

    Hop Butterscotch Wedges 110

    I Dream Of Square Cookies 112

    Love That Lemon Squares 113

    No-Fluster Clusters. 104

    Swirling Dervish Cookies 114

Corn Feed Bag, Ham &. 33

Countdown Fruit Salad 31

Crisps, Tutti-Frutti Mini- 91

Curry Fury Dip. 20

D

Dips & Spreads

    Butterscotch Me Up Dip 14

    Cheese Puck. 21

    Confusing Dip 16

    Curry Fury Dip. 20

    4 X 4 Dipping Adventure. 22

    4 O'Clock Fiesta Salsa 16

    I'm A Little Nutty Dip. 14

Dog 'N' Bean Cups. 88

Don't Box Me In Pudding 67

E

Eggs, Bronco Bull 34

El Queso Grande. 59

Ex-Cous Me Peas 45

F

Fairground Squares. 111

Fanana Of Banana Muffins 103

Flapjacks, Gold Dust. 62

Folded Pizza Subwich. 48

4 X 4 Dipping Adventure. 22

4 O'Clock Fiesta Salsa 16

Fried Funky Monkey 60

Fruit Island. 42

Fruit Salad, Countdown 31

Fruit Sipper, Swimming. 18

Fruit Sludgies 12

Fruit Soda Pop, Marshmallow. 12

Fry It!

    Cluckin' 'Za. 57

    El Queso Grande. 59

    Fried Funky Monkey 60

    Gold Dust Flapjacks 62

    Ham & Cheese Wafflewich 53

    Hit-The-Trail Mix 51

    Humpty Dumpty Burrito 65

    Kooky Zooky Coins. 56

    No Dud Spud Cakes. 63

    Quelle Surprise! 61

    Stir-Crazy Granola. 52

    UFO. 54

Fully-Loaded Potato Puffs 85

G

Garlic Toast, Big Daddy 80

Gold Dust Flapjacks 62

Gold Rush Muffins 102

Recipe Index

Granola Grab Bags . . . . . , , ... 118
Granola, Oh!-Crazy 52

H

Ham & Cheese Wafflewich 53
Ham & Corn Feed Bag 33
Ham & Pea Hide-&-Seek. 74
Herbed Micro-Chips 45
Hickory Sticks Coleslaw 38
Hit-The-Trail Mix 51
Hokey Pokey Squares. 120
Hop Butterscotch Wedges 110
Humpty Dumpty Burrito 65

I

I Dream Of Square Cookies 112
Iced Tea, Apple Of My 18
I'm A Little Nutty Dip. 14

J

Jam Tarts, Slammin' 116

K

Kooky Zooky Coins. 56

L

Lemon Pineapple Ice Bombs 107
Lemon Squares, Love That. 113
Lemonade, Milky Way Blue. 10
Lickety-Split Sundae. 25
Love That Lemon Squares 113
Luau Wow-Wow 36

M

Macaroons, Buffoon's. 42
Man-Go-Go Smoothie. 10
Marshmallow Berry Meld 70
Marshmallow Fruit Soda Pop 12
Micro-Chips. 44
Milky Way Blue Lemonade 10
Mini-Crisps, Tutti-Frutti. 91
Mix, Hit-The-Trail. 51
Mix It!
   Apple Of My Iced Tea 18
   Boastin' Toastin' Choco-Treats 28
   Bumpy Peanut Butter Balls. 26
   Cheese Puck. 21
   Curry Fury Dip. 20
   4 X 4 Dipping Adventure. 22
   Lickety-Split Sundae. 25
   Rice Cream Cones 24
   Swimming Fruit Sipper 18
   The Tower Of Trifle 28
   Yum-Yum Yogurt Layers. 27
Mix-Master Snacks-A-Lot. 32
Muffins, Fanana Of Banana 103
Muffins, Gold Rush 102

N

Neptune's Num-Nums 76
Nicely Spicy Crisps. 82
No Dud Spud Cakes. 63
No-Fluster Clusters. 104
Noodles, see Pasta & Noodles
Nutty Dip, I'm A Little 14
NYU Pizza 86

O

Omelette, Abracadabra. 77
Oodles Of Noodles Soup 71

P

Pasta & Noodles

    Ham & Pea Hide-&-Seek. 74

    Neptune's Num-Nums 76

    Oodles Of Noodles Soup 71

    Space Pod Soup. 48

Pea Hide-&-Seek, Ham & 74

Peanut Butter Balls, Bumpy 26

Peas, Ex-Cous Me 45

Pepper Micro-Chips, Salt And 45

Pies, Bird's Nest 100

Pineapple Ice Bombs, Lemon. 107

Pizza, NYU 86

Pizza Pandemonium, Surf's Up 95

Pizza Subwich, Folded 48

Pizzeria Buns, Presto 97

Plan It!

    Bird's Nest Pies. 100

    Chocolate Dollar Dippers 117

    Cinnamon Hearts 108

    Fairground Squares. 111

    Fanana Of Banana Muffins 103

    Gold Rush Muffins 102

    Granola Grab Bags 118

    Hokey Pokey Squares. 120

    Hop Butterscotch Wedges 110

    I Dream Of Square Cookies 112

    Lemon Pineapple Ice Bombs 107

    Love That Lemon Squares 113

    No-Fluster Clusters. 104

    Presto Pizzeria Buns. 97

    Samurai Sushi Rolls 98

    Señor Piquante Chili Bites 94

    Slammin' Jam Tarts 116

    Smoothie-On-A-Stick 106

    Surf's Up Pizza Pandemonium 95

    Swirling Dervish Cookies 114

Pop, Marshmallow Fruit Soda. 12

Potato Puffs, Fully-Loaded 85

Potato Soup, Smashed. 74

Presto Pizzeria Buns 97

Pudding, Don't Box Me In. 67

Q

Quelle Surprise!. 61

R

Ragin' Cajun Wedges 80

Rice Cream Cones 24

Rock-A-Hula Sauce. 69

S

Salads

    Countdown Fruit Salad 31

    Ham & Corn Feed Bag 33

    Hickory Sticks Coleslaw 38

    Luau Wow-Wow 36

Salsa, 4 O'Clock Fiesta. 16

Salt And Pepper Micro-Chips. 45

Samurai Sushi Rolls 98

Sandwich Alfredo 87

Sandwiches & Wraps

    Big Tex's Beef Dippers 83

    Chillin' Cheese Toast 79

    El Queso Grande. 59

    Folded Pizza Subwich. 48

    Fried Funky Monkey 60

    Ham & Cheese Wafflewich 53

    Humpty Dumpty Burrito 65

    Quelle Surprise!. 61

    Sandwich Alfredo 87

    Sea Wolf BBQ Sub 46

    Take 1—It's A Wrap! 36

    Tomato Tossle. 35

    Turkey-Lurkey Happy Wraps 39

Sauces

    Marshmallow Berry Meld 70

    Rock-A-Hula Sauce 69

    Wonka's Dream Sauce 70

Sea Wolf BBQ Sub 46

Seasoned Micro-Chips 45

Señor Piquante Chili Bites 94

Slammin' Jam Tarts . . . , , ... 116
Smashed Potato Soup 74
Smoothie, Man-Go-Go 10
Smoothie-On-A-Stick 106
Soda Pop, Marshmallow Fruit. 12
Soups

    Bandito's Broth 72
    Oodles Of Noodles Soup 71
    Smashed Potato Soup 74
    Space Pod Soup 48
Space Pod Soup 48
Spreads, see Dips & Spreads
Spud Cakes, No Dud 63
Squares, see Cookies & Squares
Stir-Crazy Granola. 52
Sub, Sea Wolf BBQ. 46
Subwich, Folded Pizza 48
Sundae, Lickety-Split 25
Surf's Up Pizza Pandemonium 95
Sushi Rolls, Samurai 98
Swimming Fruit Sipper 18
Swirling Dervish Cookies 114

T

Take 1—It's A Wrap! 36
Tarts, Slammin' Jam 116
Tea, Apple Of My Iced 18
The Great Apple & Cheese Squeeze 41
The Tower Of Trifle 28
Toast, Big Daddy Garlic 80
Toast, Chillin' Cheese 79
Tomato Tossle. 35
Toss It!

    Bronco Bull Eggs 34
    Countdown Fruit Salad 31
    Ham & Corn Feed Bag 33
    Hickory Sticks Coleslaw 38
    Luau Wow-Wow 36
    Mix-Master Snacks-A-Lot. 32
    Take 1—It's A Wrap! 36
    Tomato Tossle. 35

Turkey-Lurkey Happy Wraps 39
Trail Mix, Hit-The- 51
Trifle, The Tower Of. 28
Turkey-Lurkey Happy Wraps 39
Tutti-Frutti Mini-Crisps 91

U

UFO. 54

W

Wafflewich, Ham & Cheese. 53
Wonka's Dream Sauce 70
Wraps, see Sandwiches & Wraps

Y

Yogurt Layers, Yum-Yum 27
Yum-Yum Yogurt Layers. 27

Z

Zap It!

    Buffoon's Macaroons 42
    Cinnamon Micro-Chips. 45
    Ex-Cous Me Peas 45
    Folded Pizza Subwich. 48
    Fruit Island. 42
    Herbed Micro-Chips 45
    Micro-Chips. 44
    Salt And Pepper Micro-Chips. 45
    Sea Wolf BBQ Sub 46
    Seasoned Micro-Chips 45
    Space Pod Soup. 48
    The Great Apple & Cheese Squeeze 41

Recipe Notes

Recipe Notes

Company's Coming®

Kids Do BAKING

weet & savoury baked delights

Jean Paré

National Bestseller

Divider Photo

1. Mr. Squirrel's Shortbread, page 69
2. Gingerbread Kids, page 67
3. Lemon Doodles, page 66

We gratefully acknowledge the following suppliers for their generous support of our Test and Photography Kitchens:

Broil King Barbecues
Corelle®
Hamilton Beach® Canada
Lagostina®
Proctor Silex® Canada
Tupperware®

Our special thanks to the following businesses for providing props for photography:

Casa Bugatti
Cherison Enterprises Inc.
Danesco Inc.
Pyrex® Storage

Table of Contents

Attention Adults!... 4

Keeping Everything Cool in the Kitchen 5

Baking Glossary 6

Top Baking Tools... 7

On the Rise! (Breads) 8

Let Them Eat Cake! (Cakes & Squares)............................... 30

Stop, Drop & Roll! (Cookies) 50

It's a Happy Ending! (Desserts)... 70

There's Muffin to It! (Muffins & Loaves)................................. 88

Practice Makes Pie-Fect! (Pies & Pastries)........................... 106

Measurement Tables. 121

Tip Index... 122

Recipe Index 122

Attention Adults!

At Company's Coming, we love when cooking can be enjoyed by the whole family, even the kids. That's where *Kids Do Baking* comes in—a whole cookbook designed especially for them! Imagine the fun that kids will have being in charge of the kitchen (well, almost!). They'll be baking up a storm, having fun and maybe even honing natural cooking talents along the way.

Kids Do Baking was created to ease kids into the joys of baking. These 77 recipes have been crafted specifically with kids in mind—the directions are written in clear language they'll understand, and the results are deliciously kid-friendly. Kids will be able to look through the colourful photos to choose a recipe, and then bake it up all on their own—with just a little help from you.

A grown-up should always be around when kids are cookin' in the kitchen. Check over a recipe and make sure that your child is well prepared with the proper equipment and ingredients before diving into a recipe—and be available for questions, in case the young chef runs into a snag along the way! There are a few places where we've recommended that kids ask for help, with things like inverting hot pans of goodies straight from the oven.

Each of the following chapters focuses on one type of baking, so kids can choose between things like breads, cookies, desserts or muffins—whatever they feel like baking, or whatever they have the confidence to tackle. Allow kids to choose which snack they want to make for their school lunches, or which muffin they'd like for breakfast tomorrow. Encourage them to plan and

bake a special dessert for a family get-together! Getting all those compliments on their wonderful baking will make them feel ten feet tall.

Kids will love the sweet and savoury treats throughout *Kids Do Baking*—you'll love that we've used whole wheat flour and wholesome grains like oatmeal (but don't tell!). Many of the recipes substitute puréed fruit, such as applesauce, which reduces the amount of added sugar and fat.

So what are you waiting for? Get those kids into the kitchen! With *Kids Do Baking* they'll learn lifelong skills and know the value of a job well done—especially when they taste their own baking warm out of the oven! And remember, they just might share a tasty morsel or two with you.

Jean Paré

Nutrition Information Guidelines

Each recipe is analyzed using the most current version of the Canadian Nutrient File from Health Canada, which is based on the United States Department of Agriculture (USDA) Nutrient Database.

- If more than one ingredient is listed (such as "butter or hard margarine"), or if a range is given (1 – 2 tsp., 5 – 10 mL), only the first ingredient or first amount is analyzed.

- For meat, poultry and fish, the serving size per person is based on the recommended 4 oz. (113 g) uncooked weight (without bone), which is 2 – 3 oz. (57 – 85 g) cooked weight (without bone)—approximately the size of a deck of playing cards.

- Milk used is 2% M.F. (milk fat), unless otherwise stated.

- Cooking oil used is canola oil, unless otherwise stated.

- Ingredients indicating "sprinkle," "optional," or "for garnish" are not included in the nutrition information.

- The fat in recipes and combination foods can vary greatly depending on the sources and types of fats used in each specific ingredient. For these reasons, the amount of saturated, monounsaturated and polyunsaturated fats may not add up to the total fat content.

Vera C. Mazurak, Ph.D.
Nutritionist

4

Keeping Everything Cool in the Kitchen

When you want to bake, there's a lot at stake! To be a real pro in the kitchen, pay attention to following points:

Before you begin basics:

- Make sure an adult is OK with you baking and using the ingredients you need.
- If you have long hair, tie it up and out of the way.
- Roll up long sleeves and tuck in baggy shirts.
- Read the recipe all the way through before you begin.
- Wash your hands.
- Gather the proper equipment in the sizes recommended in the recipe.
- Get your ingredients ready.
- Make sure the oven rack is in the right position according to the recipe.

While you're baking basics:

- Do one recipe step at a time. The numbers beside our ingredients match the steps to keep you on track. Don't skip steps.
- Make sure to use oven mitts when handling hot pots and pans.
- When using the stove, always turn handles inward so you don't accidentally knock off any pots and pans.
- Set the timer to remind you when to check your baking.

After your baked goodies have been made basics:

- Turn off the oven.
- Clean up—or no one will ever let you bake again!

Kids Do Baking

Baking Glossary

1. **batter:** a mixture of flour, liquid and other ingredients that can be thin (like pancake batter) or thick (like muffin batter).

2. **beat:** to mix one or more ingredients with a spoon, fork or electric mixer, moving it round and round, until they are smooth.

3. **crimp:** to seal the edges of two pieces of dough with your fingers or, if you want to be fancy, with the tines of a fork.

4. **cut in:** to combine solid fat (such as butter or margarine) with dry ingredients (such as flour) until the mixture looks like crumbs the size of small peas.

5. **drain:** to strain away unwanted liquid (such as water) using a colander or strainer. Do this over the kitchen sink! Ask an adult for help especially if you're using hot ingredients—a full pot or pan can be very heavy. Never drain grease down the sink.

6. **fold in:** to gently combine ingredients by repeatedly lifting up the ingredients from the bottom of the bowl and turning them over the ingredients at the top of the bowl until the ingredients are blended. Don't mix too hard! When you're finished, the mixture shouldn't be deflated.

7. **grease:** to spray an item such as plastic wrap with cooking spray, or to rub the inside surface of a baking pan with butter, margarine or cooking oil so that what you're baking won't stick to it.

8. **invert:** to turn baked items out of the baking pan and onto a countertop or wire rack by tilting the pan over until the baking comes out. Both the pan and your baking will be hot, so make sure to ask a grown-up for help.

9. **knead:** to push and fold dough with the heels of your hands until it's smooth and elastic.

10. **make a well:** to dig a hole or well in the centre of dry ingredients, moving the dry ingredients to the outside of the mixing bowl and making room for liquid ingredients to be added to the centre.

11. **mix just until moistened:** to mix dry and wet ingredients until the dry ingredients are just wet. The mixture will still be lumpy.

12. **parchment paper:** a specially designed paper that keeps food from sticking to pans that can take high heat without burning. Waxed paper cannot be substituted for parchment paper, because waxed paper can burn and spoil your baking.

13. **process:** to mix or cut up ingredients in a blender (or food processor).

14. **punch dough down:** to smash down risen dough with your hands to force the large air pockets out of it.

15. **roll:** to form dough into a certain shape using your hands.

16. **roll out:** to roll out dough to a certain thickness using a rolling pin.

17. **sift:** to break down any lumps in dry ingredients, or to make them finer or lighter, by passing them through a sieve or sifter. If a recipe calls for an ingredient to be sifted, be sure to sift before measuring.

18. **whisk:** a tool with a handle with wire hoops attached used to beat eggs and cream lightly.

19. **yeast:** yeast reacts with the sugars in flour to ferment and form gases. These gases trigger the rising action of dough, which gives bread its soft texture. To help it rise, the dough needs to be covered and placed in a slightly warm place with no drafts.

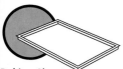

Top Baking Tools

Baking Sheet
Looks like a cookie sheet, but it has sides—so things won't roll onto the floor!

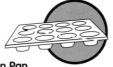

Cookie Sheet
It's the same as a baking sheet, but it doesn't have sides.

Dry Measures
Use these to measure dry ingredients. To measure dry stuff properly, spoon it into your cup, and then level off any extra with the straight side of a table knife.

Grater
Perfect for grating cheese. Go slowly so you don't accidentally grate your fingers!

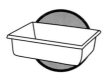

Loaf Pan
It's like a cake pan, but it's rectangular—perfect for baking a loaf of bread.

Liquid Measures
You guessed it—these measure liquids. Pour in your liquid and set on a level surface. Check at eye level to see if the liquid reaches the mark.

Measuring Spoons
Make sure ingredients are levelled off, unless the recipe calls for a "heaping" spoonful.

Muffin Pan
Mini muffin pans look almost the same—except the cups are mini-sized.

Pastry Brush
Use this to brush liquid on pastry.

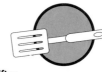

Lifter
This is handy for getting cookies off the baking sheet.

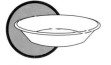

Pie Plate
A circular tin or oven-safe dish for baking.

Ramekins
Little cups that can be put in the oven.

Rolling Pin
Great for rolling out dough and pastry to get it flat.

Rubber Spatula
Great for making sure you get every last bit of batter out of the mixing bowl.

Saucepan
Sometimes called a pot. Always use the size called for in the recipe.

Serrated Knife
The rough edge makes it great for cutting soft things like bread.

Strainer
An easy way to strain liquid. Always use it over the sink.

Whisk
A tool that mixes ingredients really well and breaks up lumps.

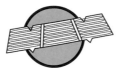

Wire Rack
Good for cooling baked items by letting air flow all around them.

Zester
Rake this tool over a lemon or orange to get small bits of rind. It works almost the same way a grater does.

Kids Do Baking

On the Rise!
Breads

Turn your kitchen into a chemistry laboratory, as you behold the wonders of yeast! In the right environment, just a little bit of yeast can make a big deal out of a small amount of dough. Fill your home with the aroma of your own bread baking in the oven, and then enjoy the results of your experiment. You'll be a glad scientist!

find 19 things you might see at a bake sale

```
A  C  S  N  U  B  R  E  N  N  I  D  P  C  B
M  C  H  E  E  S  E  C  A  K  E  U  C  H  D
E  U  F  I  G  H  E  K  A  C  D  N  U  O  P
B  I  F  J  C  K  S  L  Z  D  M  K  A  C  N
O  R  P  F  R  K  T  N  I  E  V  F  U  O  E
L  O  O  W  I  D  E  N  O  D  L  P  J  L  I
I  O  C  W  N  G  N  A  O  C  I  E  A  T  P
T  R  A  T  N  A  C  E  P  A  R  Z  U  T  N
T  S  O  F  P  I  R  G  K  O  T  A  Q  E  I
O  H  A  L  H  B  E  E  A  E  T  S  C  C  K
C  O  B  S  T  Y  S  S  R  M  T  P  W  A  P
S  Q  U  R  T  E  R  P  N  B  W  O  I  K  M
I  S  O  D  A  B  R  E  A  D  A  K  E  E  U
B  H  C  I  N  N  A  M  O  N  B  U  N  S  P
S  E  R  A  U  Q  S  N  O  M  E  L  E  Z  U
```

BISCOTTI   BROWNIES   CHEESECAKE   CHICKEN POT PIE

CHOCOLATE CAKE   CINNAMON BUNS   CUPCAKES   DINNER BUNS

LEMON SQUARES   LOAF   MACAROONS   MUFFIN

PECAN TART   POUND CAKE

PRETZEL   PUDDING

PUMPKIN PIE

SHORTBREAD

SODA BREAD

Pretzel Bun Softies

You're knot going to believe how tasty these are! Shape
the dough into giant pretzel shapes, or just tie it up in knots.

Get It Together: wire rack, measuring spoons, small bowl, baking sheet,
whisk, pastry brush, cooking spray, plastic wrap

1.	Loaf of frozen, whole-wheat bread dough, covered, thawed in refrigerator overnight	1	1
2.	Egg white (large)	1	1
	Water	1 tsp.	5 mL
	Tex-Mex seasoning	1 1/2 tsp.	7 mL

1. Divide dough into 12 equal pieces. On a slightly floured surface, roll each piece into 14 inch (35 cm) long rope. Shape each rope into loose knot (pictured at right). Pinch ends to seal. Grease baking sheet with cooking spray. Arrange knots about 1 inch (2.5 cm) apart on baking sheet. Grease plastic wrap with cooking spray. Cover knots with plastic wrap. Let stand at room temperature for about 45 minutes until doubled in size. Remove plastic wrap.

2. Place oven rack in centre position. Turn oven on to 350°F (175°C). Wait 10 minutes for oven to heat up. Put egg white and water into small bowl. Whisk. Brush knots with egg white mixture. Sprinkle with Tex-Mex seasoning. Bake knots in oven for about 20 minutes until golden. Put baking sheet on stovetop. Turn oven off. Remove knots from baking sheet and place on wire rack to cool. Makes 12 buns.

1 bun: 101 Calories; 1.6 g Total Fat (0 g Mono, 0 g Poly, 0 g Sat); 0 mg Cholesterol; 18 g Carbohydrate; 2 g Fibre; 5 g Protein; 230 mg Sodium

Pictured on page 11.

Creampuff Says: Sprinkle each bun with about 1 tsp. (5 mL) of Parmesan cheese for a cheesy version, or about 1/8 tsp. (0.5 mL) of coarse sea salt for that traditional pretzel appearance.

On the Rise!

Puffy Pockets

Watch these puff into perfect little pockets for dipping into sauces, or stuffing with tasty fillings like peanut butter and sliced bananas.

Get It Together: wire racks, dry and liquid measures, measuring spoons, mixing spoon, fork, medium bowl, 2 large bowls, plastic wrap, cooking spray, baking sheet

1.	Warm water	1/4 cup	60 mL
	Granulated sugar	2 tsp.	10 mL
	Active dry yeast	1 1/4 tsp.	6 mL
2.	Milk	1/4 cup	60 mL
	Plain yogurt	2 tbsp.	30 mL
	Large egg, fork-beaten	1	1
3.	All-purpose flour	2 cups	500 mL
	Salt	1/2 tsp.	2 mL
	Cooking spray		

1. Put water and sugar into medium bowl. Stir until sugar is dissolved. Sprinkle yeast over top. Let stand for 10 minutes. Stir until yeast is dissolved.

2. Add next 3 ingredients. Stir.

3. Put flour and salt into large bowl. Add yeast mixture. Mix until soft dough forms. Turn out onto lightly floured surface. Knead for 8 to 10 minutes until smooth and elastic. Grease large bowl with cooking spray. Place dough in bowl, turning once to grease top. Grease plastic wrap with cooking spray. Cover dough with plastic wrap. Let stand at room temperature for about 1 hour until doubled in size. Remove plastic wrap. Punch dough down. Knead for 1 to 2 minutes until smooth. Turn out onto lightly floured surface. Divide into 12 equal pieces. Roll pieces into balls. Using rolling pin, roll out 6 balls into 5 inch (12.5 cm) circles. Grease baking sheet with cooking spray. Arrange, about 1 inch (2.5 cm) apart on baking sheet. Spray with cooking spray.

(continued on next page)

Q: What can run but can't walk?

A: Water.

On the Rise!

Place oven rack in centre position. Turn oven on to Broil. Wait 10 minutes for oven to heat up. Broil for about 3 minutes until golden and puffed. Repeat with remaining 6 balls and cooking spray. Put pockets on wire racks to cool. Turn oven off. Makes 12 pockets.

1 pocket: *83 Calories; 0.7 g Total Fat (trace Mono, 0 g Poly, 0.2 g Sat); 18 mg Cholesterol; 16 g Carbohydrate; trace Fibre; 3 g Protein; 108 mg Sodium*

Pictured below.

Creampuff Says: Store extra pockets, once cooled, in a plastic bag to prevent them from drying out.

Left: Pretzel Bun Softies, page 9
Right: Puffy Pockets, left

Ape-ricot Monkey Bread

No, this isn't bread baked by monkeys—but feel free to go ape pulling off pieces of this sweet treat!

Get It Together: cutting board, serrated knife, dry measures, measuring spoons, large plate, small microwave-safe bowl, large bowl, 12 cup (3 L) Bundt pan, mixing spoon, cooking spray, plastic wrap

1. Butter, melted (see Tip, page 13)   1/2 cup   125 mL
   Apricot jam   1/2 cup   125 mL
   Ground cinnamon   1 tsp.   5 mL

2. Frozen unbaked dinner rolls, covered, 12   12
      thawed in refrigerator overnight

1. Put first 3 ingredients into large bowl. Stir well.

2. Cut each piece of dough in half. Roll into balls. Add to butter mixture. Using rubber spatula, stir gently until coated. Grease 12 cup (3 L) Bundt pan with cooking spray. Transfer balls to pan. Grease plastic wrap with cooking spray. Cover balls with plastic wrap. Let stand at room temperature for about 1 hour until doubled in size. Remove plastic wrap.

   Place oven rack in bottom position. Turn oven on to 350°F (175°C). Wait 10 minutes for oven to heat up. Bake balls in oven for about 30 minutes until golden. Put pan on stovetop. Turn oven off. Carefully invert monkey bread onto large plate (see Safety Tip). Let stand for 10 minutes to cool slightly. Makes 24 pieces.

1 piece: 97 Calories; 4.8 g Total Fat (1.0 g Mono, 0.1 g Poly, 2.4 g Sat); 10 mg Cholesterol; 13 g Carbohydrate; trace Fibre; 2 g Protein; 100 mg Sodium

Pictured on page 15.

Safety Tip: It's a good idea to ask a grown-up to help you invert the pan.

Creampuff Says: Try this recipe using other flavours of jam.

Boppin' Butterscotch Pull-Aparts

Love ooey gooey treats? You'll love these delicious pull-aparts with their sweet butterscotch glaze.

Get It Together: cutting board, sharp knife, dry measures, liquid measures, measuring spoons, large plate, small microwave-safe bowl, small bowl, 9 x 9 inch (22 x 22 cm) pan, plastic wrap, cooking spray, oven mitts

1.	Frozen, unbaked dinner rolls, covered, thawed in refrigerator overnight	12	12
2.	Butter, melted (see Tip)	1/2 cup	125 mL
	Box of butterscotch pudding powder (not instant), 6-serving size	1	1
	Milk	2 tbsp.	30 mL
	Ground cinnamon	1/2 tsp.	2 mL
3.	Sliced almonds	1/2 cup	125 mL

1. Cut each piece of dough in half. Roll into balls on lightly floured surface. Grease 9 x 9 inch (22 x 22 cm) pan with cooking spray. Arrange balls, evenly spaced, in pan.

2. Put next 4 ingredients into small bowl. Stir. Drizzle over balls.

3. Scatter almonds over balls. Grease plastic wrap with cooking spray. Cover pan with plastic wrap. Let stand at room temperature for about 1 hour until doubled in size. Remove plastic wrap. Place oven rack in centre position. Turn oven on to 350°F (175°C). Wait 10 minutes for oven to heat up.

   Bake in oven for about 30 minutes until golden. Put pan on stovetop. Turn oven off. Carefully invert pull-aparts onto large plate (see Safety Tip). Makes 24 pieces.

1 piece: 111 Calories; 5.9 g Total Fat (1.7 g Mono, 0.4 g Poly, 2.5 g Sat); 10 mg Cholesterol; 13 g Carbohydrate; trace Fibre; 2 g Protein; 118 mg Sodium

Pictured on page 15.

Safety Tip: It's a good idea to ask a grown-up to help you invert the pan.

Creampuff Tip: To melt butter, put in small microwave-safe bowl. Microwave, covered, on high (100%) for 10 seconds. Stir. Repeat steps until butter is melted.

On the Rise!

Cinnamapple Swirl Buns

These sticky-sweet cinnamon buns are glazed with yummy applesauce and butterscotch chips. Perfect for sharing at a sleepover!

Get It Together: cutting board, serrated knife, dry and liquid measures, measuring spoons, small bowl, large plate, 9 inch (22 cm) deep dish pie plate, rolling pin, rubber spatula, mixing spoon, plastic wrap, cooking spray

1.	Unsweetened applesauce	1/2 cup	125 mL
	Butterscotch chips	1/2 cup	125 mL
2.	Loaf of frozen whole-wheat bread dough, covered, thawed in refrigerator overnight	1	1
	Unsweetened applesauce	2 tbsp.	30 mL
3.	Brown sugar, packed	1/2 cup	125 mL
	Ground cinnamon	1/2 tsp.	2 mL

1. Grease 9 inch (22 cm) deep dish pie plate with cooking spray. Spread first amount of applesauce in bottom of pie plate. Sprinkle with butterscotch chips. Set aside.

2. Roll out dough on lightly floured surface to 9 x 12 inch (22 x 30 cm) rectangle. Spread second amount of applesauce over dough.

3. Put brown sugar and cinnamon into small bowl. Stir. Sprinkle over applesauce on dough. Roll up, jelly roll-style, from short side (see diagram). Pinch seam against roll to seal. Cut with serrated knife into 6 slices. Arrange slices, cut-side up, in pie plate. Grease plastic wrap with cooking spray. Cover slices with plastic wrap. Let stand at room temperature for about 75 minutes until doubled in size.

Place oven rack in centre position. Turn oven on to 375°F (190°C). Wait 10 minutes for oven to heat up. Remove plastic wrap from slices. Bake in oven for about 25 minutes until golden. Put pie plate on stovetop. Turn oven off. Let buns stand in pie plate for 10 minutes to cool slightly before carefully inverting onto large plate (see Safety Tip). Makes 6 buns.

(continued on next page)

On the Rise!

1 bun: 384 Calories; 8.4 g Total Fat (0 g Mono, 0 g Poly, 5.3 g Sat); 0 mg Cholesterol;
71 g Carbohydrate; 3 g Fibre; 10 g Protein; 445 mg Sodium

Pictured below.

Safety Tip: It's a good idea to ask a grown-up to help you invert the pan.

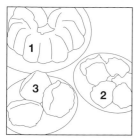

1. **Ape-ricot Monkey Bread, page 12**
2. **Boppin' Butterscotch Pull-Aparts, page 13**
3. **Cinnamapple Swirl Buns, page 14**

Left: Bottoms-Up Pizza Rustica, below
Right: Hawaiian Half-Moons, page 18

Bottoms-Up Pizza Rustica

All your favourite toppings in a pizza turned downside-up!

Get It Together: dry and liquid measures, measuring spoons, fork, small bowl, small microwave-safe bowl, 2 large bowls, 12 inch (30 cm) pizza pan, mixing spoon, rubber spatula, pastry brush, rolling pin, cooking spray, plastic wrap

QUICK PIZZA DOUGH

1.	All-purpose flour	1 1/2 cups	375 mL
	Whole-wheat flour	1/2 cup	125 mL
	Envelope of instant yeast	1/4 oz.	8 g
	(or 2 1/4 tsp., 11 mL)		
	Salt	1 tsp.	5 mL
2.	Water	3/4 cup	175 mL
	Cooking oil	2 tbsp.	30 mL

(continued on next page)

TOPPINGS

3.	Tomato sauce	1/3 cup	75 mL
	Basil pesto	1 tbsp.	15 mL
	Deli ham slices (about 8 1/2 oz., 113 g)	8	8
	Grated Italian cheese blend	2 cups	500 mL
4.	Large egg, fork-beaten	1	1

1. **Quick Pizza Dough:** Put first 4 ingredients in large bowl. Stir. Make a well in centre.

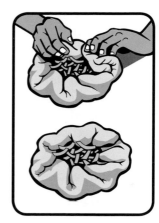

2. Put water into small, microwave-safe bowl. Microwave on high (100%) for 40 seconds. Remove bowl from microwave. Add cooking oil. Add to well. Stir until soft dough forms. Turn out onto lightly floured surface. Knead for about 4 minutes until smooth and elastic. Grease large bowl with cooking spray. Place dough in bowl, turning once to grease top. Grease plastic wrap with cooking spray. Cover dough with plastic wrap. Let stand at room temperature for 15 minutes. Remove plastic wrap. Turn out onto lightly floured surface. Roll out to 16 inch (40 cm) circle. Grease 12 inch (30 cm) pizza pan with cooking spray. Carefully transfer dough to pizza pan, allowing dough to hang over edges of pan.

3. **Toppings:** Put tomato sauce and pesto into small bowl. Stir. Spread evenly over dough to within 6 inches (15 cm) of edge. Arrange 4 slices of ham over sauce. Sprinkle with half of cheese. Repeat with remaining ham and cheese. Fold a section of border up and over edge of filling, allowing dough to overlap so that fold is created. Pinch to seal. Repeat until dough border is completely folded around filling (see diagrams).

4. Place oven rack in bottom position. Turn oven on to 425°F (220°C). Wait 10 minutes for oven to heat up. Brush dough with egg. Bake in oven for about 25 minutes until golden. Put pizza pan on stovetop. Turn oven off. Let pizza stand for 10 minutes. Transfer to cutting board. Cuts into 8 slices.

1 slice: 272 Calories; 12.6 g Total Fat (2.0 g Mono, 1.1 g Poly, 4.6 g Sat); 61 mg Cholesterol; 25 g Carbohydrate; 2 g Fibre; 17 g Protein; 983 mg Sodium

Pictured at left.

Creampuff Says: You could also try making this pizza with pepperoni and mushroom.

On the Rise!

Hawaiian Half-Moons

Turn snack time into a luau by serving up these delicious pockets!
Try them with your other favourite pizza toppings, too.

Get It Together: cutting board, wire rack, sharp knife, dry and liquid measures, measuring spoons, fork, small bowl, medium bowl, strainer, baking sheet, mixing spoon, can opener, rolling pin, whisk, pastry brush, cooking spray

1.	Grated Italian cheese blend	1/2 cup	125 mL
	Chopped deli ham	1/3 cup	75 mL
	Canned crushed pineapple, drained	1/4 cup	60 mL
	Chopped red pepper	3 tbsp.	50 mL
	Plum sauce	3 tbsp.	50 mL
2.	Frozen unbaked dinner rolls, covered, thawed in refrigerator overnight	12	12
3.	Large egg	1	1
	Water	1 tbsp.	15 mL

1. Place oven rack in centre position. Turn oven on to 350°F (175°C). Put first 5 ingredients into medium bowl. Stir.

2. On lightly floured surface, roll out each piece of dough to 5 inch (12.5 cm) circle. Place about 1 1/2 tbsp. (25 mL) ham mixture in centre of each circle.

3. Put egg and water into small bowl. Whisk. Brush edges of dough with egg mixture. Fold dough over filling. Press edges together with fork to seal. Grease baking sheet with cooking spray. Arrange pockets about 1 inch (2.5 cm) apart on baking sheet. Brush egg mixture over top. Cut 3 slits in top of each pocket to allow steam to escape. Bake in oven for about 25 minutes until golden. Put baking sheet on stovetop. Turn oven off. Remove pockets from baking sheet and place on wire rack to cool. Makes 12 pockets.

1 pocket: 132 Calories; 3.6 g Total Fat (0 g Mono, trace Poly, 0.8 g Sat); 24 mg Cholesterol; 20 g Carbohydrate; trace Fibre; 6 g Protein; 289 mg Sodium

Pictured on page 16.

Gone-To-Seed Focaccia

Not only is it fun to say (foh-CAH-chia), it's fun to eat too! You'll love the seed-and-cheese topping. Drizzle with olive oil for extra flavour and classiness!

Get It Together: cutting board, wire rack, serrated knife, dry measures, measuring spoons, baking sheet with sides, 2 small bowls, rolling pin, whisk, pastry brush, cooking spray, plastic wrap

1.	Loaf of frozen whole-wheat bread dough, covered, thawed in refrigerator overnight	1	1
2.	Egg white (large)	1	1
	Water	1 tsp.	5 mL
3.	Grated Parmesan cheese	1/4 cup	60 mL
	Salted, roasted shelled pumpkin seeds	2 tbsp.	30 mL
	Salted, roasted sunflower seeds	2 tbsp.	30 mL
	Sesame seeds	1 tbsp.	15 mL

1. Roll out dough to 10 x 14 inch (25 x 35 cm) rectangle. Grease baking sheet with sides with cooking spray. Press dough into baking sheet. Grease plastic wrap with cooking spray. Cover dough with plastic wrap. Let stand at room temperature for about 1 hour until doubled in size. Remove plastic wrap. Make dents on surface of dough with fingers.

2. Place oven rack in centre position. Turn oven on to 350°F (175°C). Put egg white and water in small bowl. Whisk. Brush over top of dough.

3. Put remaining 4 ingredients into small bowl. Stir. Sprinkle over dough. Bake in oven for about 20 minutes until golden. Put baking sheet on stovetop. Turn oven off. Remove bread from baking sheet and place on wire rack to cool. Cuts into 12 pieces.

1 piece: 135 Calories; 4.3 g Total Fat (0 g Mono, 0 g Poly, 0.7 g Sat); 2.5 mg Cholesterol; 19 g Carbohydrate; 2 g Fibre; 7 g Protein; 262 mg Sodium

Pictured on page 21.

Hot Diggity Dog Buns

No diggity! Use this handy bread dough to make hot dog or hamburger buns, and then load them up at your next picnic!

Get It Together: wire rack, dry and liquid measures, measuring spoons, small cup, 2 large bowls, small microwave-safe bowl, baking sheet, mixing spoon, whisk, pastry brush, plastic wrap, cooking spray

1.	All-purpose flour	2 3/4 cups	675 mL
	Granulated sugar	2 tbsp.	30 mL
	Envelope of instant yeast	1/4 oz.	8 g
	(or 2 1/4 tsp., 11 mL)		
	Salt	1 tsp.	5 mL
2.	Water	1/2 cup	125 mL
	Butter	2 tbsp.	30 mL
	Milk	1/2 cup	125 mL
3.	Large egg	1	1
	Water	1/2 tsp.	2 mL
	Sesame seeds	2 tbsp.	30 mL

1. Put first 4 ingredients into large bowl. Stir. Make a well in centre.

2. Put first amount of water and butter into small, microwave-safe bowl. Microwave, covered, on medium (50%) for about 2 minutes until butter is almost melted. Remove bowl from microwave. Stir butter until melted. Add milk. Stir. Add mixture to well. Stir until soft dough forms. Turn out onto lightly floured surface. Knead for 5 minutes. Grease large bowl with cooking spray. Place dough in bowl, turning once to grease top. Grease plastic wrap with cooking spray. Cover dough with plastic wrap. Let stand at room temperature for about 1 hour until doubled in size. Remove plastic wrap. Punch dough down. Turn out onto lightly floured surface. Knead for 1 to 2 minutes until smooth. Divide dough into 8 equal pieces. Shape pieces into 6 inch (15 cm) long logs. Grease baking sheet with cooking spray. Arrange logs, about 1 inch (2.5 cm) apart, on baking sheet. Grease plastic wrap with cooking spray. Cover logs with plastic wrap. Let stand at room temperature for about 30 minutes until doubled in size. Remove plastic wrap.

(continued on next page)

Top: Gone-To-Seed Focaccia, page 19
Bottom: Hot Diggity Dog Buns, above

On the Rise!

3. Place oven rack in centre position. Turn oven on to 375°F (190°C). Wait 10 minutes for oven to heat up. Put egg and second amount of water in small cup. Whisk. Brush dough with egg mixture. Sprinkle with sesame seeds. Bake in oven for about 14 minutes until golden and hollow sounding when tapped. Put baking sheet on stovetop. Turn oven off. Remove buns from baking sheet and place on wire racks to cool. Makes 8 buns.

1 bun: *206 Calories; 4.7 g Total Fat (0.8 g Mono, 0.1 g Poly, 2.1 g Sat); 35 mg Cholesterol; 35 g Carbohydrate; 1 g Fibre; 6 g Protein; 334 mg Sodium*

Pictured below.

Cravin' Cranberry Bread, below

Cravin' Cranberry Bread

If you like raisin bread, you will love this bread! If you don't like raisins, you will still love this bread! Try it as toast for breakfast, with a bit of butter.

Get It Together: cutting board, wire rack, serrated knife, dry measures, liquid measures, measuring spoons, fork, small microwave-safe cup, small cup, small heatproof bowl, medium bowl, 2 large bowls, strainer, baking sheet, mixing spoon, whisk, pastry brush, cooking spray, plastic wrap

1.	Dried cranberries	1 cup	250 mL
	Hot water	2 cups	500 mL
2.	Whole-wheat flour	1 1/2 cups	375 mL
	All-purpose flour	1 cup	250 mL
	Instant yeast	1 1/4 tsp.	6 mL
	Salt	1 tsp.	5 mL
	Ground cinnamon	1/2 tsp.	2 mL

(continued on next page)

3.	Cooking oil	2 tbsp.	30 mL
	Granulated sugar	2 tbsp.	30 mL
	Water	1/2 cup	125 mL
	Large egg, fork-beaten	1	1
4.	All-purpose flour, approximately	1/4 cup	60 mL
5.	Large egg	1	1
	Water	1/2 tsp.	2 mL

1. Put cranberries into small heatproof bowl. Add hot water. Stir. Let stand for about 15 minutes until softened. Drain. Set aside.

2. Put next 5 ingredients in large bowl. Stir.

3. Put oil and sugar into medium bowl. Stir. Pour water into small microwave-safe cup. Microwave on high (100%) for 30 seconds. Remove bowl from microwave. Add water to oil mixture. Add egg. Stir. Add to flour mixture. Stir until soft dough starts to form. Add cranberries. Mix well.

4. Turn out onto lightly floured surface. Knead for 8 to 10 minutes until smooth and elastic, adding second amount of all-purpose flour 1 tbsp. (15 mL) at a time, if necessary, to prevent sticking. Grease large bowl with cooking spray. Place dough in bowl, turning once to grease top. Grease plastic wrap with cooking spray. Cover dough with plastic wrap. Let stand at room temperature for about 1 hour until doubled in size. Remove plastic wrap. Punch dough down. Knead for 1 to 2 minutes until smooth. Shape into round loaf. Grease baking sheet with cooking spray. Transfer dough to baking sheet. Grease plastic wrap with cooking spray. Cover dough with plastic wrap. Let stand at room temperature for about 1 hour until doubled in size. Remove plastic wrap.

5. Place oven rack in centre position. Turn oven on to 375°F (190°C). Wait 10 minutes for oven to heat up. Put egg and second amount of water in small cup. Whisk. Brush over top of loaf. Bake in oven for about 25 minutes until golden and hollow sounding when tapped. Put baking sheet on stovetop. Turn oven off. Remove bread from baking sheet and place on wire rack to cool. Cuts into 16 slices.

1 slice: 118 Calories; 2.5 g Total Fat (1.0 g Mono, 0.6 g Poly, 0.4 g Sat); 27 mg Cholesterol; 22 g Carbohydrate; 2 g Fibre; 3 g Protein; 154 mg Sodium

Pictured at left.

Cheeztastic Buns

Tasty buns topped with crispy cheese—great for dipping into a bowl of your favourite soup, or taking along for school lunches.

Get It Together: wire rack, dry and liquid measures, measuring spoons, small cup, 2 large bowls, whisk, mixing spoon, grater, pastry brush, cooking spray, plastic wrap

1.	Warm water	3/4 cup	175 mL
	Granulated sugar	1/2 tsp.	2 mL
	Active dry yeast	1 1/2 tsp.	7 mL
2.	Large egg	1	1
	Cooking oil	1 tbsp.	15 mL
	Salt	1/2 tsp.	2 mL
	Whole-wheat flour	2 1/2 cups	625 mL
	Grated sharp Cheddar cheese	1 1/2 cups	375 mL
3.	Whole-wheat flour, approximately	1 tbsp.	15 mL
4.	Large egg	1	1
	Water	1/2 tsp.	2 mL
	Grated sharp Cheddar cheese	1 cup	250 mL

1. Put water and sugar into large bowl. Stir until sugar is dissolved. Sprinkle yeast over top. Let stand for 10 minutes. Stir until yeast is dissolved.

2. Add next 3 ingredients. Whisk until smooth. Add flour, 1/2 cup (125 mL) at a time, stirring constantly until stiff dough forms. Add first amount of cheese. Stir. Turn out onto lightly floured surface.

3. Knead dough for 8 to 10 minutes until smooth and elastic, adding second amount of flour, if necessary, to prevent sticking. Grease large bowl with cooking spray. Place dough in bowl, turning once to grease top.

(continued on next page)

Q: What animal makes the most of its food?

A: The giraffe. It makes a little go a long way.

On the Rise!

Grease plastic wrap with cooking spray. Cover dough with plastic wrap. Let stand at room temperature for 1 hour until doubled in size. Remove plastic wrap. Punch down dough. Knead for about 1 minute until smooth. Divide into 12 equal pieces. Roll into balls. Grease 9 x 13 inch (22 x 33 cm) baking pan with cooking spray. Arrange balls in pan. Grease plastic wrap with cooking spray. Cover balls with plastic wrap. Let stand at room temperature for about 45 minutes until doubled in size. Remove plastic wrap.

4. Place oven rack in centre position. Turn oven on to 350°F (175°C). Wait 10 minutes for oven to heat up. Put egg and water in small cup. Whisk. Brush over tops of balls. Sprinkle with second amount of cheese. Bake in oven for about 30 minutes until golden and hollow sounding when tapped. Put pan on stovetop. Turn oven off. Remove buns from pan and place on wire rack to cool. Makes 12 buns.

1 bun: 64 Calories; 5.1 g Total Fat (1.6 g Mono, 0.4 g Poly, 2.3 g Sat); 46 mg Cholesterol; 1 g Carbohydrate; trace Fibre; 4 g Protein; 166 mg Sodium

Pictured below.

Cheeztastic Buns, left

Pepperoni Hideaways

Bake a batch to have after-school snacks
for the whole week—if they last that long!

Get It Together: cutting board, wire rack, sharp knife, dry and liquid
measures, measuring spoons, small bowl, 2 large bowls, baking sheets,
mixing spoon, cooking spray, plastic wrap

1.	Warm water	2/3 cup	150 mL
	Granulated sugar	1/2 tsp.	2 mL
	Active dry yeast	1 tsp.	5 mL
2.	All-purpose flour	1 1/2 cups	375 mL
	Powdered Cheddar cheese product	1/2 cup	125 mL
	Salt	1/2 tsp.	2 mL
	Cooking oil	2 tbsp.	30 mL
	All-purpose flour, approximately	1 tbsp.	15 mL
3.	Deli pepperoni sticks (6 inch, 15 cm, length), cut in half crosswise	6	6

1. Put water and sugar into small bowl. Stir until sugar is dissolved.
    Sprinkle yeast over top. Let stand for 10 minutes. Stir until yeast
    is dissolved.

2. Put next 3 ingredients into large bowl. Stir. Add cooking oil and yeast
    mixture. Mix until soft dough forms. Turn out onto lightly floured surface.
    Knead for 8 to 10 minutes until smooth and elastic, adding second
    amount of flour, if necessary, to prevent sticking. Grease large bowl with
    cooking spray. Place dough in bowl, turning once to grease top. Grease
    plastic wrap with cooking spray. Cover dough with plastic wrap. Let
    stand at room temperature for about 75 minutes until doubled in size.
    Remove plastic wrap. Punch dough down. Knead for 1 to 2 minutes
    until smooth. Turn out onto lightly floured surface. Divide dough in half.
    Roll 1 half into 12 inch (30 cm) long rope. Cut into 6 pieces. Roll out
    each piece to 3 inch (7.5 cm) oval. Repeat steps with other half.

(continued on next page)

3. Place oven rack in centre position. Turn oven on to 450°F (230°C). Place 1 pepperoni piece in centre of 1 dough oval. Bring up edges of dough to enclose pepperoni. Pinch edges to seal (pictured at right). Repeat with remaining dough and pepperoni. Grease baking sheets with cooking spray. Arrange buns, seam-side down, about 1 inch (2.5 cm) apart on baking sheets. Bake in oven, 1 sheet at a time, for about 10 minutes until golden. Put baking sheets on stovetop. Turn oven off. Let buns stand on baking sheets for 20 minutes before removing to wire rack to cool. Makes 12 buns.

1 bun: *261 Calories; 19.0 g Total Fat (8.9 g Mono, 2.0 g Poly, 7.0 g Sat); 33 mg Cholesterol; 13 g Carbohydrate; trace Fibre; 9 g Protein; 934 mg Sodium*

Pictured below.

Pepperoni Hideaways, left

Twisted Tuna Melts, below

Twisted Tuna Melts

Tired of tuna sandwiches? Try this tasty tuna-and-cheese combo—spiral style!

Get It Together: cutting board, wire rack, sharp knife, serrated knife, dry measures, measuring spoons, small bowl, strainer, small saucepan, baking sheet, mixing spoon, grater, can opener, rolling pin, cooking spray, plastic wrap

1.	Cooking oil	1 tsp.	5 mL
	Chopped fresh white mushrooms	1/2 cup	125 mL
	Chopped celery	1/4 cup	60 mL
	Chopped onion	1/4 cup	60 mL
2.	All-purpose flour	1 tbsp.	15 mL
	Dry mustard	1/4 tsp.	1 mL

(continued on next page)

3.	Can of flaked white tuna in water, drained	6 oz.	170 g
	Grated sharp Cheddar cheese	1 cup	250 mL
4.	Loaf of frozen white bread dough, covered, thawed in refrigerator overnight	1	1

1. Heat cooking oil in small saucepan on medium. Add next 3 ingredients. Cook for 8 to 10 minutes, stirring occasionally, until vegetables are softened and starting to brown.

2. Add flour and mustard. Heat and stir for 1 minute. Transfer to small bowl. Turn burner off.

3. Add tuna. Stir. Let stand for about 10 minutes to cool slightly. Add cheese. Stir well.

4. Roll out dough to 10 x 14 inch (25 x 35 cm) rectangle. Spread tuna mixture over dough, to within 1/2 inch (12 mm) of edge on all sides. Roll up, jelly roll-style, from long side (see diagram). Pinch seam against roll to seal. Cut into 12 slices, using serrated knife. Grease baking sheet with cooking spray. Place spirals, cut-side up, about 1 inch (2.5 cm) apart on baking sheet.

Grease plastic wrap with cooking spray. Cover spirals with plastic wrap. Let stand at room temperature for about 70 minutes until doubled in size. Remove plastic wrap.

Place oven rack in centre position. Turn oven on to 375°F (190°C). Wait 10 minutes for oven to heat up. Bake spirals in oven for about 25 minutes until golden. Put baking sheet on stovetop. Turn oven off. Let spirals stand on baking sheet for 5 minutes before removing to wire rack to cool. Makes 12 spirals.

1 spiral: 170 Calories; 5.5 g Total Fat (1.2 g Mono, 0.4 g Poly, 2.1 g Sat); 16 mg Cholesterol; 19 g Carbohydrate; 2 g Fibre; 10 g Protein; 326 mg Sodium

Pictured at left.

On the Rise!

Let Them Eat Cake!
Cakes & Squares

When your friends and family see you baking these cakes, cupcakes and squares, you may have no choice but to let them sample. Make sure you let your creations cool a little before you taste them…and make plenty—or there may be cake pan-demonium!

find 22 baking tools

```
C  T  E  L  Z  C  D  R  X  C  V  B  N  M  K
O  M  B  A  K  S  D  F  E  G  K  Y  I  E  R
O  A  H  N  C  J  I  L  P  M  Q  X  A  A  O
K  N  I  I  A  O  V  E  N  M  I  T  T  S  F
I  F  H  D  R  A  O  B  G  N  I  T  T  U  C
E  A  U  S  E  O  R  R  G  R  E  T  A  R  G
C  E  I  P  R  O  L  B  U  E  W  A  Q  E  B
U  T  N  A  I  E  O  L  H  H  R  U  M  S  N
T  T  A  T  W  W  T  S  I  E  S  L  U  I  E
T  J  P  U  L  E  G  S  T  N  R  P  K  E  P
E  R  E  L  N  N  K  F  E  L  G  E  O  T  H
R  S  C  A  I  Y  I  E  L  Z  M  P  X  O  N
S  L  U  K  R  S  X  W  B  A  O  R  I  I  N
E  P  A  S  T  R  Y  B  R  U  S  H  L  N  M
A  B  S  T  R  A  I  N  E  R  A  I  E  I  A
```

BAKING SHEET	COOKIE CUTTERS	CUTTING BOARD
FORK	GRATER	KNIFE
MIXER	MEASURES	MIXING BOWL
OVEN MITTS	PASTRY BRUSH	RAMEKIN
ROLLING PIN	SAUCEPAN	SIFTER
SPATULA	SPOON	
STRAINER	TIMER	
WHISK	WIRE RACK	
ZESTER		

Tropical Twist Snack Cake

When snack time rolls around, you'll want to put on your flip-flops
and sunglasses to enjoy this tropically delicious cake!

Get It Together: cutting board, sharp knife, liquid and dry measures,
measuring spoons, fork, small microwave-safe bowl, 9 x 9 inch (22 x 22 cm)
pan, mixing spoon, cooking spray

1.	Pineapple juice	1/2 cup	125 mL
	Coarsely chopped, dried pineapple	1/2 cup	125 mL
	Dark raisins	1/4 cup	60 mL
	Lemon juice	1 tbsp.	15 mL
2.	Large eggs, fork-beaten	2	2
	Vanilla extract	1 tsp.	5 mL
3.	Whole-wheat flour	1 1/3 cups	325 mL
	Brown sugar, packed	3/4 cup	175 mL
	Medium, unsweetened coconut	1/2 cup	125 mL
	Salt	1/2 tsp.	2 mL
	Baking soda	1/4 tsp.	1 mL
	Cold butter, cut up	1/3 cup	75 mL

1. Put first 4 ingredients into small microwave-safe bowl. Stir. Microwave,
    covered, on high (100%) for about 1 minute until hot. Let stand
    in microwave for 10 minutes. Remove cover. Let stand for about
    15 minutes until cool. Remove bowl from microwave.

2. Place oven rack in centre position. Turn oven on to 350°F (175°C).
    Add eggs and vanilla to pineapple mixture. Stir.

3. Put next 5 ingredients into large bowl. Stir. Cut in butter until mixture
    resembles coarse crumbs. Add pineapple mixture. Stir until no dry flour
    remains. Grease 9 x 9 inch (22 x 22 cm) pan with cooking spray. Spread
    mixture evenly in pan. Bake in oven for about 25 to 30 minutes until
    golden. Put pan on stovetop. Turn oven off. Let cake stand in pan until
    cool. Cuts into 16 tropical squares.

1 square: 156 Calories; 6.0 g Total Fat (1.1 g Mono, 0.2 g Poly, 3.9 g Sat); 37 mg Cholesterol;
24 g Carbohydrate; 2 g Fibre; 2 g Protein; 135 mg Sodium

Pictured on page 34.

Yum-Gummy Pound Cake

This is the kind of "fruitcake" you'll really enjoy—a rainbow of sweet, chewy gummies are hiding inside!

Get It Together: cutting board, wire rack, serrated knife, dry measures, measuring spoons, table knife, large bowl, medium bowl, 12 cup (3 L) Bundt pan, mixing spoon, wooden pick, electric mixer

1.	Butter, softened (see Tip, page 42)	1 cup	250 mL
	Granulated sugar	1 1/2 cups	375 mL
	Sour cream	1 cup	250 mL
	Vanilla extract	1 tsp.	5 mL
	Large eggs	4	4
2.	All-purpose flour	3 cups	750 mL
	Baking powder	1/2 tsp.	2 mL
	Salt	1/2 tsp.	2 mL
3.	Baking gums (see Tip)	1 1/2 cups	375 mL

1. Place oven rack in centre position. Turn oven on to 325°F (160°C). Put first 4 ingredients in large bowl. Beat until light and fluffy. Add eggs, 1 at a time, beating well after each addition.

2. Put next 3 ingredients into medium bowl. Stir. Add half of flour mixture to butter mixture. Mix well. Add remaining flour mixture. Mix well until no dry flour remains.

3. Add baking gums. Stir well. Grease 12 cup (3 L) Bundt pan with cooking spray. Spread mixture evenly in pan. Bake in oven for about 70 minutes until wooden pick inserted in centre of cake comes out clean. Put pan on stovetop. Turn oven off. Let cake stand in pan for 10 minutes. Run knife around inside edge of pan to loosen cake before inverting onto wire rack to cool (see Safety Tip). Cuts into 16 "fruity" wedges.

1 wedge: 381 Calories; 15.0 g Total Fat (2.9 g Mono, 0.4 g Poly, 9.3 g Sat); 94 mg Cholesterol; 57 g Carbohydrate; trace Fibre; 4 g Protein; 201 mg Sodium

Pictured on page 34.

Safety Tip: It's a good idea to ask a grown-up to help you invert the pan.

Cookbot 3000 Tip: Regular gumdrops cannot be used for this recipe because they will melt. Baking gums can be found in the baking aisle of most grocery stores.

Let Them Eat Cake!

Rainbow Sparks Cheesecake

Creamy cheesecake just like grown-ups eat, but this one has a fun rainbow of colours. Top a slice with whipped cream and your favourite colour of sprinkles!

Get It Together: sharp knife, dry measures, measuring spoons, large bowl, medium saucepan, 9 inch (22 cm) deep dish pie plate, mixing spoon, cooking spray, wire rack, electric mixer, food processor

1.	Finely crushed vanilla wafers (about 40 wafers)	1 1/3 cup	325 mL
	Butter	1/3 cup	75 mL
2.	Cream cheese, softened (see Tip)	16 oz.	454 g
	Granulated sugar	3/4 cup	175 mL
	Large eggs	2	2
	Candy sprinkles	1/4 cup	60 mL

1. Place oven rack in centre position. Turn oven on to 350°F (175°C). Put wafers into food processor. Cover with lid. Process until fine crumbs form. Melt butter in medium saucepan on low. Remove from heat. Turn burner off. Add crumbs. Mix well. Grease 9 inch (22 cm) deep dish pie plate with cooking spray. Press crumb mixture firmly in bottom and up sides of pie plate.

2. Put cream cheese and sugar into large bowl. Beat until smooth. Add eggs, 1 at a time, beating after each addition until just mixed. Add sprinkles. Stir. Spread evenly in crust. Bake in oven for about 30 minutes until centre is almost set. Put pan on wire rack. Turn oven off. Let pie stand in pan for about 2 hours until cool. Chill for 3 hours. Cuts into 12 colourful wedges.

1 wedge: 322 Calories; 21.1 g Total Fat (1.3 g Mono, 0.2 g Poly, 12.9 g Sat); 90 mg Cholesterol; 30 g Carbohydrate; 0 g Fibre; 5 g Protein; 259 mg Sodium

Pictured on page 34.

 Cookbot 3000 Tip: To soften cream cheese, let stand at room temperature until a knife can pass easily through it.

Let Them Eat Cake!

1. Yum-Gummy Pound Cake, page 32
2. Nuts-About-Cocoa Cake, at right
3. Tropical Twist Snack Cake, page 31
4. Rainbow Sparks Cheesecake, page 33

Nuts-About-Cocoa Cake

Here's a cake that frosts itself! If you love brownies, you'll love this no-egg cake with nutty, chocolatey flavour in every bite.

Get It Together: cutting board, wire rack, sharp knife, dry and liquid measures, measuring spoons, small bowl, large bowl, sifter, 9 x 9 inch (22 x 22 cm) pan, mixing spoon, cooking spray, wooden pick

1.	Whole-wheat flour	1 1/2 cups	375 mL
	Granulated sugar	1 cup	250 mL
	Cocoa, sifted if lumpy	3 tbsp.	50 mL
	Baking soda	1 tsp.	5 mL
	Salt	1/2 tsp.	2 mL
2.	Water	1 cup	250 mL
	Cooking oil	6 tbsp.	100 mL
	White vinegar	1 tbsp.	15 mL
	Vanilla extract	1 tsp.	5 mL
3.	Chopped pecans	1/3 cup	75 mL
	Semi-sweet chocolate chips	1/3 cup	75 mL
4.	Chopped pecans	1/2 cup	125 mL
	Semi-sweet chocolate chips	1/2 cup	125 mL

1. Place oven rack in centre position. Turn oven on to 350°F (175°C). Put first 5 ingredients into large bowl. Stir. Make a well in centre.

2. Put next 4 ingredients into small bowl. Stir. Add to well. Stir until just moistened.

3. Add first amount of pecans and chocolate chips. Stir.

4. Grease 9 x 9 inch (22 x 22 cm) pan with cooking spray. Spread mixture evenly in pan. Sprinkle with second amount of pecans and chocolate chips. Bake in oven for about 35 minutes until wooden pick inserted in centre of cake comes out clean. Put pan on wire rack. Turn oven off. Let cake stand in pan until cool. Cuts into 16 nutty squares.

1 square: 222 Calories; 12.7 g Total Fat (6.5 g Mono, 3.0 g Poly, 2.4 g Sat); 0 mg Cholesterol; 28 g Carbohydrate; 3 g Fibre; 3 g Protein; 153 mg Sodium

Pictured at left.

Sweet-Spot Baby Cakes

These cutie cupcakes will be the star of the show with their lemony flavour and pretty pink frosting—plus cherries on top! You'll have more icing than you need, but having extra helps with decorating.

Get It Together: wire racks, dry and liquid measures, measuring spoons, fork, 2 medium bowls, large bowl, muffin pan, mixing spoon, zester, piping bag with medium star tip, muffin pan liners, wooden pick, electric mixer

1.	All-purpose flour	1 cup	250 mL
	Baking powder	1 1/2 tsp.	7 mL
	Grated lemon zest (see Tip, page 43)	1 tsp.	5 mL
	Salt	1/8 tsp.	0.5 mL
2.	Butter, softened (see Tip, page 42)	1/3 cup	75 mL
	Granulated sugar	1/2 cup	125 mL
	Large egg	1	1
	Vanilla yogurt	1/2 cup	125 mL

CHERRY BUTTERCREAM ICING

3.	Unsweetened cherry drink powder	1/2 tsp.	2 mL
	Milk	2 tbsp.	30 mL
4.	Icing (confectioner's) sugar	3 cups	750 mL
	Butter, softened (see Tip, page 42)	1/2 cup	125 mL
5.	Cocktail cherries with stems	8	8

1. Place oven rack in centre position. Turn oven on to 350°F (175°C). Put first 4 ingredients into medium bowl. Stir. Set aside.

2. Put butter and sugar into medium bowl. Beat until light and fluffy. Add egg. Beat well. Add half of flour mixture to butter mixture. Stir until just mixed. Add yogurt. Stir until just mixed. Add remaining flour mixture. Stir until just mixed. Fill 8 paper lined muffin cups 3/4 full. Bake in oven for about 18 minutes until wooden pick inserted in centre of a cupcake comes out clean. Put pan on stovetop. Turn oven off. Let cupcakes stand in pan for 10 minutes before removing to wire racks to cool completely.

3. **Cherry Buttercream Icing:** Put drink powder and milk into large bowl. Stir until dissolved.

(continued on next page)

Let Them Eat Cake!

Sweet-Spot Baby Cakes, left

4. Add icing sugar and butter. Beat on low for about 30 seconds until mixed. Beat on high for about 3 minutes until light and fluffy. Spoon into piping bag fitted with medium star tip (see Tip). Pipe onto cupcakes.

5. Top each cupcake with 1 cocktail cherry. Makes 8 cupcakes.

1 cupcake: 481 Calories; 20.1 g Total Fat (5.1 g Mono, 0.8 g Poly, 12.5 g Sat); 79 mg Cholesterol; 75 g Carbohydrate; trace Fibre; 3 g Protein; 295 mg Sodium

Pictured above.

 Cookbot 3000 Tip: If you don't have a piping bag, fill a resealable freezer bag with icing, then snip off one corner.

Mud Puddle Cake

You don't need your rubber boots for this mud puddle! If you want pebbles on your puddle, try sprinkling this shiny cake with tiny toffee bits and chopped nuts.

Get It Together: cutting board, sharp knife, dry and liquid measures, measuring spoons, large bowl, 9 x 13 inch (22 x 33 cm) pan, shallow frying pan, mixing spoon, wooden pick, wooden spoon/chopsticks, cooking spray, electric mixer

1.	Chopped pecans	1/2 cup	125mL
	Box of chocolate cake mix (2 layer size)	1	1
	Toffee bits (such as Skor)	1/2 cup	125 mL
2.	Chocolate ice cream topping	1/2 cup	125 mL
	Caramel ice cream topping	1/2 cup	125 mL

1. Place pecans in a medium frying pan. Heat on medium for 3 to 5 minutes, stirring often, until golden. Set aside. Turn burner off. Place oven rack in centre position. Turn oven on to 350°F (175°C). Prepare cake mix according to package directions in large bowl. Add pecans and toffee bits. Stir. Grease 9 x 13 inch (22 x 33 cm) pan with cooking spray. Spread mixture evenly in pan. Bake in oven for about 35 minutes until wooden pick inserted in centre of cake comes out clean. Put pan on stovetop. Turn oven off. Let cake stand in pan for 5 minutes.

2. Poke cake randomly with chopsticks or wooden spoon handle to create holes. Drizzle chocolate and caramel topping over cake to fill the holes and make puddles. Let stand until cool. Cuts into 20 mud puddle pieces.

1 piece: 205 Calories; 8.6 g Total Fat (3.1 g Mono, 2.0 g Poly, 2.3 g Sat); 4 mg Cholesterol; 32 g Carbohydrate; 1 g Fibre; 2 g Protein; 289 mg Sodium

Pictured on page 41.

Q: What kind of cup doesn't hold water?

A: A cupcake.

Confetti Graham Squares

These squares are like s'mores in upside-down land—they've got a graham cookie base, a layer of white chocolate and colourful marshmallows on top.

Get It Together: sharp knife, dry measures, measuring spoons, mixing spoon, medium bowl, large bowl, 9 x 13 inch (22 x 33 cm) pan, cooking spray, oven mitts, electric mixer

1. All-purpose flour	1 cup	250 mL
Graham cracker crumbs	1 cup	250 mL
Baking powder	1 tsp.	5 mL
Salt	1/2 tsp.	2 mL
2. Butter, softened (see Tip, page 42)	1/2 cup	125 mL
Brown sugar, packed	2/3 cup	150 mL
Large eggs	2	2
Vanilla extract	1 tsp.	5 mL
3. White chocolate chips	1 1/3 cups	325 mL
Miniature multi-coloured marshmallows	4 cups	1 L

1. Place oven rack in centre position. Turn oven on to 350°F (175°C). Put first 4 ingredients into medium bowl. Stir. Set aside.

2. Put butter and brown sugar into large bowl. Beat until light and fluffy. Add eggs, 1 at a time, beating well after each addition. Add vanilla and flour mixture. Beat until soft dough forms. Grease 9 x 13 inch (22 x 33 cm) pan with cooking spray. Spread dough evenly in pan. Bake in oven for about 15 minutes until golden and set. Put pan on stovetop.

3. Sprinkle chocolate chips evenly over bottom layer. Let stand for about 2 minutes until softened. Spread evenly. Sprinkle marshmallows over chocolate in single layer. Press down lightly. Bake in oven for about 1 minute until marshmallows begin to soften. Put pan on stovetop. Turn oven off. Let cake stand in pan until cool and chocolate is set. Cuts into 24 soft and sweet squares.

1 square: 189 Calories; 8.8 g Total Fat (1.1 g Mono, 0.3 g Poly, 5.1 g Sat); 32 mg Cholesterol; 27 g Carbohydrate; trace Fibre; 2 g Protein; 147 mg Sodium

Pictured on page 41.

Pictured on page 41.

Caramel Candy Brownies

How *do* you get caramel-filled candy squares into these brownies? Make this delicious recipe and find out! (There should be two leftover candy squares to nibble on while you're waiting for these to bake!)

Get It Together: dry measures, measuring spoons, fork, large bowl, small saucepan, 9 x 9 inch (22 x 22 cm) pan, mixing spoon, cooking spray, wooden pick

1.	Butter	1/2 cup	125 mL
	Unsweetened chocolate baking squares (1 oz., 28 g, each), coarsely chopped	2	2
2.	Large eggs, fork-beaten	2	2
	Granulated sugar	1 1/2 cups	375 mL
3.	All-purpose flour	3/4 cup	175 mL
4.	Caramel-filled candy bar, separated into 16 squares	3 1/2 oz.	100 g

1. Place oven rack in centre position. Turn oven on to 350°F (175°C). Heat butter and chocolate in small heavy saucepan on lowest heat, stirring often until chocolate is almost melted. Remove from heat. Turn burner off. Stir chocolate mixture until smooth. Pour into large bowl.

2. Add eggs and sugar. Stir until well mixed.

3. Add flour. Stir until just mixed. Grease 9 x 9 inch (22 x 22 cm) pan with cooking spray. Spread batter evenly in pan.

4. Arrange chocolate squares over batter, evenly spaced, in 4 rows of 4 (see diagram).

   Gently press squares down until partially covered with batter. Bake in oven for 25 to 30 minutes until wooden pick inserted in centre of brownie comes out moist but not wet. Put pan on stovetop. Turn oven off. Let brownies cool completely. Cuts into 36 caramel brownies.

1 square: 85 Calories; 3.7 g Total Fat (1.0 g Mono, 0.1 g Poly, 2.2 g Sat); 19 mg Cholesterol; 13 g Carbohydrate; trace Fibre; 1 g Protein; 23 mg Sodium

Pictured at right.

1. Mud Puddle Cake, page 38
2. Confetti Graham Squares, page 39
3. Caramel Candy Brownies, page 40

41

Gold-Dust Lemon Bars

Sweet lemony custard covers tasty, buttery shortbread. Dust these delicious bars with icing sugar for a treat that's sure to impress Mom, Dad and your friends. It's gold!

Get It Together: sharp knife, wire rack, dry and liquid measures, measuring spoons, small bowl, large bowl, 9 x 9 inch (22 x 22 cm) pan, zester, whisk, cooking spray, electric mixer

1.	Butter, softened (see Tip)	1/2 cup	125 mL
	All-purpose flour	1 1/4 cups	300 mL
	Granulated sugar	3 tbsp.	50 mL
	Salt	1/4 tsp.	1 mL
2.	Granulated sugar	1 cup	250 mL
	Large eggs	3	3
	Lemon juice	1/4 cup	60 mL
	All-purpose flour	3 tbsp.	50 mL
	Grated lemon zest (see Tip, page 43)	1 tsp.	5 mL
	Baking powder	1/2 tsp.	2 mL

1. Place oven rack in centre position. Turn oven on to 350°F (175°C). Put first 4 ingredients into large bowl. Beat until mixed. Grease 9 x 9 inch (22 x 22 cm) pan with cooking spray. Press dough into bottom of pan. Bake in oven for about 20 minutes until just golden. Put pan on stovetop.

2. Put remaining 6 ingredients into small bowl. Whisk until smooth. Pour over bottom layer. Bake in oven for about 20 minutes until set. Put pan on wire rack. Turn oven off. Let bars stand in pan on wire rack until cool. Cuts into 36 golden bars.

1 bar: 70 Calories; 2.9 g Total Fat (0.7 g Mono, 0.1 g Poly, 1.7 g Sat); 25 mg Cholesterol; 10 g Carbohydrate; trace Fibre; 1 g Protein; 47 mg Sodium

Pictured on page 44.

Cookbot 3000 Tip: To soften butter, let stand at room temperature until a knife can pass easily through it.

Let Them Eat Cake!

Orange 'N' Berry Blondies

Blondies are a lot like brownies except more fun—sweet cranberries and zippy orange zest will start a party on your tongue!

Get It Together: wire rack, sharp knife, dry measures, measuring spoons, fork, large bowl, medium saucepan, 9 x 9 inch (22 x 22 cm) baking pan, mixing spoon, zester, cooking spray, wooden pick

1.	Butter	1/2 cup	125 mL
	White chocolate chips	1/2 cup	125 mL
2.	Brown sugar, packed	1 cup	250 mL
	Dried cranberries	3/4 cup	175 mL
	Large eggs, fork-beaten	2	2
	Grated orange zest (see Tip)	2 tsp.	10 mL
	Vanilla extract	2 tsp.	10 mL
3.	All-purpose flour	1 1/2 cups	375 mL
	Salt	1/4 tsp.	1 mL

1. Place oven rack in centre position. Turn oven on to 350°F (175°C). Put butter and chocolate chips into medium heavy saucepan on lowest heat. Heat, stirring often until chocolate is almost melted. Remove from heat. Turn burner off. Stir chocolate mixture until smooth. Pour into large bowl.

2. Add next 5 ingredients. Stir well.

3. Add flour and salt. Stir until just moistened. Grease 9 x 9 inch (22 x 22 cm) baking pan with cooking spray. Spread mixture evenly in pan. Bake in oven for about 25 minutes until wooden pick inserted in centre of blondies comes out clean. Put pan on wire rack. Turn oven off. Let blondies stand in pan until cool. Cuts into 36 fun-filled squares.

1 square: 91 Calories; 3.8 g Total Fat (0.7 g Mono, 0.1 g Poly, 2.3 g Sat); 20 mg Cholesterol; 14 g Carbohydrate; trace g Fibre; 1 g Protein; 43 mg Sodium

Pictured on page 44.

Cookbot 3000 Tip: It's a good idea to ask a grown-up to help you with zesting because you only want the coloured part of the peel. The white part is very bitter.

Candy-Apple Cake

Create the taste of a summer carnival in your kitchen with this toffee-covered apple cake. Perfect for an after-dinner treat with your family!

Get It Together: wire rack, sharp knife, dry measures, measuring spoons, fork, small bowl, large saucepan, 8 x 8 inch (20 x 20 cm) pan, mixing spoon, cooking spray, wooden pick

1.	All-purpose flour	2 cups	500 mL
	Baking powder	1 tsp.	5 mL
	Ground cinnamon	1/4 tsp.	1 mL
	Salt	1/4 tsp.	1 mL
2.	Butter	1/4 cup	60 mL
	Brown sugar, packed	1/2 cup	125 mL
	Granulated sugar	1/2 cup	125 mL
	Large egg, fork-beaten	1	1
	Vanilla extract	1 tsp.	5 mL
3.	Grated, peeled cooking apple	1 cup	250 mL
	Toffee bits (such as Skor)	1/4 cup	60 mL
4.	Toffee bits (such as Skor)	1/4 cup	60 mL

1. Place oven rack in centre position. Turn oven on to 350°F (175°C). Put first 4 ingredients into small bowl. Stir. Set aside.

2. Heat butter in large saucepan until melted. Remove from heat. Add brown and granulated sugars. Stir. Add egg and vanilla. Stir well.

3. Add apple, first amount of toffee bits and flour mixture. Stir until no dry flour remains. Grease 8 x 8 inch (20 x 20 cm) pan with cooking spray. Spread evenly in pan.

4. Sprinkle with second amount of toffee bits. Bake in oven for about 35 minutes until wooden pick inserted in centre of cake comes out clean. Put pan on wire rack. Turn oven off. Let cake stand in pan until cool. Cuts into 16 toffee-topped pieces.

1 piece: 170 Calories; 5 g Total Fat (1 g Mono, trace g Poly, 3.1 g Sat); 26 mg Cholesterol; 29 g Carbohydrate; trace g Fibre; 2 g Protein; 128 mg Sodium

Pictured on page 47.

Top: Gold-Dust Lemon Bars, page 42
Bottom: Orange 'N' Berry Blondies, page 43

Peanut Butter Banana Cake

The flavours of peanut butter and banana come together in a tender, tasty cake! Makes a beautiful birthday cake.

Get It Together: cutting board, wire rack, sharp knife, dry and liquid measures, measuring spoons, small bowl, large bowl, 9 x 13 inch (22 x 33 cm) pan, potato masher, cooking spray, aluminum foil, wooden pick, electric mixer

1.	Overripe medium bananas, cut up	2	2
	Milk	2/3 cup	150 mL
	Large eggs	3	3
	Smooth peanut butter	1/2 cup	125 mL
	Cooking oil	2 tbsp.	30 mL
2.	Box of vanilla cake mix (2 layer size)	1	1
3.	Container of vanilla frosting	16 oz.	450 g
	Smooth peanut butter	1/2 cup	125 mL
	Chopped salted peanuts	2 tbsp.	30 mL
	Banana chips	1/2 cup	125 mL

1. Place oven rack in centre position. Turn oven on to 350°F (175°C). Put bananas into large bowl. Mash. Add next 4 ingredients. Beat on low for about 1 minute until well mixed.

2. Add cake mix. Beat on medium for about 2 minutes until smooth. Line 9 x 13 inch (22 x 33 cm) pan with aluminum foil. Grease foil with cooking spray. Spread batter evenly in pan. Bake in oven for about 35 minutes until golden and wooden pick inserted in centre of cake comes out clean. Put pan on stovetop. Turn oven off. Let cake stand in pan for 10 minutes. Loosen foil from pan. Invert cake and foil onto serving platter or tray. Peel off and discard foil.

3. Put frosting and peanut butter in small bowl. Stir until smooth. Frost top and sides of cake. Sprinkle with peanuts. Decorate with banana chips. Cuts into 20 tender pieces.

1 piece: 354 Calories; 18.6 g Total Fat (1.4 g Mono, 0.4 g Poly, 3.8 g Sat); 33 mg Cholesterol; 44 g Carbohydrate; 1 g Fibre; 5 g Protein; 270 mg Sodium

Pictured at right.

Top: Peanut Butter Banana Cake, above
Bottom: Candy-Apple Cake, page 45

Let Them Eat Cake!

Creamy Orange Roll-Up, below

Creamy Orange Roll-Up

The flavours of a creamy orange ice pop in a jelly roll! Try using whipped cream instead of the frosting for a flavour twist.

Get It Together: cutting board, wire racks, serrated knife, dry and liquid measures, measuring spoons, table knife, large plate, medium bowl, large bowl, strainer, sifter, 11 x 17 inch (28 x 43 cm) baking sheet with sides, zester, rubber spatula, mixing spoon, parchment paper, plastic wrap, wooden pick, waxed paper, cooking spray, electric mixer

1.	Box of angel food cake mix	15 oz.	430 g
	Orange juice	1 1/4 cups	300 mL
	Grated orange zest (see Tip, page 43)	1/2 tsp.	2 mL
2.	Icing (confectioner's) sugar	3 tbsp.	50 mL
3.	Container of vanilla frosting	16 oz.	450 g
	Can of mandarin orange segments, drained, 12 segments reserved	10 oz.	284 mL

(continued on next page)

Let Them Eat Cake!

1. Place oven rack in centre position. Turn oven on to 375°F (190°C). Grease 11 x 17 inch (28 x 43 cm) baking sheet with sides with cooking spray. Line bottom of baking sheet with parchment (not waxed) paper, extending paper 2 inches (5 cm) over long sides. Prepare cake mix in large bowl according to package directions, using orange juice instead of water. Add zest. Stir. Spread evenly in prepared baking sheet. Bake in oven for about 15 minutes until golden and wooden pick inserted in centre of cake comes out clean. Put baking sheet on wire rack. Turn oven off. Let cake stand in baking sheet for 5 minutes. Run knife along inside edges of pan to loosen cake.

2. Sift icing sugar over cake. Cover with sheet of waxed paper and tea towel. Invert onto cutting board. Remove baking sheet. Carefully peel off and discard parchment paper from bottom of cake. Roll up cake from short side (see diagram), using towel and waxed paper as guide. Let stand until cool.

3. Put frosting and orange segments into medium bowl. Stir. Unroll cake. Spread frosting mixture evenly over cake, to within 1/2 inch (12 mm) of edges. Roll up gently from short side, discarding waxed paper. Place roll, seam-side down, on large plate. Chill, covered, until firm. Serve 1 orange segment with each slice of roll. Cuts into 12 creamy slices.

1 slice: 336 Calories; 9.8 g Total Fat (0.1 g Mono, 0.2 g Poly, 1.7 g Sat); 0 mg Cholesterol; 59 g Carbohydrate; 1 g Fibre; 4 g Protein; 387 mg Sodium

Pictured at left.

Stop, Drop and Roll!
Cookies

There's so much you can do with cookie dough, but resist the urge to eat it raw—the egg needs to be cooked before it's safe to eat. Have a glass of milk handy for when your baked goodies come out of the oven!

fill in the blanks to reveal common cookie phrases

1. COOKIE J __ __
2. COOKIE C R __ __ B__
3. T O __ __ H COOKIE
4. COOKIE M O __ S __ E __
5. COOKIE S __ E E __
6. F O __ T __ N __ COOKIE
7. COOKIE C __ T __ __ R

answers:
7. cutter
6. fortune
5. sheet
4. monster
3. tough
2. crumbs
1. jar

Rainbow Peanut Cookies

Rainbow-coloured peanuts? Nope—these cookies just have a lot of peanutty flavour, and a candied rainbow of chocolatey crunch!

Get It Together: wire racks, dry measures, measuring spoons, fork, large bowl, cookie sheets, mixing spoon, lifter, cooking spray, electric mixer

1.			
Butter, softened (see Tip, page 42)	1/4 cup	60 mL
Peanut butter	1 cup	250 mL
Granulated sugar	1/2 cup	125 mL
Brown sugar, packed	1/4 cup	60 mL
Large egg	1	1
Vanilla extract	1 tsp.	5 mL
Salt	1/4 tsp.	1 mL
2.			
All-purpose flour	1 cup	250 mL
Mini candy-coated chocolate candies	3/4 cup	175 mL

1. Place oven rack in centre position. Turn oven on to 350°F (175°C). Grease cookie sheets with cooking spray. Set aside. Put first 4 ingredients into large bowl. Beat until light and fluffy. Add next 3 ingredients. Beat well.

2. Add about half of flour and half of candies to butter mixture. Mix well. Add remaining flour and candies. Mix until no dry flour remains. Roll into 1 inch (2.5 cm) balls. Arrange balls about 2 inches (5 cm) apart on cookie sheets. Flatten slightly with fork. Bake in oven, 1 sheet at a time, for about 12 minutes until golden. Let cookies stand on cookie sheets for 5 minutes before removing to wire racks to cool. Put last sheet of cookies on stovetop for 5 minutes. Turn oven off. Makes about 44 colourful cookies.

1 cookie: 115 Calories; 6.5 g Total Fat (0.3 g Mono, 0.1 g Poly, 2.4 g Sat); 11 mg Cholesterol; 13 g Carbohydrate; 1 g Fibre; 3 g Protein; 66 mg Sodium

Pictured on cover and on page 53.

Cookbot 3000 Says: Freeze cooled cookies for up to 2 months in a resealable freezer bag or airtight container.

Choc-A-Lot Trail Mix Cookies

Sweet chocolate, crunchy pecans and chewy cranberries—perfect for a trek to the tree fort!

Get It Together: cutting board, wire racks, serrated knife, sharp knife, dry measures, measuring spoons, large bowl, cookie sheets, shallow frying pan, mixing spoon, lifter, plastic wrap, cooking spray, electric mixer

1.			
Chopped pecans	1/2 cup	125 mL
Butter, softened (see Tip, page 42)	3/4 cup	175 mL
Brown sugar, packed	1/3 cup	75 mL
Granulated sugar	1/3 cup	75 mL
Large egg	1	1
Vanilla extract	1/2 tsp.	2 mL

2.		
All-purpose flour	2 cups	500 mL
Baking soda	1/2 tsp.	2 mL
Salt	1/4 tsp.	1 mL

3.		
Dried cranberries	1/2 cup	125 mL
Mini semi-sweet chocolate chips	1/2 cup	125 mL

1. Put pecans into a medium frying pan. Heat on medium for 3 to 5 minutes, stirring often, until golden. Set aside to cool completely. Turn burner off. Put next 3 ingredients into large bowl. Beat until light and fluffy. Add egg and vanilla. Beat well.

2. Put next 3 ingredients into medium bowl. Stir. Add half of flour mixture to butter mixture. Mix well. Add remaining flour mixture. Mix until no dry flour remains.

3. Add cranberries, chocolate chips, and pecans. Mix well. Divide dough in half. Roll each half into 12 inch (30 cm) long log. Wrap each log with plastic wrap. Chill for about 1 hour until firm. Cut into 1/4 inch (6 mm) slices with serrated knife. Grease cookie sheets with cooking spray. Arrange slices about 1 inch (2.5 cm) apart on cookie sheets.

   Place oven rack in centre position. Turn oven on to 375°F (190°C). Wait 10 minutes for oven to heat up. Bake cookies in oven, 1 sheet at a time, for about 8 minutes until golden. Let cookies stand on cookie sheets for 5 minutes before removing to wire racks to cool. Put last sheet of cookies on stovetop for 5 minutes. Turn oven off. Makes about 80 cookies.

(continued on next page)

Stop, Drop & Roll!

1 cookie: *45 Calories; 2.6 g Total Fat (0.9 g Mono, 0.2 g Poly, 1.3 g Sat); 7 mg Cholesterol; 5 g Carbohydrate; trace Fibre; 1 g Protein; 29 mg Sodium*

Pictured below.

Cookbot 3000 Says: Keep half the dough for these in the fridge (keeps for 1 week) and half in the freezer (keeps for 3 months) and bake them for an after school treat with your friends.

Left: Rainbow Peanut Cookies, page 51
Right: Choc-A-Lot Trail Mix Cookies, left

Hopscotch Cookies

Any party would be hoppin' with these chewy butterscotch cookies around!
Make up a batch of these for your next sleepover.

Get It Together: wire racks, dry measures, measuring spoons, medium
bowl, large bowl, cookie sheets, mixing spoon, lifter, parchment paper,
electric mixer

1.	Butter, softened (see tip, page 42)	1/2 cup	125 mL
	Brown sugar, packed	1 cup	250 mL
	Large egg	1	1
	Buttermilk	1/4 cup	60 mL
2.	All-purpose flour	2/3 cup	150 mL
	Whole-wheat flour	2/3 cup	150 mL
	Quick-cooking rolled oats	1/2 cup	125 mL
	Baking powder	1/2 tsp.	2 mL
	Salt	1/2 tsp.	2 mL
3.	Butterscotch chips	1/2 cup	125 mL

1. Place oven rack in centre position. Turn oven on to 375°F (190°C). Put
   butter and brown sugar into large bowl. Beat until light and fluffy. Add
   egg and buttermilk. Beat well.

2. Put next 5 ingredients into medium bowl. Stir. Add half of flour mixture
   to butter mixture. Mix well. Add remaining flour mixture. Mix well until
   no dry flour remains.

3. Add butterscotch chips. Mix well. Line cookie sheets with parchment
   paper. Drop mixture, using 1 tbsp. (15 mL) for each, about 2 inches
   (5 cm) apart onto cookie sheets. Bake in oven, 1 sheet at a time for
   about 10 minutes until golden. Put cookie sheet on stovetop. Let
   cookies stand on cookie sheet for 5 minutes before removing to wire
   racks to cool. Put last sheet of cookies on stovetop for 5 minutes. Turn
   oven off. Makes about 30 cookies.

1 cookie: 103 Calories; 4.4 g Total Fat (0.8 g Mono, 0.1 g Poly, 3.1 g Sat); 15 mg Cholesterol;
15 g Carbohydrate; 1 g Fibre; 1 g Protein; 79 mg Sodium

Pictured on page 57.

Open Sesame Cookies

Just like magic, these cookies will disappear from the cookie jar! These taste like sesame snaps—try some with chocolate hazelnut spread or peanut butter on top!

Get It Together: wire racks, serrated knife, dry and liquid measures, measuring spoons, large bowl, cookie sheets, shallow frying pan, mixing spoon, lifter, cooking spray, plastic wrap, electric mixer

1.	Sesame seeds	1/2 cup	125 mL
2.	Butter, softened (see Tip, page 42)	1/2 cup	125 mL
	Brown sugar, packed	1/2 cup	125 mL
	Large egg	1	1
	Liquid honey	1/4 cup	60 mL
3.	All-purpose flour	1 1/4 cups	300 mL
	Whole-wheat flour	3/4 cup	175 mL
	Baking powder	1/2 tsp.	2 mL
	Salt	1/2 tsp.	2 mL

1. Put sesame seeds in an ungreased, shallow frying pan. Heat on medium for 3 to 5 minutes, stirring often, until golden. Cool completely. Set aside. Put butter and brown sugar into large bowl. Beat until light and fluffy. Add egg and honey. Beat well.

2. Put remaining 4 ingredients and sesame seeds into medium bowl. Stir. Add half of flour mixture to butter mixture. Mix well. Add remaining flour mixture. Mix until no dry flour remains. Roll into 11 inch (28 cm) long log. Wrap with plastic wrap. Chill for about 2 hours until firm. Cut into 1/4 inch (6 mm) slices with serrated knife. Grease cookie sheets with cooking spray. Arrange slices about 1 inch (2.5 cm) apart on cookie sheets.

3. Place oven rack in centre position. Turn oven on to 375°F (190°C). Wait 10 minutes for oven to heat up. Bake in oven, 1 sheet at a time, for about 8 minutes until golden. Put cookie sheets on stovetop. Let cookies stand on cookie sheets for 5 minutes before removing to wire racks to cool completely. Put last sheet of cookies on stovetop for 5 minutes. Turn oven off. Makes about 40 magical cookies.

1 cookie: 71 Calories; 3.3 g Total Fat (0.6 g Mono, 0.1 g Poly, 1.5 g Sat); 11 mg Cholesterol; 9 g Carbohydrate; trace Fibre; 1 g Protein; 55 mg Sodium

Pictured on page 57.

Hazelnut Sugar Sammies

You'll love these sparkling sugar cookies, with creamy chocolate hazelnut filling sandwiched in between.

Get It Together: wire rack, dry measures, measuring spoons, large bowl, cookie sheets, 2 1/2 inch (6.4 cm) round cookie cutter pastry brush, mixing spoon, lifter, rolling pin, plastic wrap, cooking spray, electric mixer

1.	Butter, softened (see Tip, page 42)	1/2 cup	125 mL
	Granulated sugar	1/2 cup	125 mL
	Salt	1/4 tsp.	1 mL
	Large egg	1	1
	Vanilla extract	1/2 tsp.	2 mL
2.	All-purpose flour	1 1/2 cups	375 mL
3.	Water	1 tsp.	5 mL
	Gold sanding (decorating) sugar (see Tip, page 65)	1 tbsp.	15 mL
4.	Chocolate hazelnut spread	1/2 cup	125 mL

1. Put first 3 ingredients into large bowl. Beat until light and fluffy. Add egg and vanilla. Beat well.

2. Add half of flour to butter mixture. Mix well. Add remaining flour. Mix until no dry flour remains. Shape into ball. Flatten ball into disc and wrap in plastic wrap. Chill for at least 1 hour or overnight. Remove dough from fridge. Let stand for 10 minutes. Discard plastic wrap. Roll out dough on lightly floured surface to 1/4 inch (6 mm) thickness. Cut out circles with lightly floured 2 1/2 inch (6.4 cm) round cookie cutter. Roll out scraps to cut more circles. Grease cookie sheets with cooking spray. Arrange circles about 1 inch (2.5 cm) apart on cookie sheets.

3. Place oven rack in centre position. Turn oven on to 350°F (175°C). Wait 10 minutes for oven to heat up. Lightly brush 10 circles with water. Sprinkle with sanding sugar. Bake in oven, 1 sheet at a time, for about 10 minutes until golden. Put cookie sheets on stovetop. Let stand on cookie sheets for 5 minutes before removing to wire rack to cool completely. Put last sheet of cookies on stovetop for 5 minutes. Turn oven off. Makes about 20 cookies.

(continued on next page)

Stop, Drop & Roll!

4. Spread 2 tsp. (10 mL) chocolate hazelnut spread on bottom of each undecorated cookie. Place decorated cookies, sugar-side up, over spread. Makes about 10 sandwich cookies.

1 sandwich cookie: 254 Calories; 12.9 g Total Fat (4.2 g Mono, 1.1 g Poly, 6.5 g Sat); 46 mg Cholesterol; 32 g Carbohydrate; 1 g Fibre; 3 g Protein; 134 mg Sodium

Pictured below.

Cookbot 3000 Says: If you don't have a cookie cutter, the mouth of a small glass or cup will do the job nearly as well.

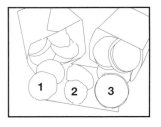

1. **Open Sesame Cookies, page 55**
2. **Hopscotch Cookies, page 54**
3. **Hazelnut Sugar Sammies, left**

Chip Chip Hooray Cookies

Just one taste and you'll be cheering for these chewy cookies full of two kinds of chips—chocolate *and* butterscotch!

Get It Together: wire racks, dry measures, measuring spoons, small bowl, large bowl, cookie sheets, mixing spoon, lifter, cooking spray, electric mixer

1.			
Butter, softened (see Tip, page 42)	1 cup	250 mL
Brown sugar, packed	1/2 cup	125 mL
Granulated sugar	1/2 cup	125 mL
Large egg	1	1
Vanilla extract	1 tsp.	5 mL
Salt	1/8 tsp.	0.5 mL
2. Whole-wheat flour	2 cups	500 mL
Baking powder	1 tsp.	5 mL
Baking soda	1/2 tsp.	2 mL
3. Butterscotch chips	1 cup	250 mL
Large flake rolled oats	1 cup	250 mL
Semi-sweet chocolate chips	1 cup	250 mL

1. Place oven rack in centre position. Turn oven on to 350°F (175°C). Put first 3 ingredients in large bowl. Beat until light and fluffy. Add next 3 ingredients. Beat well.

2. Put next 3 ingredients into small bowl. Stir. Add half of flour mixture to butter mixture. Mix well. Add remaining flour mixture. Mix until no dry flour remains.

3. Add remaining 3 ingredients. Mix well. Grease cookie sheets with cooking spray. Drop mixture, using 1 tbsp. (15 mL) at a time, about 2 inches (5 cm) apart onto cookie sheets. Bake in oven, 1 sheet at a time, for about 10 minutes until bottoms are golden. Let cookies stand on cookie sheets for 5 minutes before removing to wire rack to cool. Put last sheet of cookies on stovetop for 5 minutes. Turn oven off. Makes about 50 cookies.

1 cookie: 115 Calories; 6.3 g Total Fat (1.3 g Mono, 0.2 g Poly, 4.2 g Sat); 14 mg Cholesterol; 14 g Carbohydrate; 1 g Fibre; 2 g Protein; 61 mg Sodium

Pictured on page 60.

(continued on next page)

Stop, Drop & Roll!

Cookbot 3000 Says: If you don't want to bake the dough all at once, you can drop the dough into cookies, close together onto a baking sheet with sides, and freeze until hard. Once they're frozen, transfer them to a freezer bag or air-tight container and keep them in the freezer for up to 3 months. Bake them right from frozen on a greased baking sheet in a 350°F (175°C) oven for about 15 minutes. You can have fresh-baked cookies any time with almost no clean-up!

Full-Moon Macaroons

These chewy treats are almost as easy to make as they are to eat. Yummy rolled oats and coconut give these macaroons a bumpy surface—just like the real moon!

Get It Together: dry measures, measuring spoons, medium bowl, cookie sheets, mixing spoon, lifter, cooking spray, electric mixer

1.	Egg whites (large), room temperature	2	2
	Granulated sugar	3/4 cup	175 mL
	Vanilla extract	1/2 tsp.	2 mL
2.	Quick-cooking rolled oats	1 cup	250 mL
	Medium sweetened coconut	1/2 cup	125 mL

1. Place oven rack in centre position. Turn oven on to 350°F (175°C). Grease 2 cookie sheets with cooking spray. Set aside. Put egg whites into medium bowl. Beat until soft peaks form. Gradually add sugar, beating at the same time, until smooth and glossy. Add vanilla. Beat well.

2. Fold in oats and coconut. Drop mixture, using 1 tbsp. (15 mL) at a time, about 2 inches (5 cm) apart onto cookie sheets. Bake in oven, 1 sheet at a time, for about 12 minutes until bottoms are golden. Place cookie sheets on stovetop. Turn oven off. Let macaroons cool completely. Makes about 25 macaroons.

1 macaroon: 45 Calories; 0.7 g Total Fat (trace Mono, trace Poly, 0.4 g Sat); 0 mg Cholesterol; 9 g Carbohydrate; trace Fibre; 1 g Protein; 8 mg Sodium

Pictured on page 60.

1. Chip Chip Hooray Cookies, page 58
2. Choco-Lots O' Love Cookies, below
3. Full-Moon Macaroons, page 59

Choco-Lots O' Love Cookies

Make yummy Valentines for your friends, or treats for your classroom's Valentine's Day party.

Get It Together: wire racks, dry and liquid measures, measuring spoons, fork, large bowl, medium bowl, sifter, mixing spoon, lifter, cookie sheets, rolling pin, 3 inch (7.5 cm) heart-shaped cookie cutter, 1 1/2 inch (3.8 cm) heart shaped cookie cutter, plastic wrap, waxed paper, cooking spray, electric mixer

1.	Butter, softened (see Tip, page 42)	1 1/3 cups	325 mL
	Icing (confectioner's) sugar	1 1/2 cups	375 mL
	Large egg	1	1
	Vanilla extract	1 tsp.	5 mL
2.	All-purpose flour	2 1/2 cups	625 mL
	Cocoa, sifted if lumpy	1/2 cup	125 mL
	Baking soda	1 tsp.	5 mL
	Salt	1/2 tsp.	2 mL
3.	Raspberry jam	1 cup	250 mL

(continued on next page)

Stop, Drop & Roll!

1. Put butter and icing sugar into large bowl. Beat until smooth. Add egg and vanilla. Beat well.

2. Put next 4 ingredients into medium bowl. Stir. Add half of flour mixture to butter mixture. Mix well. Add remaining flour mixture. Mix until no dry flour remains. Divide dough in half. Shape each half into a ball. Flatten balls into discs and wrap in plastic wrap. Chill for about 1 hour until firm.

3. Place oven rack in centre position. Turn oven on to 350°F (175°C). Roll out 1 dough disk between 2 sheets of waxed paper to 1/4 inch (6 mm) thickness. Remove top sheet of waxed paper. Cut out hearts with large cookie cutter. Chill scraps for about 10 minutes. Roll out to cut more hearts. Repeat with remaining disc. Cut out hearts from centres of half of heart shapes with small cookie cutter (see diagram).

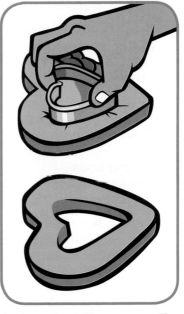

Grease cookie sheets with cooking spray. Arrange dough shapes about 2 inches (5 cm) apart on cookie sheets. Bake in oven, 1 sheet at a time, for about 10 minutes until set. Let cookies stand on cookie sheets for 5 minutes before removing to wire racks to cool completely. Put last sheet of cookies on stovetop for 5 minutes. Cool. Turn oven off. Spread 1 tbsp. (15 mL) jam on bottom of each whole heart. Place hearts with cut-out centres over jam. Makes about 20 lovely sandwich cookies.

1 sandwich cookie: *244 Calories; 12.5 g Total Fat (3.1 g Mono, 0.5 g Poly, 7.8 g Sat); 43 mg Cholesterol; 32 g Carbohydrate; 1 g Fibre; 2 g Protein; 210 mg Sodium*

Pictured at left.

Cookbot 3000 Says: Once you have cut out 10 complete hearts and 10 hearts with the middle cut out, you can chill the scraps and cut out any shapes you want with the rest of the dough.

This cookie dough can be cut into different shapes for other special days, like Christmas, Easter or Halloween.

Use marshmallow cream instead of jam and sprinkle with your favourite colour of sanding sugar.

Spicy Big Daddies

These cookies are all puffed up and full of flavour. Bake some up for a great after-school snack!

Get It Together: wire racks, dry and liquid measures, measuring spoons, fork, medium bowl, large bowl, cookie sheets, mixing spoon, lifter, cooking spray, electric mixer

1.	Brown sugar, packed	1 cup	250 mL
	Butter, softened (see Tip, page 42)	3/4 cup	175 mL
	Large eggs	2	2
	Unsweetened applesauce	2/3 cup	150 mL
2.	All-purpose flour	2 cups	500 mL
	Ground cinnamon	2 tsp.	10 mL
	Baking powder	1 tsp.	5 mL
	Salt	1 tsp.	5 mL
	Baking soda	1/2 tsp.	2 mL
	Ground allspice	1/2 tsp.	2 mL
	Ground nutmeg	1/4 tsp.	1 mL
3.	Crisp rice cereal	1 1/2 cups	375 mL
	Quick-cooking rolled oats	1 cup	250 mL
	Medium unsweetened coconut	1/2 cup	125 mL

1. Place oven rack in centre position. Turn oven on to 350°F (175°C). Put brown sugar and butter into large bowl. Beat until light and fluffy. Add eggs and applesauce. Beat well.

2. Put next 7 ingredients in medium bowl. Stir. Add half of flour mixture to butter mixture. Mix well. Add remaining flour mixture. Mix until no dry flour remains.

3. Add remaining 3 ingredients. Stir until mixed. Grease cookie sheets with cooking spray. Drop mixture, using 2 tbsp. (30 mL) at a time, about 2 inches (5 cm) apart onto cookie sheets. Bake in oven, 1 sheet at a time, for about 12 minutes until golden. Let cookies stand on cookie sheets for 5 minutes before removing to wire racks to cool. Place last sheet of cookies on stovetop for 5 minutes. Turn oven off. Makes about 30 cookies.

1 cookie: 127 Calories; 5.8 g Total Fat (1.2 g Mono, 0.2 g Poly, 3.7 g Sat); 26 mg Cholesterol; 17 g Carbohydrate; 1 g Fibre; 2 g Protein; 169 mg Sodium

Pictured on page 65.

Cookbot 3000 Says: Freeze cooled cookies for up to 2 months in a resealable freezer bag or airtight container.

Meringue Clouds

Have you ever wondered what clouds taste like? These billowy-sweet meringues will have you convinced that clouds taste like candy! Spread your favourite filling between two meringues to make star- and cloud-shaped sandwiches.

Get It Together: dry measures, measuring spoons, cookie sheets, piping bag with large star tip, mixing spoon, lifter, parchment paper, electric mixer

1.
Egg white (large), room temperature	1	1
Cream of tartar	1/4 tsp.	1 mL
Granulated sugar	1/4 cup	60 mL

1. Place oven racks in centre and bottom positions. Turn oven on to 200°F (95°C). Put egg white and cream of tartar into small bowl. Beat on medium until soft peaks form. Add sugar, 1 tbsp. (15 mL) at a time, beating constantly for about 5 minutes until smooth and glossy. Spoon mixture into piping bag fitted with large star tip (see Tip, page 37). Line bottoms of greased cookie sheets with parchment paper. Pipe mixture into star and cloud shapes (about 1 inch, 2.5 cm, for stars, and 2 inches, 5 cm, long for clouds), about 2 inches (5 cm) apart onto cookie sheets (see diagrams). Bake in oven, switching position of sheets at halftime for about 60 minutes until dry. Turn oven off. Let clouds stand in oven until cooled completely. Makes about 25 clouds.

1 cloud: 9 Calories; 0 g Total Fat (0 g Mono, 0 g Poly, 0 g Sat); 0 mg Cholesterol; 2 g Carbohydrate; 0 g Fibre; trace Protein; 2 mg Sodium

Pictured on page 65.

Cookbot 3000 Says: Spread 1 tsp. (5 mL) chocolate hazelnut spread, lemon curd or jam onto bottom of 1 cookie. Press bottom of second cookie onto filling.

Holiday Hideaway Cookies

Surprise—each of these cookies is hiding a gumdrop inside! Lots of cool colours can be used to decorate them for *any* holiday. Have fun experimenting.

Get It Together: wire racks, dry measures, measuring cups, shallow bowl, medium bowl, large bowl, cookie sheets, mixing spoon, lifter, cooking spray, electric mixer

1.	Butter, softened (see Tip, page 42)	1 cup	250 mL
	Icing (confectioner's) sugar	3/4 cup	175 mL
	Large egg	1	1
	Vanilla extract	1 tsp.	5 mL
2.	All-purpose flour	2 cups	500 mL
	Quick-cooking rolled oats	1 1/4 cups	300 mL
	Salt	1/4 tsp.	1 mL
3.	Red baking gums (see Tip, page 32)	42	42
4.	Red sanding (decorating) sugar (see Tip, next page)	1/2 cup	125 mL

1. Place oven rack in centre position. Turn oven on to 325°F (160°C). Put butter and icing sugar into large bowl. Beat until smooth. Add egg and vanilla. Beat well.

2. Put next 3 ingredients into medium bowl. Stir. Add half of flour mixture to butter mixture. Mix well. Add remaining flour mixture. Mix until no dry flour remains. Roll into balls, using 1 tbsp. (15 mL) for each.

3. Push 1 baking gum into centre of each ball. Roll balls to enclose baking gums.

4. Put sanding sugar into shallow bowl. Roll each ball in sanding sugar until coated. Grease cookie sheets with cooking spray. Arrange balls, about 1 inch (2.5 cm) apart, on cookie sheets. Bake in oven, 1 sheet at a time, for about 15 minutes until firm. Let cookies stand on cookie sheets for 5 minutes before removing to wire racks to cool. Put last sheet of cookies on stovetop for 5 minutes. Turn oven off. Makes about 42 holiday cookies.

1 cookie: 101 Calories; 4.6 g Total Fat (1.1 g Mono, 0.2 g Poly, 2.8 g Sat); 17 mg Cholesterol; 14 g Carbohydrate; trace Fibre; 1 g Protein; 48 mg Sodium

Pictured at right.

(continued on next page)

Stop, Drop & Roll!

Cookbot 3000 Tip: Sanding sugar is a coarse decorating sugar that comes in white and various colours. It's available at specialty kitchen stores.

Cookbot 3000 Says: Freeze cooled cookies for up to 2 months in a resealable freezer bag or airtight container.

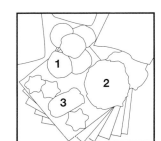

1. **Holiday Hideaway Cookies, left**
2. **Spicy Big Daddies, page 62**
3. **Meringue Clouds, page 63**

Lemon-Doodles

Tart lemon zest will put a pucker on your face when you eat these cookies! They have a tasty flavour combination of sweet *and* sour.

Get It Together: wire racks, dry measures, measuring spoons, mixing spoon, 2 small bowls, medium bowl, cookie sheets, lifter, zester, electric mixer

1.			
Butter, softened (see Tip, page 42)	1/2 cup	125 mL
Granulated sugar	3/4 cup	175 mL
Large egg	1	1
Grated lemon zest (see Tip, page 43)	1 tsp.	5 mL
2. All-purpose flour	1 cup	250 mL
Baking powder	1/2 tsp.	2 mL
Salt	1/8 tsp.	0.5 mL
3. Granulated sugar	2 tbsp.	30 mL
Ground cinnamon	2 tsp.	10 mL

1. Place oven rack in centre position. Turn oven on to 375°F (190°C). Put butter and first amount of sugar into medium bowl. Beat until light and fluffy. Add egg and lemon zest. Beat well.

2. Put next 3 ingredients into small bowl. Stir. Add half of flour mixture to butter mixture. Mix well. Add remaining flour mixture. Mix until no dry flour remains. Roll into 1 inch (2.5 cm) balls.

3. Put second amount of sugar and cinnamon into small bowl. Stir. Roll each ball in cinnamon mixture until coated. Arrange about 2 inches (5 cm) apart on ungreased cookie sheets. Bake in oven, 1 sheet at a time, for about 10 minutes until golden. Let cookies stand on cookie sheets for 5 minutes before removing to wire racks to cool. Put last sheet of cookies on stovetop. Turn oven off. Makes about 30 cookies.

1 cookie: 66 Calories; 3.2 g Total Fat (0.8 g Mono, 0.1 g Poly, 2.0 g Sat); 15 mg Cholesterol; 9 g Carbohydrate; trace Fibre; 1 g Protein; 43 mg Sodium

Pictured on front cover and on page 68.

Cookbot 3000 Says: Freeze cooled cookies for up to 2 months in a resealable freezer bag or airtight container.

Gingerbread Kids

Want to play dress-up? Use candies or dried fruit to give these kids some style! Use peanut butter or chocolate hazelnut spread as "glue" to stick on your accessories.

Get It Together: dry and liquid measures, measuring spoons, small bowl, medium bowl, cookie sheets, mixing spoon, lifter, rolling pin, 3 inch (7.5 cm) cookie cutter, cooking spray, wire racks, electric mixer

1.	Butter, softened (see Tip, page 42)	1/4 cup	60 mL
	Brown sugar, packed	1/4 cup	60 mL
	Large egg	1	1
	Fancy (mild) molasses	1/4 cup	60 mL
2.	All-purpose flour	1 1/4 cups	300 mL
	Whole-wheat flour	1/4 cup	60 mL
	Baking soda	1/2 tsp.	2 mL
	Ground ginger	1/2 tsp.	2 mL
	Ground cinnamon	1/4 tsp.	1 mL
	Salt	1/4 tsp.	1 mL
	Ground cloves	1/8 tsp.	0.5 mL

1. Place oven rack in centre position. Turn oven on to 350°F (175°C). Grease cookie sheets with cooking spray. Set aside. Put butter and brown sugar into medium bowl. Beat until light and fluffy. Add egg and molasses. Beat well.

2. Put next 7 ingredients into small bowl. Stir. Add half of flour mixture to butter mixture. Mix well. Add remaining flour mixture. Mix until no dry flour remains. Roll out dough on lightly floured surface to 10 inch (25 cm) square. Cut out shapes with 3 inch (7.5 cm) cookie cutter. Roll out scraps to cut more shapes. Arrange about 2 inches (5 cm) apart on cookie sheets. Bake in oven, 1 sheet at a time, for about 9 minutes until firm. Let cookies stand on cookie sheets for 5 minutes before removing to wire racks to cool. Put last sheet of cookies on stovetop for 5 minutes. Turn oven off. Makes about 20 gingerbread kids.

1 cookie: 76 Calories; 2.5 g Total Fat (0.6 g Mono, 0.1 g Poly, 1.5 g Sat); 17 mg Cholesterol; 12 g Carbohydrate; trace Fibre; 1 g Protein; 83 mg Sodium

Pictured on front cover and page 68.

Stop, Drop & Roll!

1. Lemon-Doodles, page 66
2. Gingerbread Kids, page 67
3. Mr. Squirrel's Shortbread, right

68

Mr. Squirrel's Shortbread

Crazy for nuts? These are tasty shortbread cookies with a punch of nutty flavour.

Get It Together: cutting board, wire rack, sharp knife, dry measures, measuring spoons, small bowl, medium bowl, cookie sheet, shallow frying pan, mixing spoon, lifter, cooking spray, electric mixer

1.	**Finely chopped pecans**	1/4 cup	60 mL
	Butter, softened (see Tip, page 42)	1/2 cup	125 mL
	Brown sugar, packed	1/4 cup	60 mL
2.	**All-purpose flour**	3/4 cup	175 mL
	Cornstarch	2 tbsp.	30 mL
3.	**Pecan halves**	15	15

1. Put first amount of pecans in a small frying pan. Heat on medium for 3 to 5 minutes, stirring often, until golden. Set aside to cool completely. Turn burner off. Place oven rack in centre position. Turn oven on to 350°F (175°C). Grease cookie sheet with cooking spray. Set aside. Put butter and brown sugar into medium bowl. Beat until light and fluffy.

2. Put flour, cornstarch and toasted pecans into small bowl. Stir. Add half of flour mixture to butter mixture. Mix well. Add remaining flour mixture. Mix until no dry flour remains. Drop mixture, using 1 tbsp. (15 mL) at a time, about 1 inch (2.5 cm) apart onto cookie sheet.

3. Press 1 pecan half gently onto each cookie. Bake in oven for about 10 minutes until just golden. Put cookie sheet on stovetop. Turn oven off. Let cookies stand on cookie sheet for 5 minutes before removing to wire rack to cool. Makes about 15 nutty cookies.

1 cookie: 115 Calories; 8.5 g Total Fat (3.0 g Mono, 1.0 g Poly, 4.1 g Sat); 16 mg Cholesterol; 9 g Carbohydrate; trace Fibre; 1 g Protein; 45 mg Sodium

Pictured on front cover and at left.

Q: What kind of tree do you find in the kitchen?

A: A pantry

It's a Happy Ending
Desserts

Eat all your vegetables at mealtime, but save a little room for dessert.
Remember, sharing your masterpieces makes them extra sweet!

find 30 baking instructions used in this book

```
S  A  L  A  M  U  X  S  L  P  P  D  R  S  E
W  P  L  L  I  H  C  E  S  W  H  I  S  K  R
Q  O  R  B  T  Y  S  O  U  E  I  O  P  N  A
R  U  D  E  R  C  G  F  O  S  R  F  J  E  R
I  R  M  A  A  E  R  N  O  L  L  P  T  A  K
J  I  V  T  X  D  E  I  S  L  M  Y  U  D  F
X  L  T  C  T  D  A  T  P  I  D  A  E  H  S
D  E  T  M  E  A  S  U  R  E  D  I  G  G  G
R  R  R  D  F  T  E  C  I  E  Z  G  N  B  R
I  I  A  J  F  A  Q  P  N  H  S  J  A  K  E
T  Z  N  I  X  E  I  W  K  C  B  E  R  N  M
S  K  S  M  N  H  M  E  L  Z  Z  I  R  D  O
O  B  F  H  W  G  E  K  E  O  O  D  A  V  V
N  M  E  N  I  B  M  O  C  E  V  B  A  K  E
Y  S  R  O  L  L  O  U  T  P  S  L  A  R  O
```

ADD	ARRANGE	BAKE	BEAT	CHILL	COOL
COMBINE	CRIMP	CUT IN	DRAIN	DRIZZLE	
GREASE	HEAT	FOLD IN	KNEAD		
MEASURE	MIX	POUR			
PRESS	MOVE	RESERVE			
ROLL OUT	SCATTER	SIFTSPREAD			
SPRINKLE	STIR	TRANSFER			
WHIP	WHISK				

Pearrific Bread Pudding

This dessert is made extra scrumptious by drizzling caramel ice cream topping over top, whether you eat it warm or cold. And look—no raisins!

Get It Together: cutting board, serrated knife, sharp knife, dry and liquid measures, measuring spoons, small microwave-safe bowl, large bowl, strainer, 9 x 9 inch (22 x 22 cm) pan, can opener, mixing spoon, cooking spray, electric mixer

1.	Butter, melted (see Tip, page 13)	1/4 cup	60 mL
	Brown sugar, packed	2/3 cup	150 mL
	Milk	2 cups	500 mL
	Large eggs	4	4
	Ground cinnamon	1 tsp.	5 mL
	Salt	1/4 tsp.	1 mL
2.	White bread cubes	8 cups	2 L
	Diced canned pears, drained	2 cups	500 mL
3.	Caramel ice cream topping	1/4 cup	60 mL

1. Place oven rack in centre position. Turn oven on to 350°F (175°C). Put first 6 ingredients into large bowl. Beat until smooth.

2. Add bread cubes and pears. Stir until coated. Grease 9 x 9 inch (22 x 22 cm) pan with cooking spray. Spread mixture evenly in pan. Bake in oven for about 55 minutes until golden and knife inserted in centre of pudding comes out clean. Put pan on stovetop. Turn oven off. Let pudding stand in pan for 10 minutes.

3. Drizzle with ice cream topping. Serves 12.

1 serving: Calories; 226 g Total Fat (1.3 g Mono, 0.5 g Poly, 3.3 g Sat); 84 mg Cholesterol; 37 g Carbohydrate; 2 g Fibre; 6 g Protein; 308 mg Sodium

Pictured on page 74.

Monsieur Auk-Auk Says: Try this with canned peaches instead of pears, and chocolate ice cream topping instead of caramel.

It's a Happy Ending!

S'more Dessert Anyone?

All the flavours of your favourite campfire treat! Try some warm with butterscotch ripple ice cream!

Get It Together: cutting board, sharp knife, dry and liquid measures, measuring spoons, fork, large bowl, sifter, small saucepan, 9 inch (22 cm) deep dish pie plate, mixing spoon, cooking spray, wooden pick

1.	All-purpose flour	1 cup	250 mL
	Granulated sugar	3/4 cup	175 mL
	Graham cracker crumbs	1/2 cup	125 mL
	Baking soda	1/2 tsp.	2 mL
	Salt	1/4 tsp.	1 mL
2.	Water	1/2 cup	125 mL
	Cooking oil	1/4 cup	60 mL
	Cocoa, sifted if lumpy	3 tbsp.	50 mL
3.	Large egg, fork-beaten	1	1
	Buttermilk	1/3 cup	75 mL
	Vanilla extract	1/2 tsp.	2 mL
4.	Miniature marshmallows	1 cup	250 mL
	Milk chocolate bar, chopped	3 1/2 oz.	100 g
5.	Whole graham crackers, broken into small pieces	4	4

1. Place oven rack in centre position. Turn oven on to 375°F (190°C). Put first 5 ingredients into large bowl. Stir. Make a well in centre.

2. Put next 3 ingredients into small saucepan. Heat and stir on medium for about 3 minutes until mixture comes to a boil. Turn burner off. Carefully pour cocoa mixture into well. Stir until smooth.

3. Add next 3 ingredients. Stir well. Grease 9 inch (22 cm) deep dish pie plate with cooking spray. Pour mixture evenly into pie plate. Bake in oven for about 30 minutes until wooden pick inserted in centre of cake comes out clean. Put pie plate on stovetop. Turn oven to broil.

4. Scatter marshmallows and chocolate pieces over cake. Broil in oven on same rack for about 2 minutes until marshmallows are golden. Put pie plate on stovetop. Turn oven off.

(continued on next page)

It's a Happy Ending!

5. Scatter graham cracker pieces over top. Let stand in pie plate for 10 minutes before cutting. Cuts into 8 wedges.

1 wedge: 322 Calories; 12.6 g Total Fat (4.4 g Mono, 2.3 g Poly, 3.4 g Sat); 31 mg Cholesterol; 50 g Carbohydrate; 1 g Fibre; 4 g Protein; 223 mg Sodium

Pictured on page 74.

Berry Cobbler Gobbler

Juicy, bubbling berries and a golden biscuit topping make this look (and taste!) oh-so-good.

Get It Together: dry and liquid measures, measuring spoons, small bowl, medium bowl, 8 x 8 inch (20 x 20 cm) baking dish, baking sheet with sides, mixing spoon, cooking spray, wooden pick

1.	Frozen mixed berries, thawed	3 cups	750 mL
	Granulated sugar	1/4 cup	60 mL
	Cornstarch	1 tbsp.	15 mL
	Lemon juice	1 tsp.	5 mL
2.	All-purpose flour	1 cup	250 mL
	Granulated sugar	1/3 cup	75 mL
	Baking powder	1 1/2 tsp.	7 mL
	Salt	1/2 tsp.	2 mL
3.	Milk	1/2 cup	125 mL
	Cooking oil	2 tbsp.	30 mL

1. Spread frozen berries on baking sheet. Let stand for 30 minutes until thawed. Place oven rack in centre position. Turn oven on to 400°F (205°C). Put berries and next 3 ingredients into medium bowl. Stir gently. Grease 8 x 8 inch (20 x 20 cm) baking dish with cooking spray. Spoon mixture evenly into dish.

2. Put next 4 ingredients into small bowl. Stir. Make a well in centre.

3. Add milk and cooking oil to well. Stir until just moistened. Drop batter onto fruit mixture, using about 2 tbsp. (30 mL) for each mound. Bake in oven for 25 to 30 minutes until golden and wooden pick inserted in centre of biscuit comes out clean. Put dish on stovetop. Turn oven off. Let cobbler cool for 15 minutes. Serves 8.

1 serving: 176 Calories; 3.7 g Total Fat (2.1 g Mono, 1.0 g Poly, 0.3 g Sat); 1 mg Cholesterol; 34 g Carbohydrate; 2 g Fibre; 2 g Protein; 257 mg Sodium

Pictured on page 74.

It's a Happy Ending!

1. Berry Cobbler Gobbler, page 73
2. Pearrific Bread Pudding, page 71
3. S'more Dessert Anyone?, page 72

74

Bananarama Cheesecakes

These mini cheesecakes are so good you'll go bananas! They have tropical flavours from pineapple and coconut too—great for a summertime party!

Get It Together: dry and liquid measures, measuring spoons, fork, large bowl, muffin pan, shallow frying pan, mixing spoon, muffin pan liners, electric mixer

1.	**Medium sweetened coconut**	2 tbsp.	30 mL
	Gingersnaps	12	12
	(about 2 inch, 5 cm, diameter)		
2.	**Spreadable cream cheese**	1 1/2 cups	375 mL
	Large egg	1	1
	Box of banana cream pudding	1	1
	powder (not instant), 6-serving size		
	Milk	1/2 cup	125 mL
3.	**Pineapple jam**	3/4 cup	175 mL

1. Put coconut into a small frying pan. Heat on medium for 3 to 5 minutes, stirring often, until golden. Set aside to cool completely. Turn burner off. Place oven rack in centre position. Turn oven on to 350°F (175°C). Put 12 paper muffin pan liners into muffin pan. Put 1 gingersnap into bottom of each muffin liner.

2. Put cream cheese in large bowl. Beat until smooth. Add next 3 ingredients. Beat well. Spoon about 3 tbsp. (50 mL) over each cookie. Bake in oven for about 20 minutes until set. Put pan on stovetop. Turn oven off. Let cheesecakes stand in pan for 10 minutes.

3. Top each cheesecake with 1 tbsp. (15 mL) jam. Sprinkle with 1/2 tsp. (2 mL) coconut. Chill in pan for about 1 hour until firm. Makes 12 mini cheesecakes.

1 mini cheesecake: 224 Calories; 11.5 g Total Fat (0.4 g Mono, 0.1 g Poly, 7.7 g Sat); 49 mg Cholesterol; 28 g Carbohydrate; trace Fibre; 3 g Protein; 227 mg Sodium

Pictured on page 77.

Monsieur Auk-Auk Says: These can be eaten at room temperature or cold, but they should be stored in the fridge.

It's a Happy Ending!

Razz Pizzazz Cheesecakes

Make these pretty raspberry mini cheesecakes when you really want to show your stuff! They're perfectly kid-sized little cakes.

Get It Together: dry and liquid measures, measuring spoons, small microwave-safe bowl, small bowl, medium bowl, muffin pan, mixing spoon, muffin pan liners, electric mixer

1.	Graham cracker crumbs	3/4 cup	175 mL
	Butter, melted (see Tip, page 13)	2 tbsp.	30 mL
	Granulated sugar	2 tbsp.	30 mL
2.	Granulated sugar	1/2 cup	125 mL
	Ricotta cheese	1/2 cup	125 mL
	Cream cheese, softened (see Tip, page 33)	4 oz.	113 mL
	Large egg	1	1
	Lemon juice	1 tbsp.	15 mL
3.	Fresh raspberries	36	36

1. Place oven rack in centre position. Turn oven on to 325°F (160°C). Put first 3 ingredients into small bowl. Stir. Put 12 muffin pan liners into muffin pan. Press about 4 tsp. (20 mL) crumb mixture into bottom of each muffin cup.

2. Put next 3 ingredients in medium bowl. Beat until smooth. Add egg and lemon juice. Beat well. Spoon about 2 tbsp. (30 mL) over graham crumb mixture in each cup. Bake in oven for about 18 minutes until set. Put pan on stovetop. Turn oven off. Let cheesecakes stand in pan for about 1 hour until cool.

3. Top each cheesecake with 3 raspberries. Chill in pan for about 1 hour until firm. Makes 12 mini cheesecakes.

1 mini cheesecake: 137 Calories; 7.2 g Total Fat (0.7 g Mono, 0.3 g Poly, 4.4 g Sat); 37 mg Cholesterol; 16 g Carbohydrate; 1 g Fibre; 3 g Protein; 99 mg Sodium

Pictured at right.

It's a Happy Ending!

1. Bananarama Cheesecakes, page 75
2. Razz Pizzazz Cheescakes, left
3. Topsy-Turvy Fruit Pudding, page 78

Topsy-Turvy Fruit Pudding

It's like magic—the yummy sauce for this baked pudding starts out on top and ends up on the bottom. You'll flip for it!

Get It Together: dry and liquid measures, measuring spoons, fork, small cup, small bowl, medium bowl, strainer, 2 quart (2 L) baking dish, mixing spoon, cooking spray, wooden pick

1.			
All-purpose flour	1 cup	250 mL
Brown sugar, packed	1/2 cup	125 mL
Baking powder	1 1/2 tsp.	7 mL
Salt	1/2 tsp.	2 mL

2.			
Large egg, fork-beaten	1	1
Milk	1/2 cup	125 mL
Can of fruit cocktail	14 oz.	398 mL

3.			
Butter	3 tbsp.	50 mL
Brown sugar, packed	1/2 cup	125 mL
Boiling water	3/4 cup	175 mL

1. Place oven rack in centre position. Turn oven on to 350°F (175°C). Put first 4 ingredients into medium bowl. Stir. Make a well in centre.

2. Add egg and milk to well. Stir until smooth. Drain juice from fruit cocktail, and save in small cup. Add fruit cocktail to flour mixture. Stir gently to mix. Grease 2 quart (2 L) baking dish with cooking spray. Spread batter evenly in dish.

3. Put butter, brown sugar and reserved juice into small bowl. Carefully add boiling water. Stir until butter melts and sugar is dissolved. Slowly pour over batter. Do not stir. Bake in oven for about 30 minutes until golden and wooden pick inserted in centre of pudding comes out clean. Put dish on stovetop. Turn oven off. Let pudding stand for 10 minutes. Serve warm. Serves 8.

1 serving: 246 Calories; 5.0 g Total Fat (1.2 g Mono, 0.2 g Poly, 3.0 g Sat); 39 mg Cholesterol; 49 g Carbohydrate; 1 g Fibre; 3 g Protein; 309 mg Sodium

Pictured on page 77.

Strawberry Shortcake Pizza

You've had shortcake, you've had pizza...put them together
to make this strawberry extravaganza!

Get It Together: cutting board, sharp knife, dry and liquid measures, measuring spoons, fork, large bowl, 12 inch (30 cm) pizza pan, mixing spoon, rubber spatula, cooking spray, wooden pick

1.	All-purpose flour	1 1/2 cups	375 mL
	Brown sugar, packed	1/4 cup	60 mL
	Baking powder	1 1/2 tsp.	7 mL
	Baking soda	1/2 tsp.	2 mL
	Salt	1/2 tsp.	2 mL
	Cold butter, cut up	1/3 cup	75 mL
2.	Buttermilk	2/3 cup	150 mL
	Vanilla extract	1 tsp.	5 mL
3.	Strawberry spreadable cream cheese	1 cup	250 mL
	Sliced fresh strawberries	2 cups	500 mL
	Frozen whipped topping, thawed	2 cups	500 mL
	Sliced fresh strawberries	1/2 cup	125 mL

1. Place oven rack in centre position. Turn oven on to 400°F (205°C). Grease 12 inch (30 cm) pizza pan with cooking spray. Set aside. Put first 5 ingredients into large bowl. Stir. Cut in butter until mixture resembles coarse crumbs.

2. Add buttermilk and vanilla. Stir until soft dough forms. Turn out onto lightly floured cutting board. Knead 6 times. Press dough into pan. Bake in oven for about 12 minutes until golden and wooden pick inserted in centre of pizza crust comes out clean. Put pan on stovetop. Turn oven off. Let crust cool completely.

3. Spread cream cheese evenly over crust to within 1/2 inch (12 mm) of edge. Arrange strawberry slices in single layer over cream cheese. Spread whipped topping over strawberries. Arrange second amount of strawberries over whipped cream. Cuts into 8 wedges.

1 wedge: 349 Calories; 21.1 g Total Fat (2.1 g Mono, 0.4 g Poly, 14.1 g Sat); 47 mg Cholesterol; 38 g Carbohydrate; 1 g Fibre; 5 g Protein; 512 mg Sodium

Pictured on page 80.

Monsieur Auk-Auk Says: Try using peeled and sliced kiwi or banana instead of all or part of the strawberries.

Top: Peachy Queen Trifle, below
Bottom: Strawberry Shortcake Pizza, page 79

Peachy Queen Trifle

This dessert is not only easy and fun to make, it looks fancy and tastes great too. It's fit for a queen!

Get It Together: cutting board, wire rack, serrated knife, sharp knife, liquid measures, measuring spoons, table knife, medium bowl, large bowl, large glass bowl, strainer, two 9 x 5 x 3 inch (22 x 12.5 x 7.5 cm) loaf pans, zester, mixing spoon, can opener, plastic wrap, wooden pick, blender

1.	Box of angel food cake mix	15 oz.	430 g
	Grated lemon zest (see Tip, page 43)	1 tbsp.	15 mL

(continued on next page)

2. Cans of sliced peaches, drained (28 oz., 796 mL each)	2	2
3. Vanilla yogurt	2 cups	500 mL
Grated lemon zest (see Tip, page 43)	1 tsp.	5 mL

1. Place oven rack in centre position. Turn oven on to 350°F (175°C). Prepare cake mix in large bowl according to package directions, adding first amount of lemon zest. Spread evenly in 2 ungreased 9 x 5 x 3 inch (22 x 12.5 x 7.5 cm) loaf pans. Bake in oven for about 40 minutes until wooden pick inserted in centre of each loaf comes out clean. Put pans on stovetop. Turn oven off. Rest each loaf pan on its side on wire rack until completely cool. Run knife around inside edges of pans to loosen cakes. Invert cakes on cutting board (see Safety Tip). Cut into 1 inch (2.5 cm) cubes.

2. Save 6 peach slices for garnish. Chop remaining peaches. Put 1 cup (250 mL) chopped peaches into blender. Cover with lid. Process until smooth. Transfer to medium bowl.

3. Add yogurt and second amount of lemon zest to blended peaches. Stir. To assemble trifle, layer ingredients in large glass bowl as follows:
Half of cake pieces
Half of chopped peaches
Half of yogurt mixture
Remaining cake pieces
Remaining chopped peaches
Remaining yogurt mixture, spread evenly

Garnish with reserved peach slices. Chill, covered, for about 2 hours to blend flavours. Makes about 13 cups (3.25 L).

1 cup (250 mL): 217 Calories; 1.6 g Total Fat (0.4 g Mono, 0.2 g Poly, 0.8 g Sat); 4 mg Cholesterol; 48 g Carbohydrate; 3 g Fibre; 4 g Protein; 277 mg Sodium

Pictured at left.

Safety Tip: It's a good idea to ask a grown-up to help you invert the pans.

Monsieur Auk-Auk Says: A garnish is a food item you use to make the food you've cooked look extra special.

Try this with your favourite berries and flavoured yogurt.

It's a Happy Ending!

Apple-Pie Sponge Pudding

Apple and caramel flavours hidden under a yummy sponge topping. Dust these cute puddings with icing sugar, or serve them with ice cream!

Get It Together: dry and liquid measures, measuring spoons, six 6 oz. (170 mL) ramekins or custard cups, small bowl, medium bowl, baking sheet with sides, can opener, mixing spoon, cooking spray, electric mixer

1.	Canned apple pie filling	3/4 cup	175 mL
	Caramel ice cream topping	6 tbsp.	100 mL
2.	Large eggs	2	2
	Granulated sugar	1/2 cup	125 mL
	All-purpose flour	1/2 cup	125 mL
	Whipping cream	1 cup	250 mL

1. Place oven rack in centre position. Turn oven on to 375°F (190°C). Put pie filling and topping into small bowl. Stir. Grease six 6 oz. (170 mL) ramekins with cooking spray. Spoon about 3 tbsp. (50 mL) pie filling mixture into each ramekin. Arrange ramekins on baking sheet with sides.

2. Put eggs and sugar into medium bowl. Beat until thick and pale. Add flour and whipping cream. Beat until smooth. Pour over apple mixture in each ramekin until ramekins are 3/4 full. Bake in oven for about 30 minutes until golden and knife inserted in centre of a pudding comes out clean. Place baking sheet on stovetop. Turn oven off. Let puddings stand for 10 minutes to cool slightly. Serves 6.

1 serving: 342 Calories; 16.2 g Total Fat (4.2 g Mono, 0.6 g Poly, 9.7 g Sat); 126 mg Cholesterol; 47 g Carbohydrate; 1 g Fibre; 4 g Protein; 122 mg Sodium

Pictured on page 84.

Q: Why did the kid throw butter out the window?

A: He wanted to see a butterfly

Boggling Baked Snowballs

Ice cream baked in the oven? You bet! When you cover ice cream with a cozy layer of meringue, crazy things can happen.

Get It Together: dry and liquid measures, measuring spoons, ramekins or custard cups, spoon, medium bowl, 8 x 8 inch (20 x 20 cm) baking pan, electric mixer

1. Vanilla ice cream   2 cups   500 mL

2. Egg whites (large), room temperature   3   3
    (see Safety Tip, below)
    Vanilla extract   1/2 tsp.   2 mL
    Granulated sugar   1/3 cup   75 mL

1. Spoon 1/2 cup (125 mL) ice cream into each of four 6 oz. (170 mL) ramekins. Smooth tops. Arrange ramekins in 8 x 8 inch (20 x 20 cm) baking pan. Place in freezer. Chill for about 3 hours until firm.

2. Place oven rack in centre position. Turn oven on to 450°F (230°C). Put egg whites and vanilla into medium bowl. Beat for about 3 minutes until soft peaks form. Add sugar, 1 tbsp. (15 mL) at a time, while beating. Beat until shiny and sugar is dissolved. Remove ice cream from freezer. Quickly spoon about 1/2 cup (125 mL) egg white mixture over ice cream, making sure to completely cover ice cream. Bake in oven for about 2 minutes until golden. Put baking sheet on stovetop. Turn oven off. Serve immediately. Serves 4.

1 serving: 349 Calories; 18.0 g Total Fat (0 g Mono, 0 g Poly, 11.0 g Sat); 120 mg Cholesterol; 38 g Carbohydrate; 0 g Fibre; 8 g Protein; 112 mg Sodium

Pictured on page 84.

Safety Tip: This recipe has uncooked eggs in the final result. Make sure to start with fresh, clean, Grade A eggs—and keep them in the fridge until you need them. Eat your baking on the same day and don't save anything that's leftover. If any of your tasters is expecting a baby, or is a young child or elderly adult, they should not eat this recipe or anything that has uncooked eggs in it.

1. Boggling Baked Snowballs, page 83
2. Caramel Apple Bombs, right
3. Apple-Pie Sponge Pudding, page 82

84

Caramel Apple Bombs

Serve these with your favourite topping: ice cream, whipped cream or vanilla yogurt! Sweet apples are best for baking—get a grown-up to help you pick out Spartan, McIntosh or Jonagold apples.

Get It Together: cutting board, sharp knife, dry and liquid measures, measuring spoons, 4 serving bowls, small bowl, shallow 2 quart (2 L) casserole, mixing spoon, melon baller or corer, vegetable peeler

1.	**Butter, softened (see Tip, page 42)**	**1/4 cup**	**60 mL**
	Brown sugar, packed	**1/4 cup**	**60 mL**
	Finely chopped walnuts	**2 tbsp.**	**30 mL**
2.	**Unpeeled medium cooking apples (such as McIntosh)**	**4**	**4**
3.	**Apple juice**	**1 cup**	**250 mL**

1. Place oven rack in centre position. Turn oven on to 350°F (175°C). Put first 3 ingredients into small bowl. Stir. Set aside.

2. Carefully remove cores from apples with melon baller or corer, stopping 1/2 inch (12 mm) from bottom of apple and being careful not to pierce base (see diagram). Remove 1/2 inch (12 mm) of peel from top of each apple using vegetable peeler. Spoon about 1 tbsp. (15 mL) butter mixture into each apple. Spread any remaining butter mixture over tops of apples. Arrange in 2 quart (2 L) casserole.

3. Pour apple juice into casserole. Bake, covered, in oven for about 45 minutes until apples are tender. Put casserole on stovetop. Turn oven off. Let apples stand for 10 minutes. Transfer apples to 4 serving bowls. Spoon liquid from casserole over apples. Serves 4.

1 serving: 276 Calories; 14.0 g Total Fat (3.3 g Mono, 2.3 g Poly, 7.5 g Sat); 30 mg Cholesterol; 40 g Carbohydrate; 4 g Fibre; 1 g Protein; 87 mg Sodium

Pictured at left.

Choconana Quesadilla

This is a sweet version of the quesadilla (keh-sah-DEE-yah), with a melty-good banana and chocolate hazelnut combo. It will taste almost like a banana split if you serve it with a spoonful of ice cream!

Get It Together: cutting board, sharp knife, liquid measures, measuring spoons, small cup, small bowl, baking sheet, potato masher, rubber spatula, mixing spoon, cooking spray

1.	Chocolate hazelnut spread	1/2 cup	125 mL
	Mashed banana (about 1 small)	1/2 cup	125 mL
2.	Flour tortillas (9 inch, 22 cm, diameter)	3	3
	Cooking spray		
3.	Granulated sugar	1 tbsp.	15 mL
	Ground cinnamon	1/8 tsp.	0.5 mL

1. Place oven rack in centre position. Turn oven on to 425°F (220°C). Grease baking sheet with cooking spray. Set aside. Put hazelnut spread and banana into small bowl. Stir.

2. Spread banana mixture evenly over half of each tortilla to within 1/2 inch (12 mm) of edge. Fold tortilla in half to cover filling. Press edges down lightly. Place tortillas on baking sheet. Spray with cooking spray.

3. Put sugar and cinnamon into small cup. Stir. Sprinkle over tortillas. Bake in oven for about 10 minutes until edges start to brown. Put baking sheet on stovetop. Turn oven off. Carefully transfer tortillas to cutting board. Cut each quesadilla into 4 wedges. Serve warm. Makes 12 wedges.

1 wedge: 96 Calories; 3.9 g Total Fat (1.5 g Mono, 0.7 g Poly, 0.8 g Sat); 0 mg Cholesterol; 14 g Carbohydrate; 1 g Fibre; 1 g Protein; 81 mg Sodium

Pictured at right.

Rhuby-Strawberry Crisp

This dessert with tangy rhubarb and strawberries is so easy, and you will probably have lots of the ingredients at home already! Try it with some vanilla ice cream on the side.

Get It Together: dry and liquid measures, measuring spoons, medium bowl, strainer, 2 quart (2 L) baking dish, baking sheets with sides, mixing spoon, cooking spray

(continued on next page)

It's a Happy Ending!

Left: Choconana Quesadilla, left
Right: Rhuby-Strawberry Crisp, left

1.			
	Frozen rhubarb	3 cups	750 mL
	Container of frozen strawberries in light syrup, thawed	15 oz.	425 g
	Granulated sugar	1/2 cup	125 mL
	Minute tapioca	2 tbsp.	30 mL
2.	Butter, softened (see Tip, page 42)	1/3 cup	75 mL
	Quick-cooking rolled oats	1 cup	250 mL
	Granulated sugar	1/2 cup	125 mL
	Whole-wheat flour	1/2 cup	125 mL

1. Spread frozen rhubarb on baking sheet. Let stand for 30 minutes until thawed. Drain. Place oven rack in centre position. Turn oven on to 350°F (175°C). Grease 2 quart (2 L) baking dish with cooking spray. Put rhubarb and next 3 ingredients into dish. Stir. Let stand for 30 minutes to soften tapioca.

2. Put remaining 4 ingredients in medium bowl. Stir until crumbly. Scatter over fruit mixture. Bake in oven for about 40 minutes until topping is golden and fruit is bubbling. Put dish on stovetop. Turn oven off. Serve warm. Serves 8.

1 serving: 293 Calories; 8.6 g Total Fat (2.0 g Mono, 0.4 g Poly, 4.8 g Sat); 20 mg Cholesterol; 54 g Carbohydrate; 4 g Fibre; 3 g Protein; 56 mg Sodium

Pictured above.

Monsieur Auk-Auk Says: Strawberries can be set in a bowl of warm water, unopened, until thawed, or taken out the day before and thawed in refrigerator overnight.

It's a Happy Ending!

There's Muffin to It!
Muffins & Loaves

Any way you slice it, loafing around in the kitchen is lots of fun. "Quick breads"—such as muffins and loaves—get their name because the ingredients that make them rise do their work without the extra step of having to let the dough sit.

Help Monsieur Auk Auk get to the oven before his Yummy Yogurt Muffins get too brown.

Boatload of Oat Muffins

An oatmeal muffin with lots of nutty crunch! These are great for breakfast with jam or jelly, or as a snack for sharing with friends.

Get It Together: cutting board, wire rack, sharp knife, dry and liquid measures, measuring spoons, fork, medium bowl, large bowl, muffin pan, mixing spoon, cooking spray, wooden pick

1.

All-purpose flour	1 1/2 cups	375 mL
Brown sugar, packed	1 cup	250 mL
Large flake rolled oats	1 cup	250 mL
Chopped pecans	1/3 cup	75 mL
Slivered almonds	1/3 cup	75 mL
Raw sunflower seeds	2 tbsp.	30 mL
Baking powder	1 tsp.	5 mL
Baking soda	1/2 tsp.	2 mL
Salt	1/2 tsp.	2 mL

2.

Large egg, fork-beaten	1	1
Sour cream	1 cup	250 mL
Cooking oil	1/2 cup	125 mL
Vanilla extract	1 tsp.	5 mL

1. Place oven rack in centre position. Turn oven on to 375°F (190°C). Grease 12 muffin cups with cooking spray. Set aside. Put first 9 ingredients into large bowl. Stir. Make a well in centre.

2. Put remaining 4 ingredients into medium bowl. Stir. Add to well. Stir until just moistened. Fill muffin cups 3/4 full with batter. Bake in oven for about 20 minutes until wooden pick inserted in centre of a muffin comes out clean. Put pan on stovetop. Turn oven off. Let muffins stand in pan for 5 minutes before removing to wire rack to cool. Makes 12 muffins.

1 muffin: 325 Calories; 18.3 g Total Fat (7.6 g Mono, 3.8 g Poly, 3.5 g Sat); 31 mg Cholesterol; 36 g Carbohydrate; 2 g Fibre; 5 g Protein; 216 mg Sodium

Pictured on page 91.

Cocoa-Nut Monkey Loaf

This yummy loaf is full of delicious chocolate and banana flavours—
and coconut too! Lots of fun to serve to your monkeys—oops, I mean friends!

Get It Together: cutting board, wire rack, serrated knife, dry and liquid measures, measuring spoons, fork, medium bowl, large bowl, sifter, 9 x 5 x 3 inch (22 x 12.5 x 7.5 cm) loaf pan, potato masher, mixing spoon, cooking spray, wooden pick

1.	All-purpose flour	2 cups	500 mL
	Granulated sugar	1 cup	250 mL
	Fine coconut	1/3 cup	75 mL
	Cocoa, sifted if lumpy	1/4 cup	60 mL
	Baking powder	1 tsp.	5 mL
	Baking soda	1/2 tsp.	2 mL
	Salt	1/2 tsp.	2 mL
2.	Large eggs, fork-beaten	2	2
	Mashed, overripe banana (about 2 1/2 medium)	1 1/2 cups	375 mL
	Buttermilk (or 1/3 cup milk with 1 tsp. vinegar)	1/3 cup	75 mL
	Cooking oil	1/4 cup	60 mL
	Vanilla extract	1/2 tsp.	2 mL

1. Place oven rack in centre position. Turn oven on to 350°F (175°C). Grease 9 x 5 x 3 inch (22 x 12.5 x 7.5 cm) loaf pan with cooking spray. Set aside. Put first 7 ingredients into large bowl. Stir. Make a well in centre.

2. Put remaining 5 ingredients into medium bowl. Stir. Add to well. Stir until just moistened. Spread batter evenly in pan. Bake in oven for about 60 minutes until wooden pick inserted in centre of loaf comes out clean. Put pan on stovetop. Turn oven off. Let loaf stand in pan for 10 minutes before removing to wire rack to cool. Cuts into 16 slices.

1 slice: 172 Calories; 5.0 g Total Fat (2.1 g Mono, 1.0 g Poly, 1.1 g Sat); 27 mg Cholesterol; 30 g Carbohydrate; 1 g Fibre; 3 g Protein; 164 mg Sodium

Pictured at right.

1. Boatload Of Oat Muffins, page 89
2. Go Go GORP Muffins, page 92
3. Cocoa-Nut Monkey Loaf, left

Go Go GORP Muffins

GORP means "Good Old Raisins and Peanuts." These muffins are packed with other good stuff too, like granola and chocolate chips. They'll give you all sorts of energy to have all sorts of fun!

Get It Together: cutting board, wire racks, sharp knife, dry and liquid measures, measuring spoons, fork, small bowl, large bowl, muffin pan, mixing spoon, cooking spray, wooden pick

1.	Whole-wheat flour	1 1/2 cups	375 mL
	Granola	1 cup	250 mL
	Chopped salted peanuts	1/2 cup	125 mL
	Raisins	1/2 cup	125 mL
	Semi-sweet chocolate chips	1/2 cup	125 mL
	Brown sugar, packed	1/4 cup	60 mL
	Baking powder	2 tsp.	10 mL
	Ground cinnamon	1 tsp.	5 mL
	Salt	1/4 tsp.	1 mL
2.	Large eggs, fork-beaten	2	2
	Orange juice	3/4 cup	175 mL
	Cooking oil	1/2 cup	125 mL

1. Place oven rack in centre position. Turn oven on to 375°F (190°C). Grease 12 muffin cups with cooking spray. Set aside. Put first 9 ingredients into large bowl. Stir. Make a well in centre.

2. Put remaining 3 ingredients into small bowl. Stir. Add to well. Stir until just moistened. Fill muffin cups full with batter. Bake in oven for about 18 minutes until wooden pick inserted in centre of a muffin comes out clean. Put pan on stovetop. Turn oven off. Let muffins stand in pan for 5 minutes before removing to wire rack to cool. Makes 12 muffins.

1 muffin: 293 Calories; 17.0 g Total Fat (6.1 g Mono, 2.9 g Poly, 3.1 g Sat); 36 mg Cholesterol; 32 g Carbohydrate; 4 g Fibre; 6 g Protein; 199 mg Sodium

Pictured on page 91.

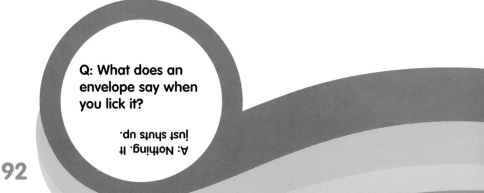

Q: What does an envelope say when you lick it?

A: Nothing. It just shuts up.

Lovely Lemonberry Muffins

Fresh lemon and raspberry flavour makes these treats so tasty to eat—and glazing them adds extra love!

Get It Together: wire rack, dry and liquid measures, measuring spoons, fork, small bowl, medium bowl, large bowl, muffin pan, zester, mixing spoon, cooking spray, wooden pick

1.			
All-purpose flour	2 cups	500 mL
Granulated sugar	3/4 cup	175 mL
Baking powder	2 tsp.	10 mL
Baking soda	1/2 tsp.	2 mL
Salt	1/2 tsp.	2 mL
2. Large eggs, fork-beaten	2	2
Buttermilk	1 cup	250 mL
Cooking oil	1/2 cup	125 mL
Grated lemon zest (see Tip, page 43)	1 tbsp.	15 mL
Fresh raspberries	1 cup	250 mL

LEMON GLAZE

3.			
Lemon juice	1 tbsp.	15 mL
Icing (confectioner's) sugar	1/2 cup	125 mL

1. Place oven rack in centre position. Turn oven on to 375°F (190°C). Grease 12 muffin cups with cooking spray. Set aside. Put first 5 ingredients into large bowl. Stir. Make a well in centre.

2. Put next 4 ingredients into medium bowl. Stir. Add to well. Add raspberries. Stir until just moistened. Fill muffin cups 3/4 full. Bake in oven for about 20 minutes until wooden pick inserted in centre of a muffin comes out clean. Put pan on stovetop. Turn oven off.

3. **Lemon Glaze:** Stir lemon juice into icing sugar in small bowl, adding more lemon juice or icing sugar, if necessary, until mixture is a pourable consistency. Spoon glaze over hot muffins. Let stand in pan for 5 minutes before removing to wire rack to cool. Makes 12 muffins.

1 muffin: 244 Calories; 10.5 g Total Fat (5.5 g Mono, 2.7 g Poly, 1.2 g Sat); 37 mg Cholesterol; 35 g Carbohydrate; trace Fibre; 4 g Protein; 269 mg Sodium

Pictured on page 95.

Sticky Spice Spirals

Sugar and spice and everything nice in a spiral biscuit—
once you flip these out of the pan, the sticky-sweet bottom will be up on top!

Get It Together: cutting board, sharp knife, dry and liquid measures, measuring spoons, fork, medium bowl, large bowl, baking sheet, muffin pan, mixing spoon, rolling pin, cooking spray, electric mixer

1.			
Butter, softened (see Tip, page 42)	1/2 cup	125 mL
Brown sugar, packed	1 cup	250 mL
Corn syrup	1 tbsp.	15 mL
Ground cinnamon	2 tsp.	10 mL
Ground cardamom	1 tsp.	5 mL
Ground ginger	1 tsp	5 mL
Pepper	1/4 tsp.	1 mL
2.			
All-purpose flour	2 1/4 cups	550 mL
Brown sugar, packed	1/4 cup	60 mL
Baking powder	1 tbsp.	15 mL
Salt	1 tsp.	5 mL
Baking soda	1/2 tsp.	2 mL
Cold butter, cut up	1/3 cup	75 mL
Milk	3/4 cup	175 mL

1. Put first 7 ingredients in medium bowl. Beat until light and fluffy. Grease 12 muffin cups with cooking spray. Spoon about 2 tsp. (10 mL) butter mixture into each muffin cup. Set remainder aside.

2. Place oven rack in centre position. Turn oven on to 400°F (205°C). Put next 5 ingredients in large bowl. Stir. Cut in second amount of butter until mixture resembles coarse crumbs. Add milk. Stir until soft dough forms. Turn out onto lightly floured surface. Knead 6 times. Roll out or pat to 12 x 8 inch (30 x 20 cm) rectangle. Spread reserved butter mixture over dough. Roll up, jelly-roll style, from long side (see diagram, page 95).

(continued on next page)

There's Muffin to It!

Pinch seam against roll to seal. Cut into 12 slices. Place slices, cut side up, in muffin cups. Bake in oven for about 15 minutes until golden. Put pan on stovetop. Turn oven off. Carefully invert pan onto baking sheet (see Tip). Let cool. Makes 12 spirals.

1 spiral: 290 Calories; 12.8 g Total Fat (3.3 g Mono, 0.5 g Poly, 8.1 g Sat); 34 mg Cholesterol; 42 g Carbohydrate; 1 g Fibre; 3 g Protein; 493 mg Sodium

Pictured below.

Safety Tip: It's a good idea to ask a grown-up to help you invert the pan.

Left: Lovely Lemonberry Muffins, page 93
Right: Sticky Spice Spirals, left

Cheesy Chili Loaf

What do get when you cross your favourite meatloaf with cheesy bread?
A super-hearty cheese loaf packed with real chili!

Get It Together: cutting board, wire rack, serrated knife, dry and
liquid measures, measuring spoons, fork, medium bowl, large bowl,
9 x 5 x 3 inch (22 x 12.5 x 7.5 cm) loaf pan, mixing spoon, can opener,
grater, cooking spray, wooden pick

1.			
Whole-wheat flour	1 1/2 cups	375 mL	
All-purpose flour	1 cup	250 mL	
Baking powder	1 tbsp.	15 mL	
Baking soda	1 tsp.	5 mL	
Chili powder	1 tsp.	5 mL	
Salt	1/4 tsp.	1 mL	
Pepper	1/4 tsp.	1 mL	
2.			
Large eggs, fork-beaten	2	2	
Milk	2/3 cup	150 mL	
Cooking oil	1/4 cup	60 mL	
Granulated sugar	1/4 cup	60 mL	
Can of chili	14 oz.	398 mL	
Grated sharp Cheddar cheese	1 cup	250 mL	

1. Place oven rack in centre position. Turn oven on to 350°F (175°C).
   Grease 9 x 5 x 3 inch (22 x 12.5 x 7.5 cm) loaf pan with cooking spray.
   Put first 7 ingredients into large bowl. Stir. Make a well in centre.

2. Put next 4 ingredients into medium bowl. Stir. Stir in chili and cheese.
   Add to well. Stir until just moistened. Spread evenly in pan. Bake in
   oven for about 50 minutes until wooden pick inserted in centre of loaf
   comes out clean. Put pan on stovetop. Turn oven off. Let loaf stand
   in pan for 10 minutes before removing to wire rack to cool. Cuts into
   16 slices.

1 slice: 170 Calories; 6.9 g Total Fat (2.7 g Mono, 1.2 g Poly, 2.0 g Sat); 35 mg Cholesterol;
22 g Carbohydrate; 3 g Fibre; 7 g Protein; 388 mg Sodium

Pictured on page 98.

Monsieur Auk-Auk Says: Store this tasty and satisfying
"meatloaf" in the fridge...if there is any left over.

There's Muffin to It!

Cheese-Please Garlic Biscuits

Like garlic bread? You'll love the herb-licious and garlicky flavour in these cheesy-good biscuits! Serve them warm with a family meal.

Get It Together: wire rack, dry and liquid measures, measuring spoons, small microwave-safe bowl, small bowl, medium bowl, baking sheet, mixing spoon, pastry brush, grater, cooking spray, wooden pick

1.	Biscuit mix	2 1/2 cups	625 mL
	Grated sharp Cheddar cheese	1 cup	250 mL
	Greek seasoning	2 tsp.	10 mL
	Garlic powder	1/4 tsp.	1 mL
2.	Milk	3/4 cup	175 mL
3.	Butter, melted (see Tip, page 13)	1/4 cup	60 mL
	Garlic powder	1/4 tsp.	1 mL

1. Place oven rack in centre position. Turn oven on to 450°F (230°C). Grease baking sheet with cooking spray. Set aside. Put first 4 ingredients into medium bowl. Stir. Make a well in centre.

2. Add milk to well. Stir until just moistened. Drop dough, using 1/3 cup (75 mL) for each biscuit, about 2 inches (5 cm) apart on baking sheet. Bake in oven for about 12 minutes until golden and wooden pick inserted in centre of a biscuit comes out clean. Put baking sheet on stovetop. Turn oven off.

3. Put butter and second amount of garlic powder in small bowl. Stir. Brush evenly over biscuits. Let stand on baking sheet for 5 minutes before removing to wire rack to cool. Makes about 8 biscuits.

1 biscuit: 265 Calories; 15.0 g Total Fat (2.9 g Mono, 0.4 g Poly, 7.7 g Sat); 31 mg Cholesterol; 25 g Carbohydrate; trace Fibre; 8 g Protein; 660 mg Sodium

Pictured on page 98.

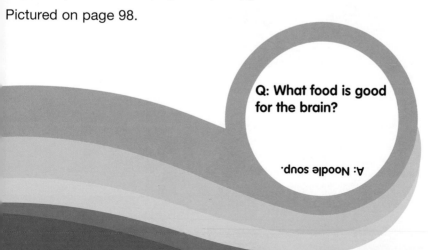

Q: What food is good for the brain?

A: Noodle soup.

1. Chili-Con-Corny Loaf, right
2. Cheesy Chili Loaf, page 96
3. Cheese-Please Garlic Biscuits, page 97
4. Hooray Olé Muffins, page 100

Chili-Con-Corny Loaf

*Everyone's favourite Mexican flavours baked into a loaf—
start a fiesta and share some hearty slices with your friends!*

Get It Together: cutting board, wire rack, serrated knife, dry and liquid
measures, large bowl, strainer, 9 x 5 x 3 inch (22 x 12.5 x 7.5 cm) loaf
pan, can opener, cooking spray, wooden pick, blender or food processor

1.			
All-purpose flour	1 1/4 cups	300 mL	
Whole-wheat flour	3/4 cup	175 mL	
Brown sugar, packed	3 tbsp.	50 mL	
Baking powder	1 tbsp.	15 mL	
Chili powder	2 tsp.	10 mL	
Salt	1 tsp.	5 mL	

2.			
Canned white kidney beans, rinsed and drained	1 cup	250 mL	
Buttermilk	3/4 cup	175 mL	
Large eggs	2	2	
Cooking oil	1/4 cup	60 mL	

3.			
Grated Mexican cheese blend	1 cup	250 mL	
Canned kernel corn, drained	1/2 cup	125 mL	

1. Place oven rack in centre position. Turn oven on to 350°F (175°C).
   Grease 9 x 5 x 3 inch (22 x 12.5 x 7.5 cm) loaf pan with cooking spray.
   Set aside. Put first 6 ingredients into large bowl. Stir. Make a well in
   centre.

2. Put next 4 ingredients into blender. Cover with lid. Process until smooth.
   Add to well.

3. Add cheese and corn. Stir until just moistened. Spread evenly in loaf
   pan. Bake in oven for about 55 minutes until wooden pick inserted in
   centre of loaf comes out clean. Put pan on stovetop. Turn oven off. Let
   loaf stand in pan for 10 minutes before removing to wire rack to cool.
   Cuts into 16 slices.

1 slice: 179 Calories; 6.8 g Total Fat (2.1 g Mono, 1.1 g Poly, 1.9 g Sat); 34 mg Cholesterol;
24 g Carbohydrate; 1 g Fibre; 7 g Protein; 338 mg Sodium

Pictured at left.

Hooray Olé Muffins

These muffins are full of cheesy-taco flavour! They'll make a salsa-licious sidekick to a big bowl of your favourite soup or chili.

Get It Together: wire rack, dry and liquid measures, measuring spoons, fork, table knife, medium bowl, large bowl, muffin pan, grater, mixing spoon, cooking spray, wooden pick

1.	All-purpose flour	1 cup	250 mL
	Whole-wheat flour	1 cup	250 mL
	Granulated sugar	2 tbsp.	30 mL
	Taco seasoning mix, stir before measuring	1 tbsp.	15 mL
	Baking powder	2 tsp.	10 mL
	Baking soda	1 tsp.	5 mL
2.	Large eggs, fork-beaten	2	2
	Milk	1/2 cup	125 mL
	Salsa	1/2 cup	125 mL
	Cooking oil	1/4 cup	60 mL
	Grated sharp Cheddar cheese	3/4 cup	175 mL

1. Place oven rack in centre position. Turn oven on to 375°F (190°C). Grease 12 muffin cups with cooking spray. Set aside. Put first 6 ingredients into large bowl. Stir. Make a well in centre.

2. Put next 4 ingredients into medium bowl. Stir. Add cheese. Stir gently. Add to well. Stir until just moistened. Fill muffin cups 3/4 full with batter. Bake in oven for about 18 minutes until wooden pick inserted in centre of a muffin comes out clean. Put pan on stovetop. Turn oven off. Let muffins stand in pan for 5 minutes. Run knife around inside edges of cups to loosen muffins before removing to wire rack to cool. Makes 12 muffins.

1 muffin: 162 Calories; 8.1 g Total Fat (3.4 g Mono, 1.5 g Poly, 2.2 g Sat); 44 mg Cholesterol; 18 g Carbohydrate; 1 g Fibre; 6 g Protein; 333 mg Sodium

Pictured on page 98.

Rainin' Chocolate-Raisin Biscuits

It's rainin' chocolate-covered raisins! These crispy, tender biscuits
are loaded with double-chocolatey flavour.

Get It Together: cutting board, wire rack, sharp knife, dry and liquid
measures, measuring spoons, fork, large bowl, small bowl, small heavy
saucepan, sifter, baking sheet, mixing spoon, parchment paper,
wooden pick

1.	All-purpose flour	2 cups	500 mL
	Granulated sugar	1/3 cup	75 mL
	Cocoa, sifted if lumpy	3 tbsp.	50 mL
	Baking powder	2 tsp.	10 mL
	Baking soda	1 tsp.	5 mL
	Salt	1/2 tsp.	2 mL
	Cold butter, cut up	1/3 cup	75 mL
2.	Milk	2/3 cup	150 mL
	Sour cream	1/2 cup	125 mL
	Chocolate-covered raisins	1 cup	250 mL
3.	Semi-sweet chocolate baking square (1 oz., 28 g), coarsely chopped	1	1

1. Place oven rack in centre position. Turn oven on to 400°F (205°C).
   Put first 6 ingredients into large bowl. Stir. Cut in butter until mixture
   resembles coarse crumbs. Make a well in centre.

2. Put milk and sour cream into small bowl. Stir. Add milk mixture
   and raisins to well. Stir until just moistened. Line baking sheet with
   parchment paper. Drop dough, using 1/4 cup (60 mL) for each biscuit,
   about 1 inch (2.5 cm) apart onto baking sheet. Bake in oven for about
   17 minutes until wooden pick inserted in centre of a biscuit comes out
   clean. Put baking sheet on stovetop. Turn oven off. Let biscuits stand
   on baking sheet for 5 minutes before removing to wire rack to cool.

3. Heat chocolate in small, heavy saucepan on lowest heat, stirring often,
   until chocolate is almost melted. Remove from heat. Turn burner off.
   Stir until smooth. Drizzle over biscuits. Makes about 12 biscuits.

1 biscuit: 251 Calories; 10.7 g Total Fat (1.5 g Mono, 0.2 g Poly, 6.5 g Sat); 21 mg Cholesterol;
37 g Carbohydrate; 2 g Fibre; 4 g Protein; 359 mg Sodium

Pictured on page 103.

There's Muffin to It!

Apple-Cot Muffins

These applesaucy muffins with apricot are so fruity-sweet!
Keep them handy for after-school snacks.

Get It Together: cutting board, wire rack, sharp knife, dry and liquid measures, measuring spoons, fork, large bowl, medium bowl, muffin pan, mixing spoon, cooking spray, wooden pick

1.			
All-purpose flour	1 1/2 cups	375 mL
Quick-cooking rolled oats	1 1/2 cups	375 mL
Baking powder	2 tsp.	10 mL
Salt	1/2 tsp.	2 mL
2.		
Large eggs, fork-beaten	2	2
Unsweetened applesauce	1 1/2 cups	375 mL
Brown sugar, packed	1/2 cup	125 mL
Cooking oil	1/3 cup	75 mL
Ground cinnamon	1 tsp.	5 mL
Vanilla extract	1 tsp.	5 mL
3.		
Chopped dried apricot	1/2 cup	125 mL

1. Place oven rack in centre position. Turn oven on to 375°F (190°C). Grease 12 muffin cups with cooking spray. Put first 4 ingredients into large bowl. Stir. Make a well in centre.

2. Put next 6 ingredients into medium bowl. Stir. Add to well.

3. Add apricot. Stir until just moistened. Fill 12 muffin cups 3/4 full with batter. Bake in oven for about 20 minutes until wooden pick inserted in centre of a muffin comes out clean. Put pan on stovetop. Turn oven off. Let muffins stand in pan for 5 minutes before removing to wire rack to cool. Makes 12 muffins.

1 muffin: 222 Calories; 7.8 g Total Fat (3.6 g Mono, 1.8 g Poly, 0.7 g Sat); 36 mg Cholesterol; 35 g Carbohydrate; 2 g Fibre; 4 g Protein; 207 mg Sodium

Pictured at right.

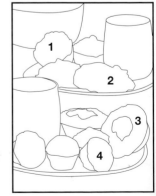

1. Apple-Cot Muffins, above
2. Rainin' Chocolate-Raisin Biscuits, page 101
3. Yummy Yogurt Muffins, page 105
4. Cinna-Mini Muffets, page 104

There's Muffin to It!

Cinna-Mini Muffets

These cute, cinnamon-sprinkled mini muffins will remind you of doughnut bites!
A lip-smackin' snack for when you're on the go.

Get It Together: wire racks, dry and liquid measures, measuring spoons,
small microwave-safe bowl, small bowl, medium bowl, large shallow bowl,
mini-muffin pan, pastry brush, zester, mixing spoon, cooking spray, wooden
pick, electric mixer

1.	Butter, softened (see Tip, page 42)	2 tbsp.	30 mL
	Granulated sugar	1/2 cup	125 mL
	Large egg	1	1
2.	Milk	3/4 cup	175 mL
	Grated orange zest (see Tip, page 43)	1 tsp.	5 mL
	Vanilla extract	1 tsp.	5 mL
3.	All-purpose flour	2 cups	500 mL
	Baking powder	1 tbsp.	15 mL
	Salt	1/4 tsp.	1 mL
4.	Butter, melted (see Tip, page 13)	2 tbsp.	30 mL
5.	Granulated sugar	1/2 cup	125 mL
	Ground cinnamon	1/2 tsp.	2 mL

1. Place oven rack in centre position. Turn oven on to 400°F (205°C).
    Grease 24 mini-muffin cups with cooking spray. Set aside. Put first
    3 ingredients into medium bowl. Beat until light and creamy.

2. Add next 3 ingredients. Beat well.

3. Put next 3 ingredients into small bowl. Stir. Add to milk mixture. Stir
    until just mixed. Fill 24 mini-muffin cups full with batter. Bake in oven for
    about 10 minutes until wooden pick inserted in centre of a muffet comes
    out clean. Put pan on stovetop. Turn oven off. Let muffets stand in pan
    for 5 minutes.

4. Brush muffet tops with butter.

5. Put second amount of sugar and cinnamon into large shallow bowl.
    Stir. Remove muffets from pan to cinnamon mixture. Toss until coated.
    Arrange on wire racks to cool. Makes 24 muffets.

1 muffet: 91 Calories; 2.2 g Total Fat (0.5 g Mono, 0.1 g Poly, 1.3 g Sat); 14 mg Cholesterol;
17 g Carbohydrate; trace Fibre; 2 g Protein; 113 mg Sodium

Pictured on page 103.

There's Muffin to It!

Yummy Yogurt Muffins

These delicious muffins will remind you of cupcakes with their sweet vanilla flavour. Each one has a dollop of strawberry jam on top—yum!

Get It Together: wire rack, dry and liquid measures, measuring spoons, fork, small bowl, large bowl, muffin pan, mixing spoon, cooking spray

1.			
All-purpose flour	2 cups	500 mL
Granulated sugar	1 cup	250 mL
Baking powder	1 tbsp.	15 mL
Salt	1/4 tsp.	1 mL
2.		
Large eggs, fork-beaten	2	2
Vanilla yogurt	1 cup	250 mL
Cooking oil	1/2 cup	125 mL
Vanilla extract	1 tsp.	5 mL
3.		
Strawberry jam	1/4 cup	60 mL

1. Place oven rack in centre position. Turn oven on to 375°F (190°C). Grease 12 muffin cups with cooking spray. Set aside. Put first 4 ingredients into large bowl. Stir. Make a well in centre.

2. Put next 4 ingredients into small bowl. Stir. Add to well. Stir until just moistened. Fill 12 muffin cups 3/4 full with batter.

3. Spoon about 1 tsp. jam over each muffin. Bake in oven for about 20 minutes until wooden pick inserted in muffin, not jam, comes out clean. Put pan on stovetop. Turn oven off. Let muffins stand in pan for 5 minutes before removing to wire rack to cool. Makes 12 muffins.

1 muffin: 264 Calories; 10.7 g Total Fat (5.5 g Mono, 2.7 g Poly, 1.3 g Sat); 38 mg Cholesterol; 39 g Carbohydrate; trace Fibre; 4 g Protein; 210 mg Sodium

Pictured on page 103.

Q: What two things can't you have for breakfast?

A: Lunch and dinner.

Practice Makes Pie-Fect!
Pies & Pastries

It's amazing how many fun and delicious things you can do with pastry—
and you can bake pastry dishes that taste great for any meal!

Personal baking profile

My name is: _____

My favourite thing to bake is: _____

My favourite kind of cookie is: _____

My favourite kind of cake is: _____

My favourite kind of pie is: _____

My favourite kind of bun is: _____

My favourite kind of pizza is: _____

The person I know who bakes the
best (next to me) is:

_____

My favourite recipe in this book is:

_____

If I owned my own bakery, I would call it:

_____

In my bakery, I would sell:

_____

Bonkers Chocolate Pie

A chocolate cake baked in a pie shell? That *is* bonkers! Serve with a scoop of vanilla ice cream, or a dollop of whipped cream.

Get It Together: dry and liquid measures, measuring spoons, small bowl, medium bowl, sifter, mixing spoon, wooden pick, electric mixer

1. Refrigerator pie crust | 1 | 1

2. All-purpose flour | 1 1/4 cups | 300 mL
   Cocoa, sifted if lumpy | 3 tbsp. | 50 mL
   Baking powder | 1/2 tsp. | 2 mL
   Baking soda | 1/2 tsp. | 2 mL
   Salt | 1/2 tsp. | 2 mL

3. Butter, softened (see Tip, see page 42) | 1/3 cup | 75 mL
   Granulated sugar | 2/3 cup | 150 mL
   Large egg | 1 | 1
   Milk | 3/4 cup | 175 mL
   Vanilla extract | 1 tsp. | 5 mL
   Mini semi-sweet chocolate chips | 1/2 cup | 125 mL

1. Let pie crust stand at room temperature for 30 minutes. Unroll pie crust. Line 9 inch (22 cm) deep dish pie plate. Roll under and press between your fingers to make crust look nice.

2. Place oven rack in bottom position. Turn oven on to 375°F (190°C). Put next 5 ingredients into small bowl. Stir.

3. Put butter and sugar into medium bowl. Beat until light and fluffy. Add next 3 ingredients. Beat well. Add flour mixture. Beat until smooth. Add chocolate chips. Stir. Pour batter into pie shell. Spread evenly. Bake in oven for about 45 minutes until wooden pick inserted in centre of pie comes out clean and pastry is golden. Put pie on stovetop. Turn oven off. Let pie stand for 10 minutes. Cuts into 8 wedges.

1 wedge: 392 Calories; 18.7 g Total Fat (3.1 g Mono, 0.4 g Poly, 10.0 g Sat); 53 mg Cholesterol; 53 g Carbohydrate; 1 g Fibre; 5 g Protein; 432 mg Sodium

Pictured on page 111.

Mango Tango Pie

It takes two to tango—peach and mango! When you find out how good these fruits taste together in the pie, you'll want to dance too!

Get It Together: wire rack, dry measures, measuring spoons, medium bowl, large bowl, strainer, 9 inch (22 cm) pie plate, mixing spoon, can opener, pastry brush

1.	Box of refrigerator pie crust (2 crusts)	15 oz.	425 g
2.	Cans of sliced mangos in syrup, (14 oz., 398 mL, each), drained	2	2
	Cans of sliced peaches in syrup, drained (14 oz., 398 mL, each)	2	2
	Lime juice	1 tsp.	5 mL
	Vanilla extract	1/2 tsp.	2 mL
3.	Granulated sugar	2/3 cup	150 mL
	All-purpose flour	1/3 cup	75 mL
4.	Cold butter, cut into small pieces	2 tbsp.	30 mL
	Milk	1 tbsp.	15 mL
	Granulated sugar	1 tbsp.	15 mL

1. Let pie crust stand at room temperature for 30 minutes. Unroll 1 pie crust. Line 9 inch (22 cm) pie plate.

2. Put next 4 ingredients into large bowl. Stir.

3. Put first amount of sugar and flour into small bowl. Stir. Add to fruit mixture. Stir well.

4. Place oven rack in bottom position. Turn oven on to 400°F (205°C). Spoon fruit mixture into crust. Drop butter randomly onto fruit, using about 1/2 tsp. (2 mL) amounts. Brush rim of bottom crust with water.

(continued on next page)

Practice Makes Pie-Fect!

Unroll remaining pie crust. Place over fruit mixture. Trim around pie plate to remove excess crust and crimp decorative edge to seal (see diagram, page 108). Brush top of pie with milk. Sprinkle with second amount of sugar. Cut several small slits in top to allow steam to escape. Bake in oven for about 50 minutes until golden. Put pie on stovetop. Turn oven off. Let pie stand on wire rack to cool. Cuts into 8 wedges.

1 wedge: *475 Calories; 16.6 g Total Fat (0.7 g Mono, 0.1 g Poly, 7.7 g Sat); 17 mg Cholesterol; 81 g Carbohydrate; 2 g Fibre; 3 g Protein; 229 mg Sodium*

Pictured on page 111.

Dappled-Apple Pecan Tarts

The nuts start a flavour party with yummy apple and butterscotch! These tiny pecan pies are sweet, nutty and so simple to make.

Get It Together: cutting board, wire rack, sharp knife, dry measures, medium bowl, baking sheet with sides, shallow frying pan, potato masher, can opener, mixing spoon

1.	Chopped pecans	2 cups	500 mL
	Can of apple pie filling	19 oz.	540 mL
	Butterscotch chips	1 cup	250 mL
2.	Unbaked tart shells	24	24

1. Put pecans into a large frying pan. Heat on medium for 5 to 8 minutes, stirring often, until golden. Set aside. Turn burner off. Transfer nuts to baking sheet with sides to cool completely. Place oven rack in centre position. Turn oven on to 375°F (190°C). Put pie filling into medium bowl. Mash until apple is in small pieces. Add pecans and butterscotch chips. Stir.

2. Arrange tart shells on baking sheet with sides. Spoon about 2 tbsp. (30 mL) pecan mixture into each tart shell. Bake in oven for about 25 minutes until pastry is golden and filling is bubbling. Put baking sheet on wire rack to cool. Turn oven off. Makes 24 tarts.

1 tart: *233 Calories; 16.0 g Total Fat (7.0 g Mono, 2.9 g Poly, 5.3 g Sat); 0 mg Cholesterol; 21 g Carbohydrate; 1 g Fibre; 2 g Protein; 132 mg Sodium*

Pictured on page 111.

Creampuff Says: Make half the tarts for this week's snacks and freeze cooled tarts for up to 2 months in a resealable freezer bag or airtight container.

Practice Makes Pie-Fect!

Pear-fect Puff Pastries

This pastry is easy and fun to work with—watch it puff up around the pear halves in the oven. Save these pretty, cream-cheesy treats for a very special party!

Get It Together: cutting board, wire rack, sharp knife, vegetable peeler, measuring spoons, spoon, small microwave-safe bowl, baking sheet with sides, rolling pin, mixing spoon, pastry brush, cooking spray

1.	Package of puff pastry (14 oz., 397 g), thawed according to package directions	1/2	1/2
2.	Fresh ripe peeled pears	2	2
	Raspberry cream cheese	8 tsp.	40 mL
3.	Apple jelly	2 tbsp.	30 mL

1. Roll out pastry on lightly floured surface to 10 inch (25 cm) square. Cut into 4 squares. Grease baking sheet with sides with cooking spray. Transfer pastry to ungreased baking sheet.

2. Place oven rack in bottom position. Turn oven on to 400°F (205°C). Cut pears in half lengthwise. Scoop out cores with spoon and discard. Fill each pear half with about 2 tsp. (10 mL) cream cheese. Place pear halves, cut-side down, in centre of pastry squares. Trim pastry into pear shape, leaving 3/4 inch (2 cm) border around each pear. Cut 4 leaf shapes from trimmings (use 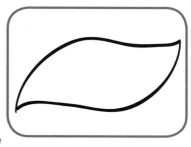 diagram as template). Press 1 leaf into pointed end of each pastry. Make 3 deep cuts into each pear, almost, but not quite through to filling. Bake in oven for about 25 minutes until pastry is puffed and golden and pear is tender. Put baking sheet on stovetop. Turn oven off.

3. Put jelly into small, microwave-safe bowl. Microwave, covered, on medium (50%) for about 45 seconds until almost melted. Remove bowl from microwave. Stir until smooth. Brush over pears. Let stand on baking sheet for 10 minutes before removing to wire rack to cool. Makes 4 pastries.

1 pastry: 278 Calories; 14.9 g Total Fat (trace Mono, trace Poly, 4.6 g Sat); 5 mg Cholesterol; 32 g Carbohydrate; 2 g Fibre; 5 g Protein; 284 mg Sodium

Pictured at right.

Creampuff Says: Position pears with their points facing in to be sure the pointy pastry leaves don't burn.

Practice Makes Pie-Fect!

1. Mango Tango Pie, page 108
2. Dappled-Apple Pecan Tarts, page 109
3. Bonkers Chocolate Pie, page 107
4. Pear-fect Puff Pastries, left

111

Mighty Meatball Pie

You'll be proud to set this mighty fine pie on the dinner table! Use your favourite kind of meatballs—they come in Italian and Swedish flavours, and even meatless!

Get It Together: sharp knife, dry measures, measuring spoons, fork, large bowl, can opener, mixing spoon, pastry brush

1.	**Can of condensed onion soup**	**10 oz.**	**284 mL**
	Minute tapioca	**1 1/2 tbsp.**	**25 mL**
	Frozen mixed vegetables	**1 cup**	**250 mL**
	Frozen cooked meatballs	**25**	**25**
2.	**Frozen 9 inch (22 cm) pie shells,**	**2**	**2**
	thawed according to		
	package instructions		
	Large egg, fork-beaten	**1**	**1**

1. Place oven rack in bottom position. Turn oven on to 375°F (190°C). Put onion soup and tapioca into large bowl. Stir. Add vegetables and meatballs. Stir until coated.

2. Brush edge of 1 pie shell with half of egg. Spoon meatball mixture into shell. Invert second pie shell on top. Carefully remove top pie plate. Crimp decorative edge to seal (see diagram). Brush top of pie with remaining egg. Cut several small slits in top to allow steam to escape. Bake in oven for about 75 minutes, until pastry is golden and filling is bubbling. Put pie on stovetop. Turn oven off. Let pie stand for 15 minutes. Cuts into 6 wedges.

1 wedge: *415 Calories; 23.7 g Total Fat (0.3 g Mono, 0.3 g Poly, 9.8 g Sat); 56 mg Cholesterol; 43 g Carbohydrate; 1 g Fibre; 6 g Protein; 821 mg Sodium*

Pictured on page 114.

> **Creampuff Says:** Not all frozen vegetables will work for this recipe. Stick to any combination of peas, corn, carrots and beans (broccoli, cauliflower and peppers are too watery).

Practice Makes Pie-Fect!

Tomato Turkey Turnovers

Fun triangles of puff pastry surround yummy turkey, cheese and tomato goodness.

Get It Together: cutting board, wire rack, sharp knife, dry measures, fork, spoon, small bowl, baking sheet with sides, rolling pin, mixing spoon, grater, pastry brush, cooking spray

1. Package of puff pastry (14 oz., 397 g), thawed according to package directions	1/2	1/2
2. Deli smoked turkey slices (about 4 oz., 113 g), chopped	4	4
Grated Monterey Jack cheese	1/2 cup	125 mL
Seeded Roma (plum) tomatoes, chopped	1/4 cup	60 mL
3. Large egg, fork-beaten	1	1

1. Place oven rack in bottom position. Turn oven on to 400°F (205°C). Roll out pastry on lightly floured surface to 10 inch (25 cm) square. Cut into 4 squares. Grease baking sheet with sides with cooking spray. Transfer pastry to baking sheet.

2. Put next 3 ingredients into small bowl. Stir. Spoon about 1/4 cup (60 mL) turkey mixture onto centre of each pastry square.

3. Brush pastry edges with egg. Fold one corner to opposite corner to form a triangle. Pinch edges to seal. Brush top of each turnover with egg. Cut 3 small slits in tops to allow steam to escape. Bake in oven for about 20 minutes until puffed and golden. Put baking sheet on stovetop. Turn oven off. Let turnovers stand in pan for 10 minutes before removing to wire rack to cool. Makes 4 turnovers.

1 turnover: 298 Calories; 18.7 g Total Fat (trace Mono, trace Poly, 6.5 g Sat); 76 mg Cholesterol; 19 g Carbohydrate; 1 g Fibre; 13 g Protein; 589 mg Sodium

Pictured on page 114.

Creampuff Says: To seed the tomatoes, cut them in half crosswise. Scoop the seeds out of the pockets with a spoon.

Practice Makes Pie-Fect!

Quiche-Me-Quick Tarts

You haven't had broccoli dressed up in a cheesy quiche tart like this before!

Get It Together: dry and liquid measures, measuring spoons, large plate, spoon, fork, grater

1.			
Frozen chopped broccoli, thawed	1/2 cup	125 mL
Unbaked tart shells	12	12
Grated sharp Cheddar cheese	3/4 cup	175 mL

2.			
Large eggs	2	2
Milk	3/4 cup	175 mL
Salt	1/4 tsp.	1 mL
Pepper, sprinkle		

1. Spread frozen broccoli on large plate. Let stand for 30 minutes until thawed. If some broccoli are big, chop into smaller pieces. Place oven rack in bottom position. Turn oven on to 375°F (190°C). Arrange tart shells on baking sheet with sides. Spoon broccoli and cheese into tart shells.

2. Put remaining 4 ingredients into 2 cup (500 mL) measure. Whisk with fork. Fill each tart shell half full with mixture. Bake in oven for about 25 minutes until set. Put baking sheet on stovetop. Turn oven off. Makes 12 tarts.

1 tart: 134 Calories; 8.2 g Total Fat (0.7 g Mono, 0.1 g Poly, 3.9 g Sat); 48 mg Cholesterol; 11 g Carbohydrate; trace Fibre; 4 g Protein; 183 mg Sodium

Pictured at left.

Creampuff Says: Use frozen broccoli because it's partially cooked already.

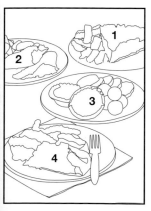

1. Mighty Meatball Pie, page 112
2. Tomato Turkey Turnovers, page 113
3. Quiche-Me-Quick Tarts, above
4. Upside-Down Chicken Pot Pie, page 116

Practice Makes Pie-Fect!

Upside-Down Chicken Pot Pie

Why did the chicken cross the road? To check out this crazy pot pie!
This is an awesome meal to serve your friends.

Get It Together: dry and liquid measures, fork, spoon, medium bowl,
baking sheet with sides, mixing spoon, pastry brush

1.	Refrigerator pie crust	1	1
2.	Chopped cooked chicken	2 cups	500 mL
	Frozen pea and carrot mix	1 cup	250 mL
	Alfredo pasta sauce	1/2 cup	125 mL
3.	Large egg, fork-beaten	1	1

1. Let pie crust stand at room temperature for 30 minutes. Unroll pie crust. Place on large ungreased baking sheet with sides. Place oven rack in bottom position. Turn oven on to 400°F (205°C).

2. Put next 3 ingredients into medium bowl. Stir. Spoon chicken mixture onto centre of pastry, leaving 3 inch (7.5 cm) border. Fold a section of border up and over edge of filling, allowing pastry to overlap so that fold is created. Pinch to seal. Repeat until pastry border is completely folded around filling (pictured at right).

3. Brush pastry with egg. Bake in oven for about 30 minutes until pastry is golden. Put baking sheet on stovetop. Turn oven off. Let pie stand for 5 minutes. Cuts into 4 wedges.

1 wedge: 481 Calories; 27.1 g Total Fat (1.9 g Mono, 1.2 g Poly, 12.2 g Sat); 151 mg Cholesterol; 31 g Carbohydrate; 1 g Fibre; 26 g Protein; 462 mg Sodium

Pictured on page 114.

Practice Makes Pie-Fect!

Nut 'N' Jam Twists

Do the twist! These jammy twists packed with peanuts are a quick, sweet treat.
These are great for a snack, or to take along for a packed lunch.

Get It Together: cutting board, sharp knife, dry and liquid measures,
baking sheet with sides, rubber spatula, cooking spray, aluminum foil

1.	**Tube of jumbo refrigerator crescent rolls (4 rolls per tube)**	**11 oz.**	**318 g**
2.	**Raspberry jam**	**1/4 cup**	**60 mL**
	Chopped salted peanuts, roasted	**1/4 cup**	**60 mL**

1. Remove dough from tube. Separate halves. Unroll each half with long side closest to you (see diagram 1). Lightly press together perforated diagonal edge on each rectangle until no holes remain (see diagram 2).

diagram 1

2. Place oven rack in centre position. Turn oven on to 350°F (175°C). Spread 2 tbsp. (30 mL) jam evenly over 1 rectangle, leaving 1/4 inch (6 mm) edge at both short sides. Sprinkle 2 tbsp. (30 mL) peanuts evenly over jam. Fold left side over right, pressing short sides together to seal. Cut rectangle horizontally into

diagram 2

4 strips. Holding both ends of each strip, twist several times. Line baking sheet with sides with aluminum foil. Grease foil with cooking spray. Arrange twists on baking sheet. Repeat with remaining dough, jam and peanuts. Bake in oven for about 20 minutes until golden. Put baking sheet on stovetop. Turn oven off. Makes 8 twists.

1 twist: 211 Calories; 11.0 g Total Fat (0 g Mono, 0 g Poly, 2.8 g Sat); 0 mg Cholesterol; 23 g Carbohydrate; trace Fibre; 4 g Protein; 336 mg Sodium

Pictured on page 119.

Razzle Dazzle Custard Tarts

Ah, tastes like summer vacation in a tart shell. Nope, not sunscreen lotion flavour
(yuck!)—fresh raspberries! These tarts make cute, delicious treats.

Get It Together: dry and liquid measures, measuring spoons, spoon,
baking sheet with sides, piping bag, blender or food processor,
electric mixer

(continued on next page)

Practice Makes Pie-Fect!

1. Unbaked tart shells	12	12
2. Fresh raspberries	1/2 cup	125 mL
Whipping cream	1/2 cup	125 mL
Granulated sugar	3 tbsp.	50 mL
Egg yolks (large)	3	3
3. Whipping cream	1/2 cup	125 mL
Granulated sugar	2 tbsp.	30 mL
Fresh raspberries	12	12

1. Place oven rack in centre position. Turn oven on to 400°F (205°C). Wait 10 minutes for oven to heat up. Arrange tart shells on baking sheet with sides. Bake in oven for about 12 minutes until golden. Put baking sheet on stovetop. Turn oven to 300°F (150°C).

2. Put next 4 ingredients into blender. Cover with lid. Process until smooth. Fill each tart shell 3/4 full with raspberry mixture. Bake in oven for about 25 minutes until set but centre still wobbles. Put baking sheet on stovetop. Turn oven off. Let tarts stand until cool. Chill for about 2 hours until set.

3. Put second amount of whipping cream and second amount of sugar into small bowl. Beat until stiff peaks form. Spoon whipped cream into piping bag (see Tip, page 37). Pipe cream onto tarts. Garnish with raspberries. Makes 12 tarts.

1 tart: 189 Calories; 13.4 g Total Fat (2.6 g Mono, 0.5 g Poly, 7.1 g Sat); 82 mg Cholesterol; 16 g Carbohydrate; trace Fibre; 2 g Protein; 80 mg Sodium

Pictured at right.

Happy Apple Pinwheels

These taste just like a bakery treat, but you make them right in your own kitchen.

Get It Together: cutting board, wire rack, sharp knife, dry and liquid measures, measuring spoons, fork, small cup, medium bowl, baking sheet with sides, mixing spoon, rolling pin, pastry brush, can opener, waxed paper, plastic wrap, parchment paper, electric mixer

(continued on page 120)

1. Nut 'N' Jam Twists, page 117
2. Happy Apple Pinwheels, left
3. Razzle Dazzle Custard Tarts, page 117

1.	Butter, softened (see Tip, page 42)	1/2 cup	125 mL
	Cream cheese, softened (see Tip, page 33)	4 oz.	113 g
	Granulated sugar	2 tbsp.	30 mL
	Whole-wheat flour	1 cup	250 mL
2.	Canned apple pie filling, chopped	1/4 cup	60 mL
3.	Large egg, fork-beaten	1	1
4.	Milk	2 tsp	10 mL
	Icing (confectioner's) sugar	1/2 cup	125 mL

1. Put butter and cream cheese into medium bowl. Beat until smooth. Add sugar. Beat until light and fluffy. Add flour. Beat until soft dough forms. Shape into ball. Form ball into disc and wrap in plastic wrap. Chill for 3 hours. Remove dough from refrigerator. Let stand for 20 minutes. Discard plastic wrap. Roll out between 2 sheets of waxed paper to 9 inch (22 cm) square. Discard top sheet of waxed paper. Cut into 4 squares. Line baking sheet with sides with parchment paper. Transfer squares from waxed paper onto baking sheet.

2. Place oven rack in centre position. Turn oven on to 375°F (190°C). Spoon 1 tbsp. (15 mL) pie filling onto centre of each square. Make 4 cuts with sharp knife from edge of filling to each corner (see picture 1, at right).

3. Brush every other pastry point with egg. Lift points and fold towards centre, pressing dough lightly onto filling and overlapping points to create a pinwheel (see picture 2, at right). Brush top of pastry with remaining egg. Bake in oven for about 17 minutes until golden. Put baking sheet on stovetop. Turn oven off.

4. Stir milk into icing sugar in small cup until smooth. Drizzle over warm pastries. Let stand in pan for 10 minutes before removing to wire rack to cool. Makes 4 pinwheels.

1 pinwheel: 507 Calories; 33.9 g Total Fat (6.0 g Mono, 1.1 g Poly, 21.5 g Sat); 142 mg Cholesterol; 47 g Carbohydrate; 4 g Fibre; 8 g Protein; 276 mg Sodium

Pictured on page 119.

Practice Makes Pie-Fect!

Measurement Tables

Throughout this book measurements are given in Conventional and Metric measure. To compensate for differences between the two measurements due to rounding, a full metric measure is not always used. The cup used is the standard 8 fluid ounce. Temperature is given in degrees Fahrenheit and Celsius. Baking pan measurements are in inches and centimetres as well as quarts and litres. An exact metric conversion is given below as well as the working equivalent (Metric Standard Measure).

Spoons

Conventional Measure	Metric Exact Conversion Millilitre (mL)	Metric Standard Measure Millilitre (mL)
1/8 teaspoon (tsp.)	0.6 mL	0.5 mL
1/4 teaspoon (tsp.)	1.2 mL	1 mL
1/2 teaspoon (tsp.)	2.4 mL	2 mL
1 teaspoon (tsp.)	4.7 mL	5 mL
2 teaspoons (tsp.)	9.4 mL	10 mL
1 tablespoon (tbsp.)	14.2 mL	15 mL

Cups

Conventional Measure	Metric Exact Conversion Millilitre (mL)	Metric Standard Measure Millilitre (mL)
1/4 cup (4 tbsp.)	56.8 mL	60 mL
1/3 cup (5 1/3 tbsp.)	75.6 mL	75 mL
1/2 cup (8 tbsp.)	113.7 mL	125 mL
2/3 cup (10 2/3 tbsp.)	151.2 mL	150 mL
3/4 cup (12 tbsp.)	170.5 mL	175 mL
1 cup (16 tbsp.)	227.3 mL	250 mL
4 1/2 cups	1022.9 mL	1000 mL (1 L)

Oven Temperatures

Fahrenheit (°F)	Celsius (°C)
175°	80°
200°	95°
225°	110°
250°	120°
275°	140°
300°	150°
325°	160°
350°	175°
375°	190°
400°	205°
425°	220°
450°	230°
475°	240°
500°	260°

Dry Measurements

Conventional Measure Ounces (oz.)	Metric Exact Conversion Grams (g)	Metric Standard Measure Grams (g)
1 oz.	28.3 g	28 g
2 oz.	56.7 g	57 g
3 oz.	85.0 g	85 g
4 oz.	113.4 g	125 g
5 oz.	141.7 g	140 g
6 oz.	170.1 g	170 g
7 oz.	198.4 g	200 g
8 oz.	226.8 g	250 g
16 oz.	453.6 g	500 g
32 oz.	907.2 g	1000 g (1 kg)

Pans

Conventional Inches	Metric Centimetres
8x8 inch	20x20 cm
9x9 inch	22x22 cm
9x13 inch	22x33 cm
10x15 inch	25x38 cm
11x17 inch	28x43 cm
8x2 inch round	20x5 cm
9x2 inch round	22x5 cm
10x4 1/2 inch tube	25x11 cm
8x4x3 inch loaf	20x10x7.5 cm
9x5x3 inch loaf	22x12.5x7.5 cm

Casseroles

CANADA & BRITAIN Standard Size Casserole	Exact Metric Measure	UNITED STATES Standard Size Casserole	Exact Metric Measure
1 qt. (5 cups)	1.13 L	1 qt. (4 cups)	900 mL
1 1/2 qts. (7 1/2 cups)	1.69 L	1 1/2 qts. (6 cups)	1.35 L
2 qts. (10 cups)	2.25 L	2 qts. (8 cups)	1.8 L
2 1/2 qts. (12 1/2 cups)	2.81 L	2 1/2 qts. (10 cups)	2.25 L
3 qts. (15 cups)	3.38 L	3 qts. (12 cups)	2.7 L
4 qts. (20 cups)	4.5 L	4 qts. (16 cups)	3.6 L
5 qts. (25 cups)	5.63 L	5 qts. (20 cups)	4.5 L

Tip Index

Baking gums, purchasing 32

Butter, melting 13

Butter, softening. 42

Citrus, zesting. 43

Pans, safely inverting 12

Cream cheese, softening 33

Piping bag, substituting 37

Sugar, sanding, about. 65

Recipe Index

A

Ape-ricot Monkey Bread 12

Apple-Cot Muffins. 102

Apple Pecan Tarts, Dappled- 109

Apple-Pie Sponge Pudding 82

Apple Pinwheels, Happy 120

Apples

    Candy-Apple Cake 45

    Caramel Apple Bombs 85

B

Bananarama Cheesecakes 75

Bananas

    Choconana Quesadilla. 86

    Cocoa-Nut Monkey Loaf 90

    Peanut Butter Banana Cake 46

Bars, see Squares & Bars

Berry Blondies, Orange 'N' 43

Berry Cobbler Gobbler 73

Biscuits

    Cheese-Please Garlic Biscuits. 97

    Rainin' Chocolate-Raisin Biscuits 101

    Sticky Spice Spirals 94

Blondies, Orange 'N' Berry 43

Boatload of Oat Muffins 89

Boggling Baked Snowballs 83

Bonkers Chocolate Pie 107

Boppin' Butterscotch Pull-Aparts 13

Bottoms-Up Pizza Rustica. 16

Bread Pudding, Pearrific. 71

Breads, see also Loaves

    Ape-ricot Monkey Bread 12

    Boppin' Butterscotch Pull-Aparts. 13

    Cravin' Cranberry Bread 22

    Gone-To-Seed Focaccia 19

    Puffy Pockets 10

Brownies, Caramel Candy. 40

Buns

    Cheeztastic Buns 24

    Cinnamapple Swirl Buns. 14

    Hawaiian Half-Moons 18

    Hot Diggity Dog Buns 20

    Pepperoni Hideaways 26

    Pretzel Bun Softies 9

    Twisted Tuna Melts. 28

Buttercream Icing, Cherry. 36

Butterscotch Pull-Aparts, Boppin' 13

C

Cakes

    Bananarama Cheesecakes 75

    Candy-Apple Cake 45

    Creamy Orange Roll-Up 48

    Mud Puddle Cake 38

Nuts-About-Cocoa Cake 35

Peanut Butter Banana Cake 46

Rainbow Sparks Cheesecake 33

Razz Pizzazz Cheesecakes 76

Sweet-Spot Baby Cakes 36

Tropical Twist Snack Cake 31

Yum-Gummy Pound Cake 32

Candy-Apple Cake 45

Candy Brownies, Caramel 40

Caramel Apple Bombs 85

Caramel Candy Brownies 40

Cheesecakes

Bananarama Cheesecakes 75

Rainbow Sparks Cheesecake 33

Razz Pizzazz Cheesecakes 76

Cheese-Please Garlic Biscuits 97

Cheesy Chili Loaf 96

Cheeztastic Buns 24

Cherry Buttercream Icing 36

Chicken Pot Pie, Upside-Down 116

Chili-Con-Corny Loaf 99

Chili Loaf, Cheesy 96

Chip Chip Hooray Cookies 58

Choc-A-Lot Trail Mix Cookies 52

Chocolate

Bonkers Chocolate Pie 107

Caramel Candy Brownies 40

Chip Chip Hooray Cookies 58

Choc-A-Lot Trail Mix Cookies 52

Choco-Lots O' Love Cookies 60

Choconana Quesadilla 86

Cocoa-Nut Monkey Loaf 90

Confetti Graham Squares 39

Go Go GORP Muffins 92

Hazelnut Sugar Sammies 56

Mud Puddle Cake 38

Nuts-About-Cocoa Cake 35

Orange 'N' Berry Blondies 43

Rainbow Peanut Cookies 51

Rainin' Chocolate-Raisin Biscuits 101

S'more Dessert Anyone? 72

Choco-Lots O' Love Cookies 60

Choconana Quesadilla 86

Cinnamapple Swirl Buns 14

Cinna-Mini Muffets 104

Cobbler Gobbler, Berry 73

Cocoa Cake, Nuts-About- 35

Cocoa-Nut Monkey Loaf 90

Confetti Graham Squares 39

Cookies

Chip Chip Hooray Cookies 58

Choc-A-Lot Trail Mix Cookies 52

Choco-Lots O' Love Cookies 60

Full-Moon Macaroons 59

Gingerbread Kids 67

Hazelnut Sugar Sammies 56

Holiday Hideaway Cookies 64

Hopscotch Cookies 54

Lemon-Doodles 66

Meringue Clouds 63

Mr. Squirrel's Shortbread 69

Open Sesame Cookies 55

Rainbow Peanut Cookies 51

Spicy Big Daddies 62

Corny Loaf, Chili-Con- 99

Cranberry Bread, Cravin' 22

Cravin' Cranberry Bread 22

Creamy Orange Roll-Up 48

Crisp, Rhuby-Strawberry 86

Custard Tarts, Razzle Dazzle 118

Recipe Index

D

Dappled-Apple Pecan Tarts 109

Dessert Anyone?, S'more 72

Dough, Quick Pizza. 16

F

Focaccia, Gone-To-Seed. 19

Fruit Pudding, Topsy-Turvy. 78

Full-Moon Macaroons. 59

G

Garlic Biscuits, Cheese-Please 97

Gingerbread Kids 67

Glaze, Lemon 93

Go Go GORP Muffins. 92

Gold-Dust Lemon Bars 42

Gone-To-Seed Focaccia 19

Graham Squares, Confetti. 39

H

Happy Apple Pinwheels 120

Hawaiian Half-Moons 18

Hazelnut Sugar Sammies 56

Holiday Hideaway Cookies 64

Hooray Olé Muffins. 100

Hopscotch Cookies. 54

Hot Diggity Dog Buns 20

I

Icing, Cherry Buttercream. 36

J

Jam Twists, Nut 'N' 117

L

Lemon Bars, Gold-Dust. 42

Lemonberry Muffins, Lovely 93

Lemon-Doodles 66

Lemon Glaze. 93

Loaves, see also Breads

    Cheesy Chili 96

    Chili-Con-Corny 99

    Cocoa-Nut Monkey 90

Lovely Lemonberry Muffins. 93

M

Macaroons, Full-Moon 59

Mango Tango Pie 108

Meatball Pie, Mighty. 112

Meringue Clouds. 63

Mighty Meatball Pie 112

Monkey Bread, Ape-ricot 12

Mr. Squirrel's Shortbread 69

Mud Puddle Cake. 38

Muffins

    Apple-Cot Muffins. 102

    Boatload of Oat Muffins 89

    Cinna-Mini Muffets 104

    Go Go GORP Muffins. 92

    Hooray Olé Muffins 100

    Lovely Lemonberry Muffins. 93

    Yummy Yogurt Muffins 105

N

Nut 'N' Jam Twists. 117

Nuts

   Boatload of Oat Muffins 89

   Boppin' Butterscotch Pull-Aparts. 13

   Caramel Apple Bombs 85

   Choc-A-Lot Trail Mix Cookies 52

   Choconana Quesadilla. 86

   Dappled-Apple Pecan Tarts. 109

   Go Go GORP Muffins. 92

   Hazelnut Sugar Sammies 56

   Mr. Squirrel's Shortbread 69

   Mud Puddle Cake 38

   Nut 'N' Jam Twists 117

   Nuts-About-Cocoa Cake 35

   Peanut Butter Banana Cake 46

   Rainbow Peanut Cookies. 51

Nuts-About-Cocoa Cake 35

O

Oat Muffins, Boatload of. 89

Open Sesame Cookies 55

Orange 'N' Berry Blondies. 43

Orange Roll-Up, Creamy. 48

P

Pastries, Savoury

   Pear-fect Puff Pastries 110

   Tomato Turkey Turnovers. 113

Pastries, Sweet

   Happy Apple Pinwheels. 120

Nut 'N' Jam Twists. 117

Peachy Queen Trifle 80

Peanut Butter Banana Cake 46

Peanut Cookies, Rainbow. 51

Pear-fect Puff Pastries 110

Pearrific Bread Pudding 71

Pecan Tarts, Dappled-Apple. 109

Pepperoni Hideaways 26

Pies, Savoury

   Mighty Meatball 112

   Upside-Down Chicken Pot. 116

Pies, Sweet

   Bonkers Chocolate 107

   Mango Tango 108

Pinwheels, Happy Apple 120

Pizza Dough, Quick. 16

Pizza Rustica, Bottoms-Up 16

Pizza, Strawberry Shortcake. 79

Pockets, Puffy. 10

Pot Pie, Upside-Down Chicken 116

Pound Cake, Yum-Gummy 32

Pretzel Bun Softies. 9

Puddings

   Apple-Pie Sponge 82

   Pearrific Bread 71

   Topsy-Turvy Fruit 78

Puffy Pockets 10

Pull-Aparts, Boppin' Butterscotch 13

Q

Quesadilla, Choconana 86

Quiche-Me-Quick Tarts. 115

Quick Pizza Dough 16

Recipe Index   **125**

R

Rainbow Peanut Cookies 51

Rainbow Sparks Cheesecake 33

Rainin' Chocolate-Raisin Biscuits 101

Raisin Biscuits, Rainin' Chocolate- 101

Razz Pizzazz Cheesecakes 76

Razzle Dazzle Custard Tarts 118

Rhuby-Strawberry Crisp 86

S

Sesame Cookies, Open. 55

Shortbread, Mr. Squirrel's. 69

Shortcake Pizza, Strawberry. 79

S'more Dessert Anyone? 72

Spice Spirals, Sticky. 94

Spicy Big Daddies. 62

Sponge Pudding, Apple-Pie 82

Squares & Bars

　　Caramel Candy Brownies 40

　　Confetti Graham Squares 39

　　Gold-Dust Lemon Bars 42

　　Orange 'N' Berry Blondies. 43

Sticky Spice Spirals 94

Strawberry Crisp, Rhuby- 86

Strawberry Shortcake Pizza 79

Sugar Sammies, Hazelnut. 56

Sweet-Spot Baby Cakes 36

T

Tarts

　　Dappled-Apple Pecan 109

　　Quiche-Me-Quick 115

　　Razzle Dazzle Custard. 118

Tomato Turkey Turnovers. 113

Topsy-Turvy Fruit Pudding 78

Trail Mix Cookies, Choc-A-Lot 52

Trifle, Peachy Queen. 80

Tropical Twist Snack Cake 31

Tuna Melts, Twisted 28

Turkey Turnovers, Tomato 113

Turnovers, Tomato Turkey 113

Twisted Tuna Melts 28

U

Upside-Down Chicken Pot Pie. 116

Y

Yogurt Muffins, Yummy 105

Yum-Gummy Pound Cake. 32

Yummy Yogurt Muffins 105

Recipe Notes